Himouto (干物妹)

A lazy little sister who never lifts a finger around the house.
"At home, Umaru is a himouto."
Origin: a portmanteau of imouto (little sister) and himono (a woman who is elegant and polished in public, but secretly a slob at home).

From Shueisha's *Imouto Dictionary*.

HIMOUTO! ♥ ⑤

Characters Inside

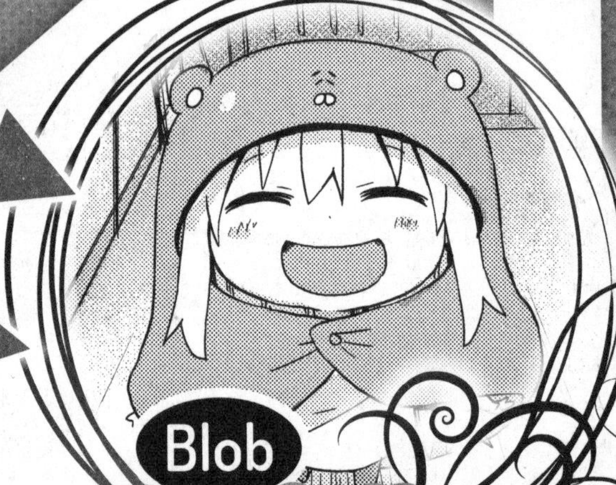

Blob

Inside Umaru

Taihei's little sister. Once she steps through the front door, she turns into an irresponsible slob whose motto is, "Eat, sleep (Zzz...), play!"♪

Master

Siblings

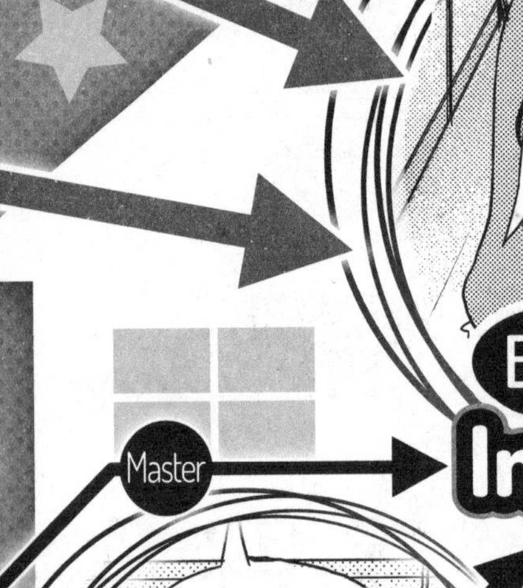

Taihei

Umaru's big brother. He has an office job, but he also works a second job doing chores and generally being a "house-husband."

Story

Inside, Taihei's little sister Umaru is a lazy little sloth the whole year round, spending her days indulging in snacks and video games, with a cola ever in one hand. ♪ But once she steps outside, she turns into a super-perfect, super-popular overachiever! These days, our little himouto's world is slowly but steadily expanding... There's Ebina, Umaru's neighbor and friend; ♥ Kirie, who looks up to Inside Umaru as her master; ♪ and Sylphynford, Outside Umaru's frenemy--and UMR's actual friend! How are the three different worlds of Umaru coming together and changing...?

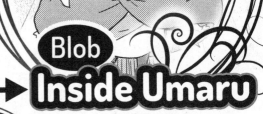

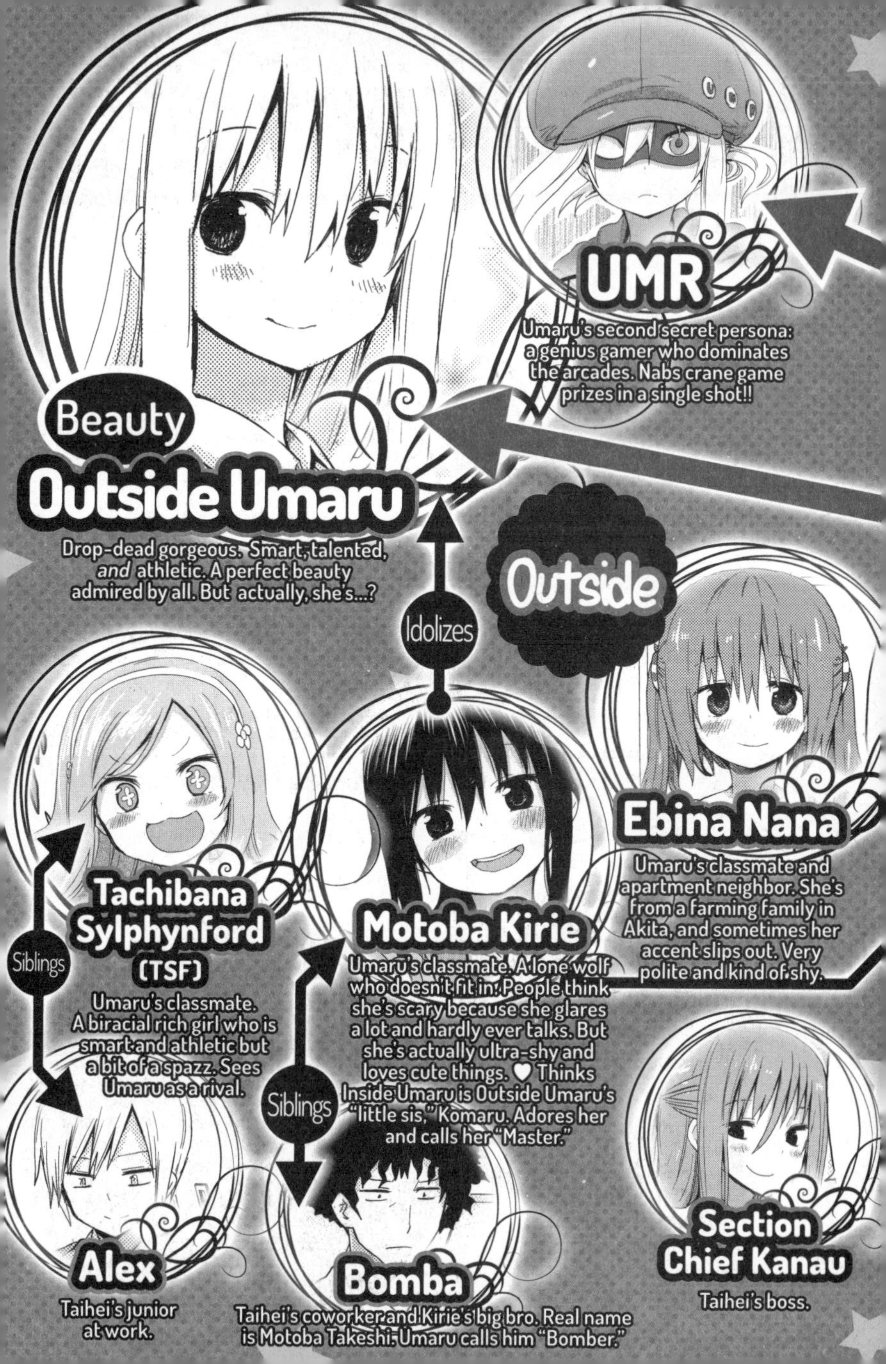
UMR
Umaru's second secret persona: a genius gamer who dominates the arcades. Nabs crane game prizes in a single shot!!
Beauty
Outside Umaru
Drop-dead gorgeous. Smart, talented, *and* athletic. A perfect beauty admired by all. But actually, she's...?
Idolizes
Outside
Ebina Nana
Umaru's classmate and apartment neighbor. She's from a farming family in Akita, and sometimes her accent slips out. Very polite and kind of shy.
Motoba Kirie
Umaru's classmate. A lone wolf who doesn't fit in. People think she's scary because she glares a lot and hardly ever talks. But she's actually ultra-shy and loves cute things. ♥ Thinks Inside Umaru is Outside Umaru's "little sis," Komaru. Adores her and calls her "Master."
Tachibana Sylphynford
(TSF)
Umaru's classmate. A biracial rich girl who is smart and athletic but a bit of a spazz. Sees Umaru as a rival.
Siblings
Siblings
Section Chief Kanau
Taihei's boss.
Bomba
Taihei's coworker and Kirie's big bro. Real name is Motoba Takeshi. Umaru calls him "Bomber."
Alex
Taihei's junior at work.

HIMOUTO! UMARU-CHAN 5

CONTENTS

No. 72 Umaru & the New Game

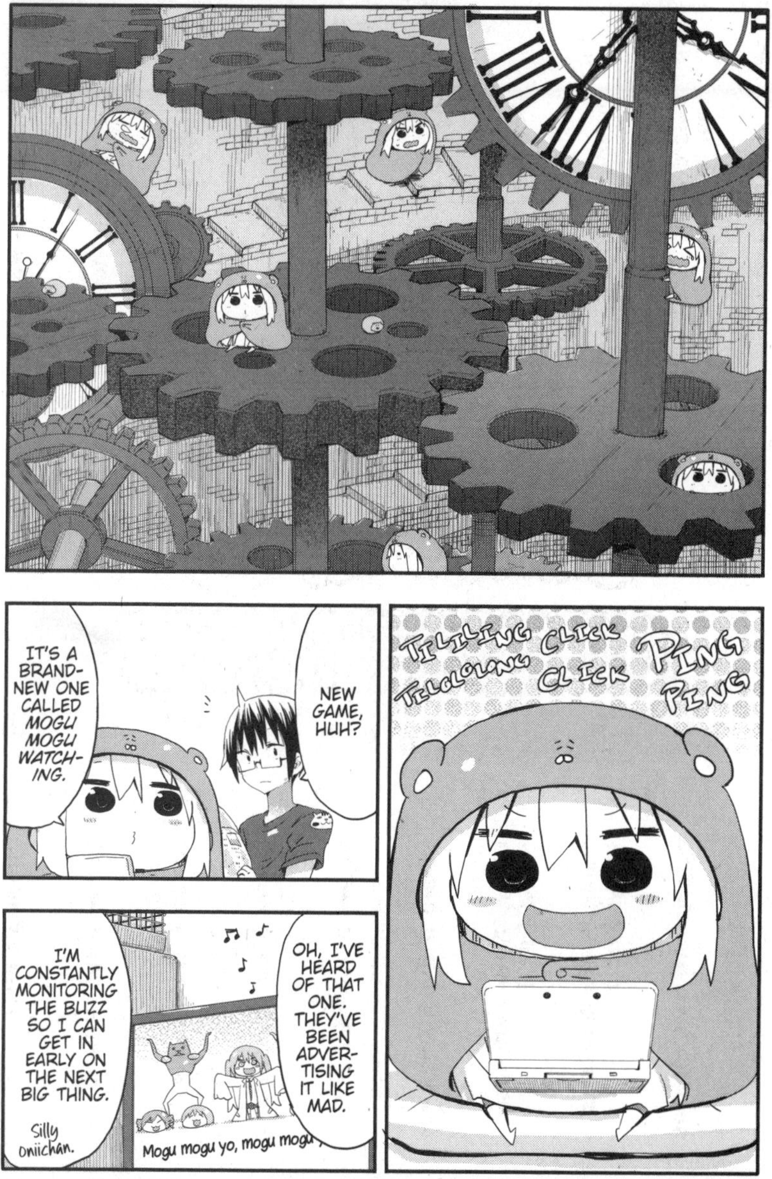
TILILING CLICK
TELOLOLONG CLICK
PING PING
NEW GAME, HUH?
IT'S A BRAND-NEW ONE CALLED MOGU MOGU WATCHING.
OH, I'VE HEARD OF THAT ONE. THEY'VE BEEN ADVERTISING IT LIKE MAD.
Mogu mogu yo, mogu mogu
I'M CONSTANTLY MONITORING THE BUZZ SO I CAN GET IN EARLY ON THE NEXT BIG THING.
Silly oniichan.

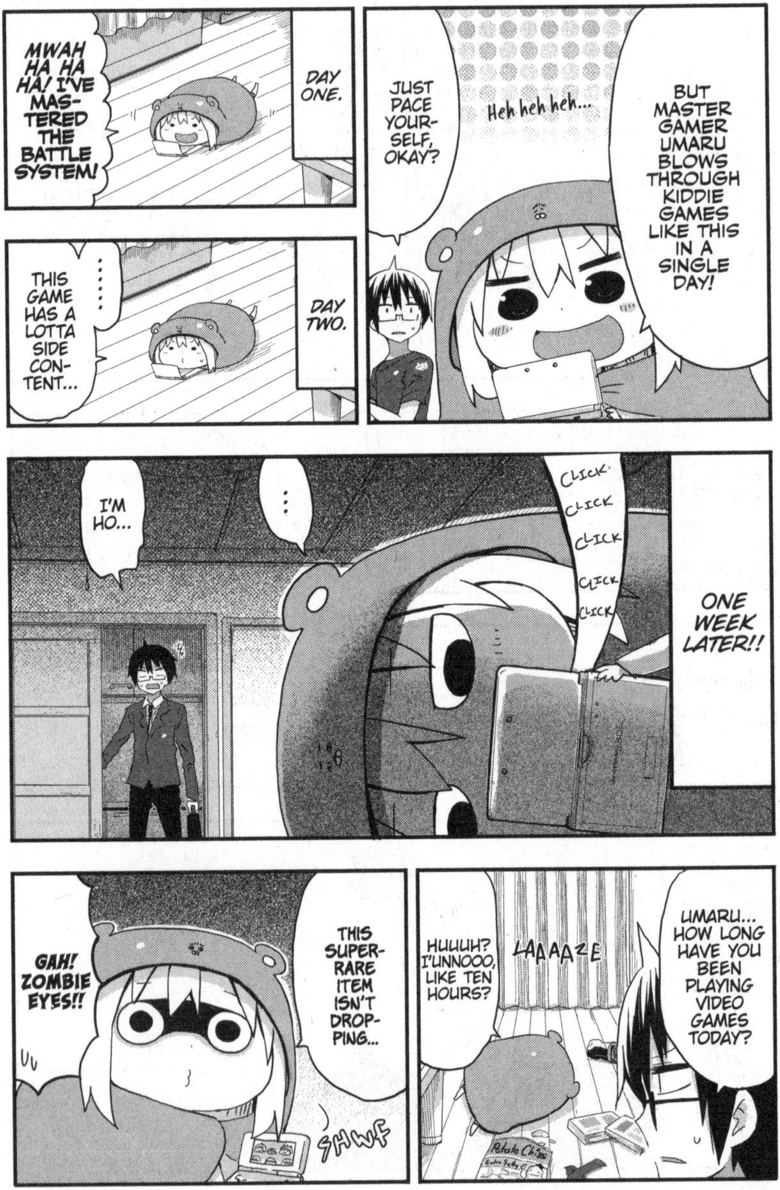
BUT MASTER GAMER UMARU BLOWS THROUGH KIDDIE GAMES LIKE THIS IN A SINGLE DAY!
Heh heh heh...
JUST PACE YOUR-SELF, OKAY?
DAY ONE.
MWAH HA HA HA! I'VE MAS-TERED THE BATTLE SYSTEM!
DAY TWO.
......
THIS GAME HAS A LOTTA SIDE CON-TENT...
ONE WEEK LATER!!
CLICK
CLICK
CLICK
CLICK
CLICK
...
I'M HO...
UMARU... HOW LONG HAVE YOU BEEN PLAYING VIDEO GAMES TODAY?
LAAAAZE
HUUUH? I'UNNOOO, LIKE TEN HOURS?
THIS SUPER-RARE ITEM ISN'T DROP-PING...
GAH! ZOMBIE EYES!!
SHWF

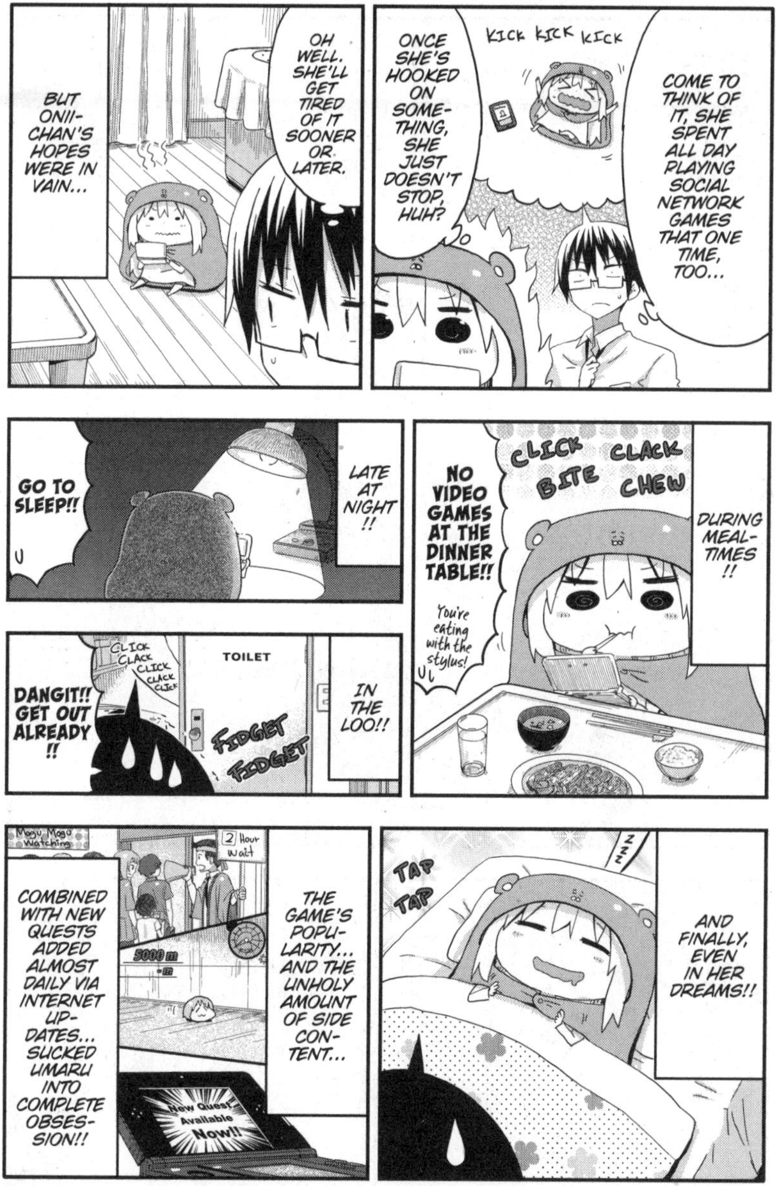
COME TO THINK OF IT, SHE SPENT ALL DAY PLAYING SOCIAL NETWORK GAMES THAT ONE TIME, TOO...
KICK KICK KICK
ONCE SHE'S HOOKED ON SOMETHING, SHE JUST DOESN'T STOP, HUH?
OH WELL. SHE'LL GET TIRED OF IT SOONER OR LATER.
BUT ONII-CHAN'S HOPES WERE IN VAIN...
DURING MEALTIMES!!
CLICK CLACK
BITE CHEW
NO VIDEO GAMES AT THE DINNER TABLE!!
You're eating with the stylus!
LATE AT NIGHT!!
GO TO SLEEP!!
IN THE LOO!!
TOILET
CLICK CLACK CLICK CLACK CLICK
FIDGET FIDGET
DANGIT!! GET OUT ALREADY!!
AND FINALLY, EVEN IN HER DREAMS!!
ZZZ
TAP TAP
THE GAME'S POPULARITY... AND THE UNHOLY AMOUNT OF SIDE CONTENT...
2 Hour wait
Mogu Mogu Watching
5000
New Quest Available Now!!
COMBINED WITH NEW QUESTS ADDED ALMOST DAILY VIA INTERNET UPDATES... SUCKED UMARU INTO COMPLETE OBSESSION!!

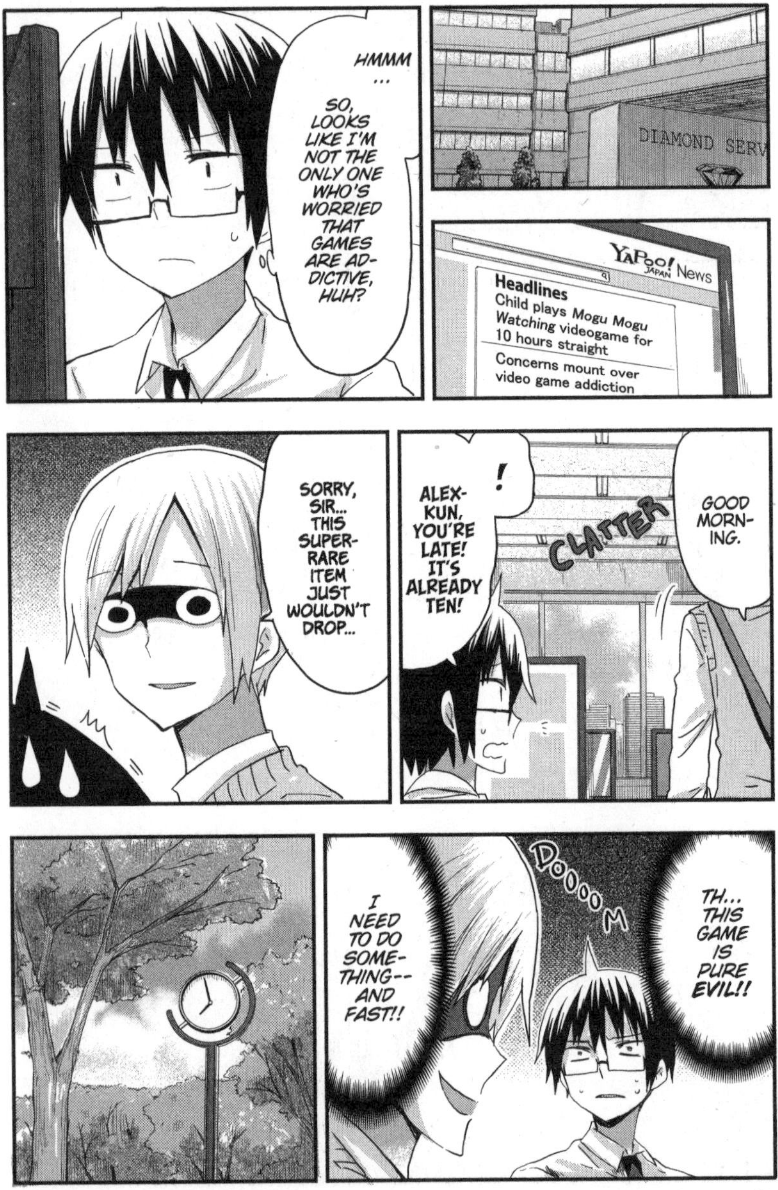
DIAMOND SERV
YAPOO! JAPAN News
Headlines
Child plays Mogu Mogu Watching videogame for 10 hours straight
Concerns mount over video game addiction
HMMM...
SO, LOOKS LIKE I'M NOT THE ONLY ONE WHO'S WORRIED THAT GAMES ARE ADDICTIVE, HUH?
GOOD MORNING.
CLATTER
!
ALEX-KUN, YOU'RE LATE! IT'S ALREADY TEN!
SORRY, SIR... THIS SUPER-RARE ITEM JUST WOULDN'T DROP...
TH... THIS GAME IS PURE EVIL!!
DOOOOOM
I NEED TO DO SOMETHING--AND FAST!!

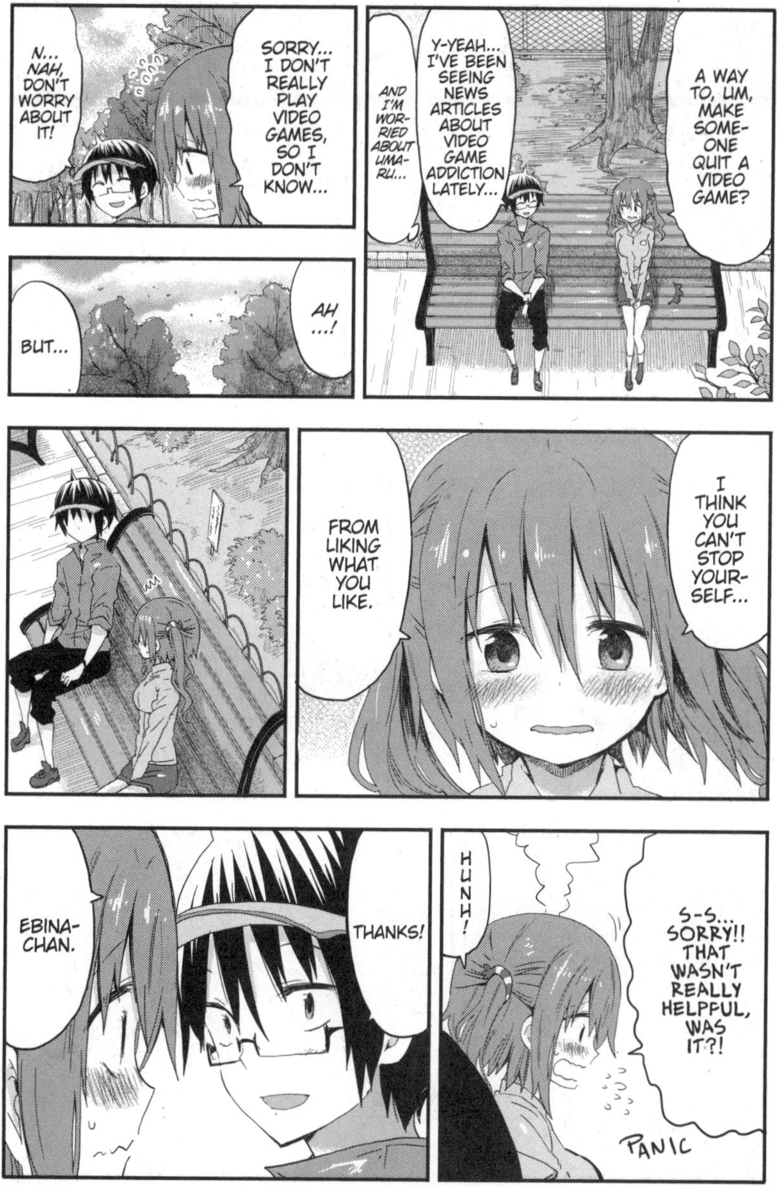
A WAY TO, UM, MAKE SOMEONE QUIT A VIDEO GAME?
Y-YEAH... I'VE BEEN SEEING NEWS ARTICLES ABOUT VIDEO GAME ADDICTION LATELY...
AND I'M WORRIED ABOUT UMARU...
SORRY... I DON'T REALLY PLAY VIDEO GAMES, SO I DON'T KNOW...
N... NAH, DON'T WORRY ABOUT IT!
AH ...!
BUT...
I THINK YOU CAN'T STOP YOURSELF...
FROM LIKING WHAT YOU LIKE.
HUNH!
S-S... SORRY!! THAT WASN'T REALLY HELPFUL, WAS IT?!
PANIC
THANKS!
EBINA-CHAN.

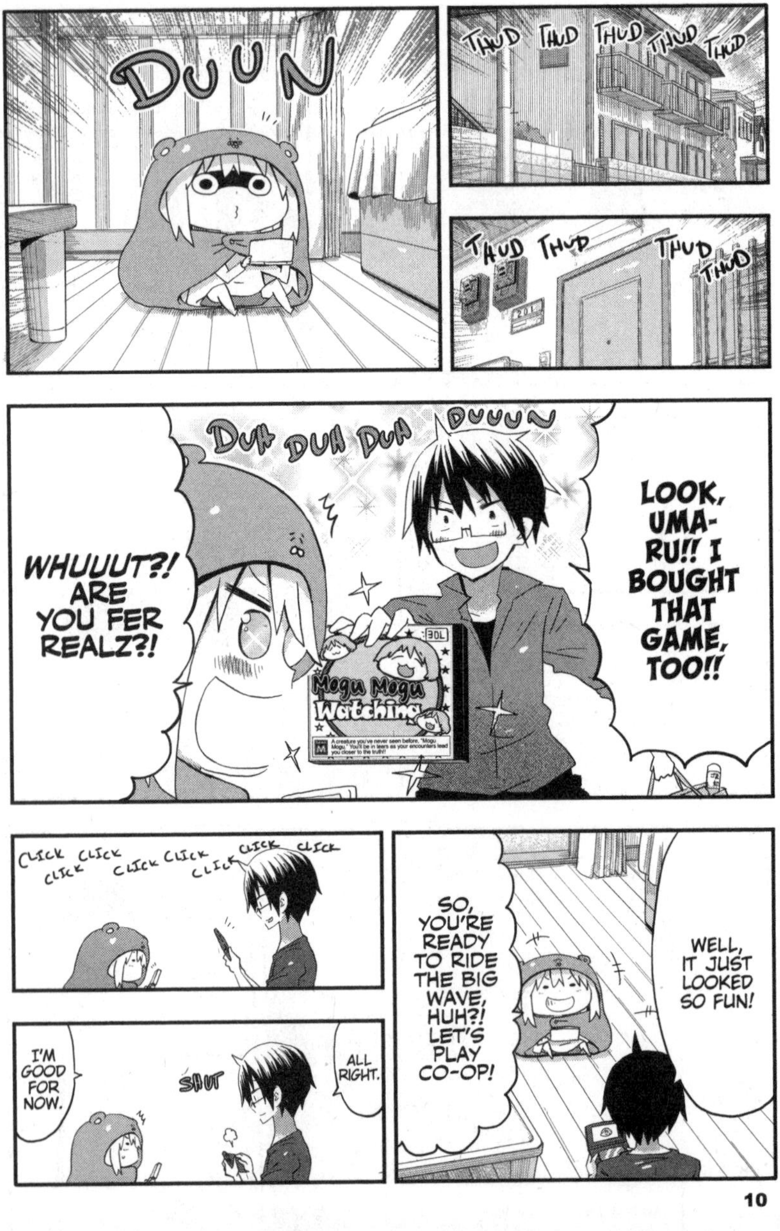
THUD THUD THUD THUD THUD
THUD THUD THUD THUD
DUUN
LOOK, UMA-RU!! I BOUGHT THAT GAME, TOO!!
DUUUN
DUH DUH DUH
3DL
Mogu Mogu Watching
A creature you've never seen before, "Mogu Mogu." You'll be in tears as your encounters lead you closer to the truth!!
WHUUUT?! ARE YOU FER REALZ?!
WELL, IT JUST LOOKED SO FUN!
SO, YOU'RE READY TO RIDE THE BIG WAVE, HUH?! LET'S PLAY CO-OP!
CLICK CLICK CLICK CLICK CLICK CLICK CLICK CLICK
ALL RIGHT.
SHUT
I'M GOOD FOR NOW.

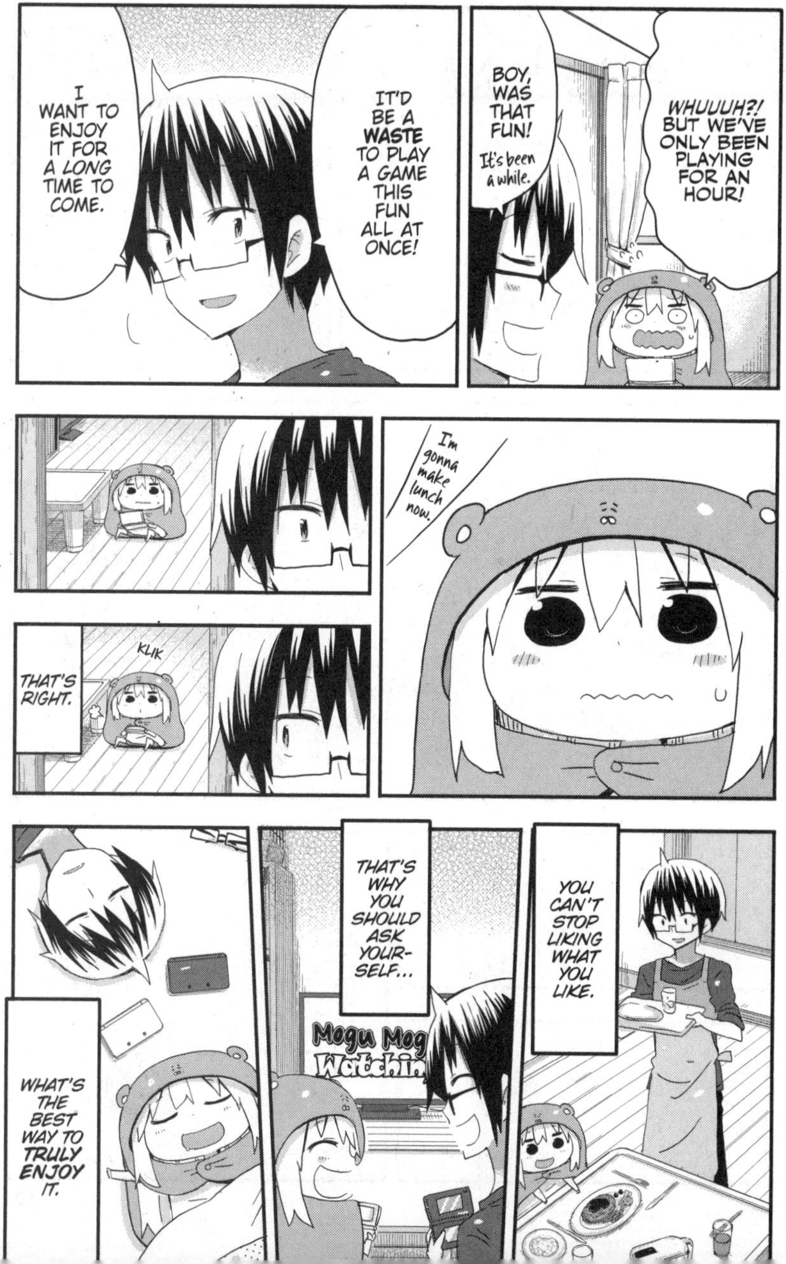
BOY, WAS THAT FUN!
It's been a while.
WHUUUH?! BUT WE'VE ONLY BEEN PLAYING FOR AN HOUR!
IT'D BE A WASTE TO PLAY A GAME THIS FUN ALL AT ONCE!
I WANT TO ENJOY IT FOR A LONG TIME TO COME.
I'm gonna make lunch now.
KLIK
THAT'S RIGHT.
YOU CAN'T STOP LIKING WHAT YOU LIKE.
THAT'S WHY YOU SHOULD ASK YOURSELF...
Mogu Mog
Watchin
WHAT'S THE BEST WAY TO TRULY ENJOY IT.

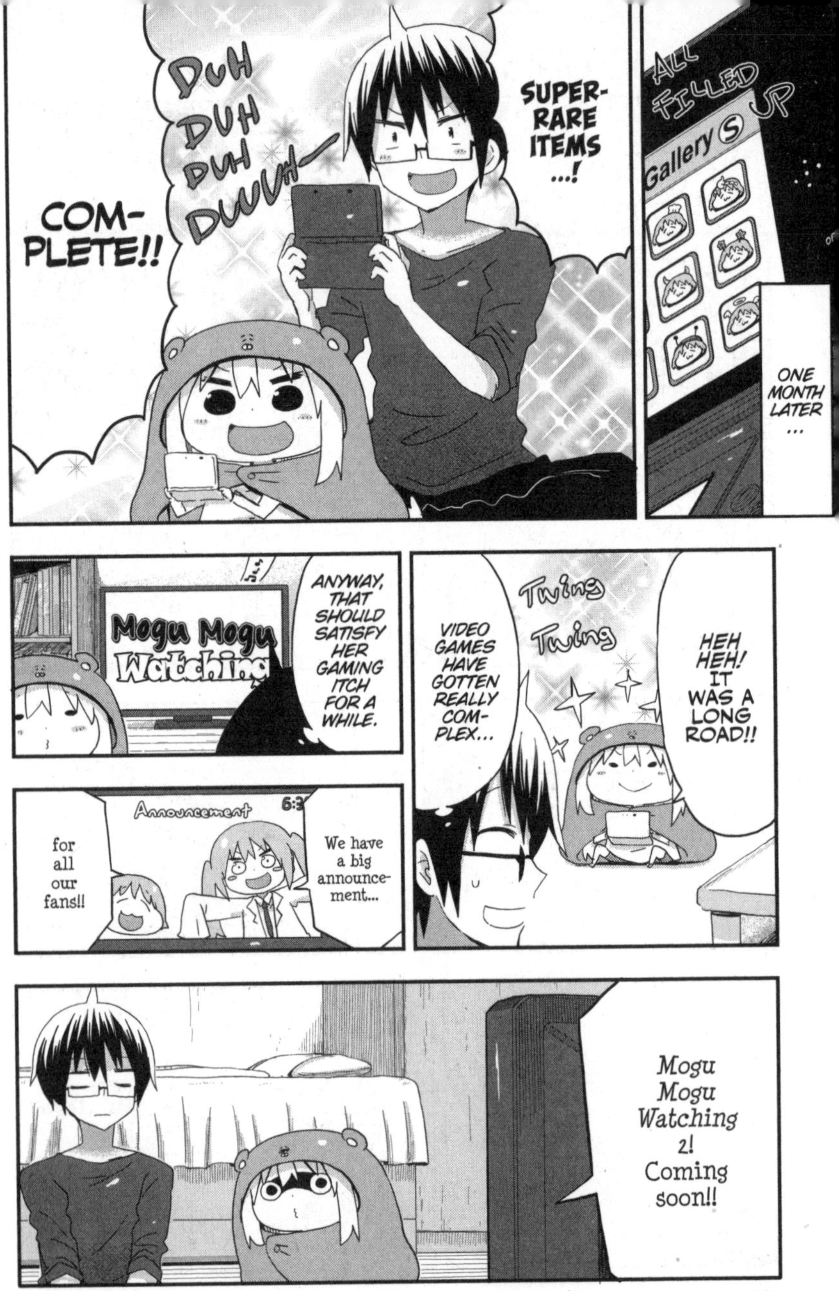

ALL FILLED UP
Gallery S
ONE MONTH LATER...
SUPER-RARE ITEMS...!
DUH DUH DUH DUUUH—
COMPLETE!!
HEH HEH! IT WAS A LONG ROAD!!
Twing Twing
VIDEO GAMES HAVE GOTTEN REALLY COMPLEX...
ANYWAY, THAT SHOULD SATISFY HER GAMING ITCH FOR A WHILE.
Mogu Mogu Watching
Announcement
We have a big announcement...
for all our fans!!
Mogu Mogu Watching 2! Coming soon!!

No. 73 **Umaru & the Hot Day**

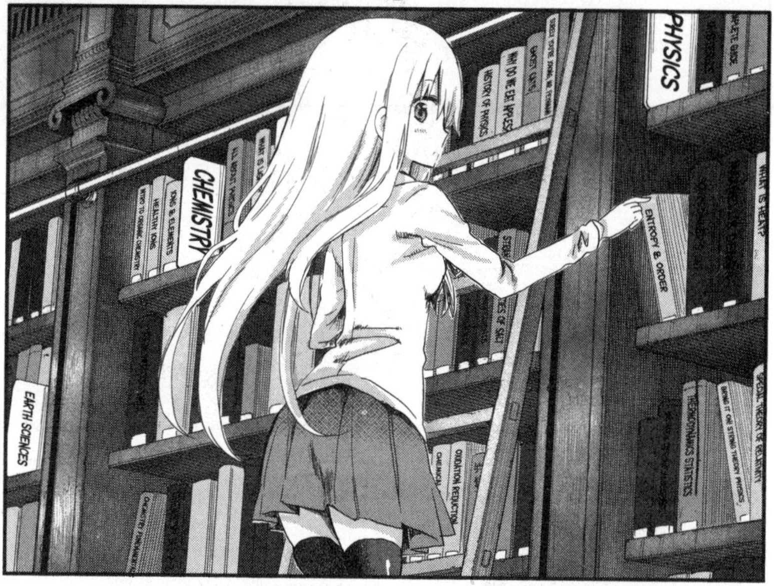
PHYSICS
HISTORY OF PHYSICS
CHEMISTRY
INTRO TO ORGANIC CHEMISTRY
HEALTHY IONS
IONS & ELEMENTS
ENTROPY & ORDER
WHAT IS HEAT?
EARTH SCIENCES
OXIDATION REDUCTION
THERMODYNAMICS STATISTICS
SPECIAL THEORY OF RELATIVITY

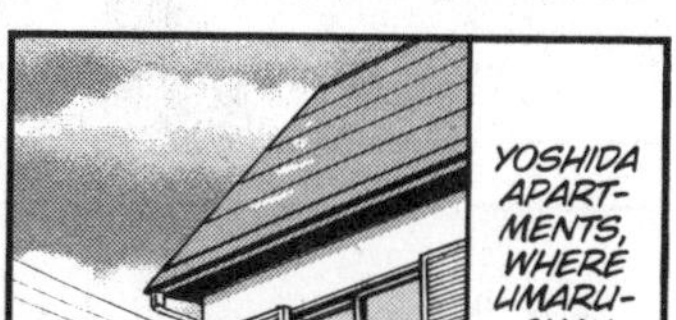
YOSHIDA APARTMENTS, WHERE UMARU-CHAN LIVES.

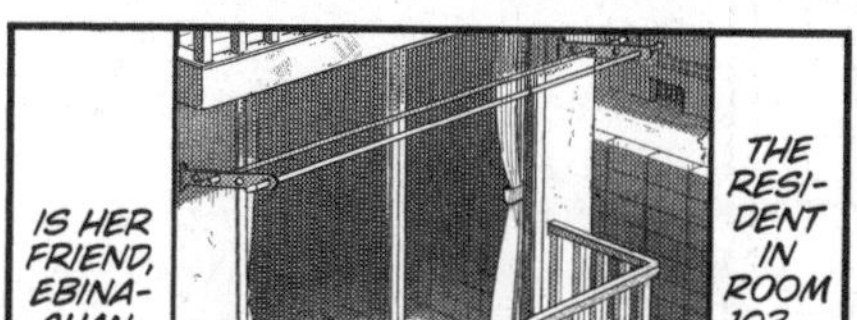
THE RESIDENT IN ROOM 103...
IS HER FRIEND, EBINA-CHAN.

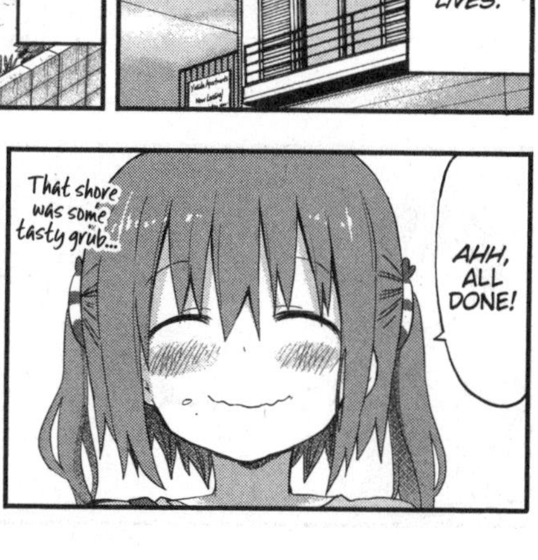
AHH, ALL DONE!
That shore was some tasty grub...

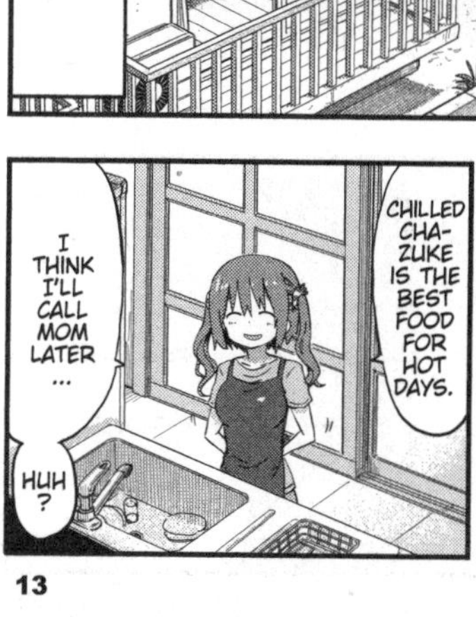
CHILLED CHAZUKE IS THE BEST FOOD FOR HOT DAYS.
I THINK I'LL CALL MOM LATER...
HUH?

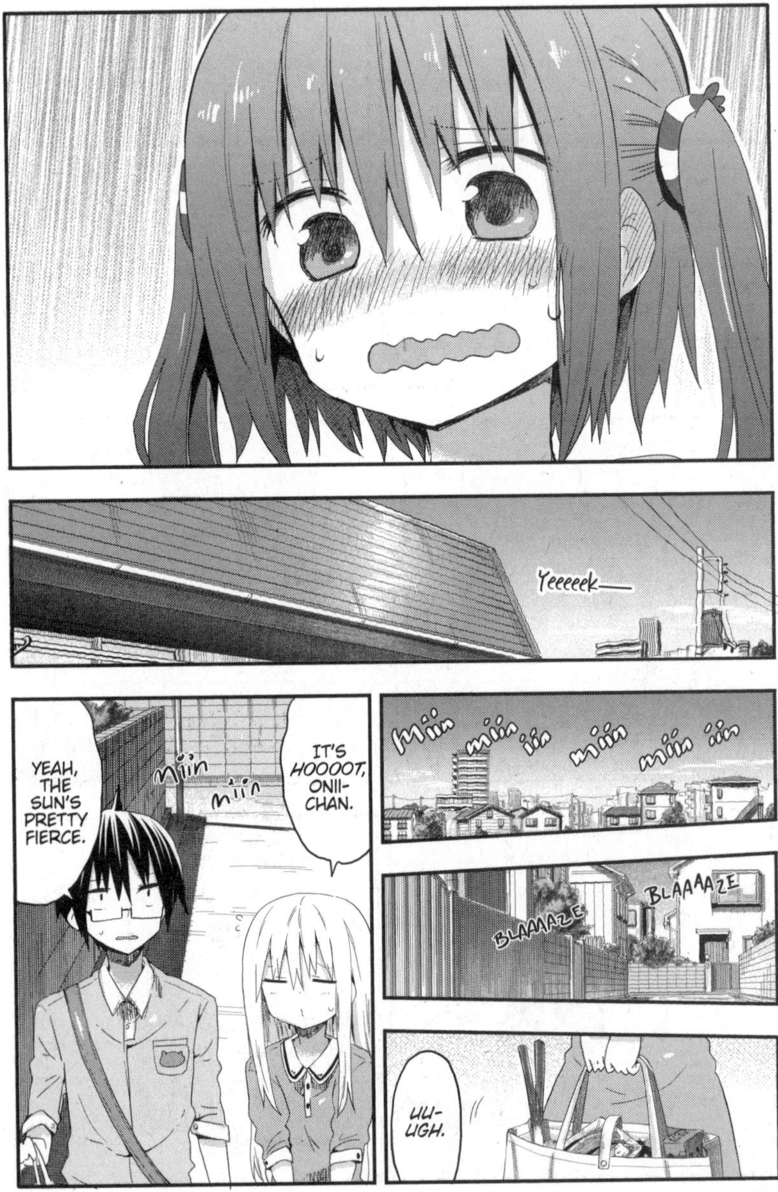
Yeeeeek—
Miin miin iin miin miin iin
BLAAAAZE
BLAAAAZE
UU-UGH.
IT'S HOOOOT, ONII-CHAN.
YEAH, THE SUN'S PRETTY FIERCE.
miin miin

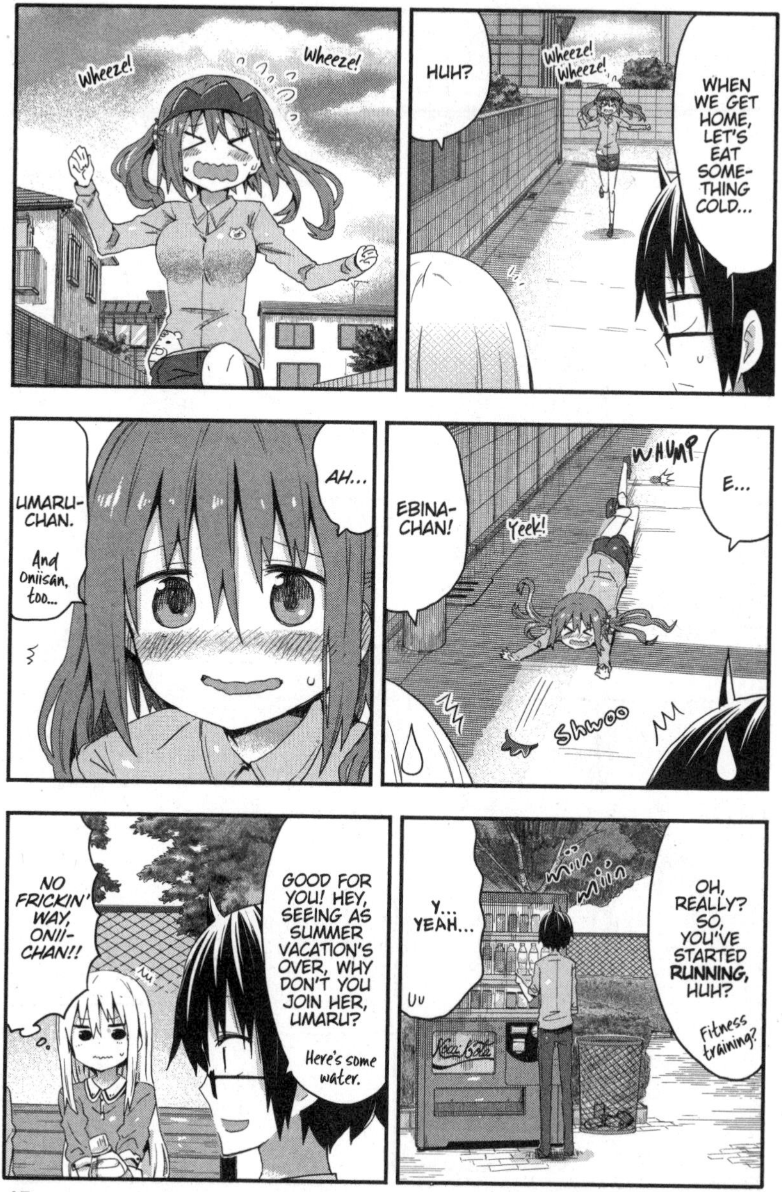
WHEN WE GET HOME, LET'S EAT SOMETHING COLD...
Wheeze! Wheeze!
HUH?
Wheeze!
Wheeze!
E...
WHUMP
EBINA-CHAN!
Yeek!
Shwoo
AH...
UMARU-CHAN.
And oniisan, too...
OH, REALLY? SO, YOU'VE STARTED **RUNNING**, HUH?
Fitness training?
miin miin
Y... YEAH...
GOOD FOR YOU! HEY, SEEING AS SUMMER VACATION'S OVER, WHY DON'T YOU JOIN HER, UMARU?
Here's some water.
NO FRICKIN' WAY, ONII-CHAN!!

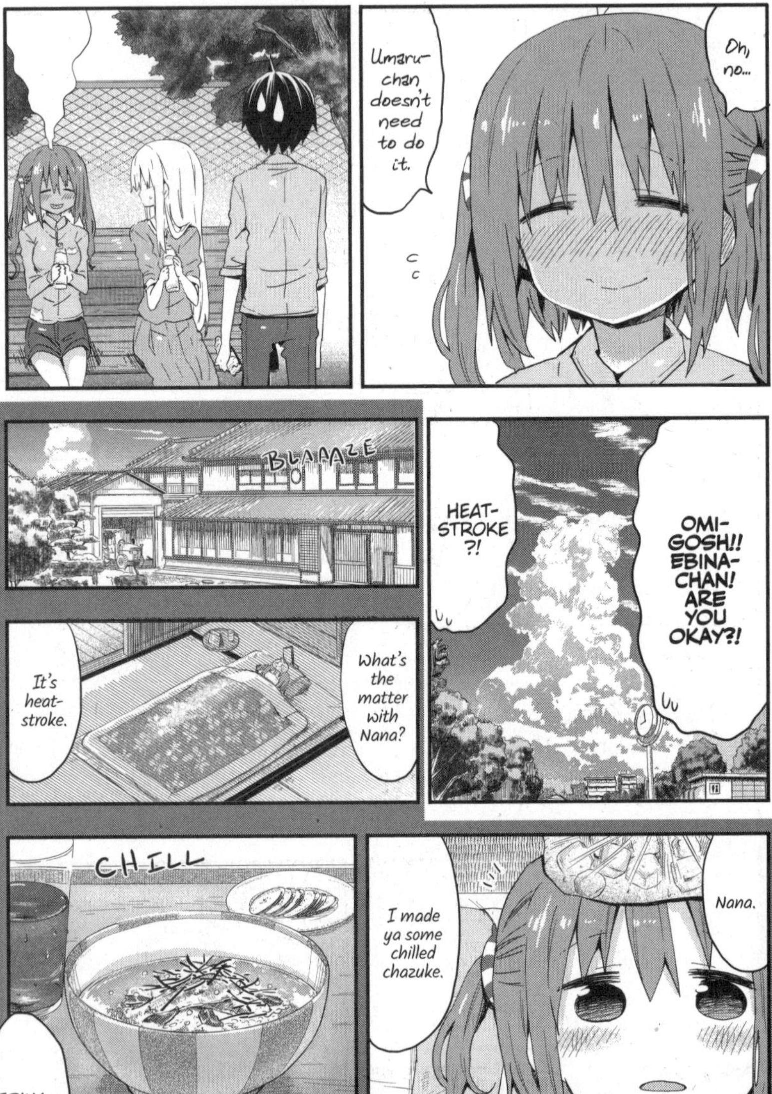

Oh, no...
Umaru-chan doesn't need to do it.
OMIGOSH!! EBINA-CHAN! ARE YOU OKAY?!
HEAT-STROKE?!
BLAAAZE
What's the matter with Nana?
It's heat-stroke.
Nana.
I made ya some chilled chazuke.
CHILL
EBINA-CHAN.

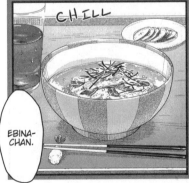

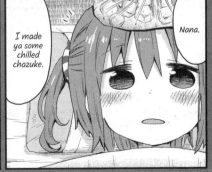

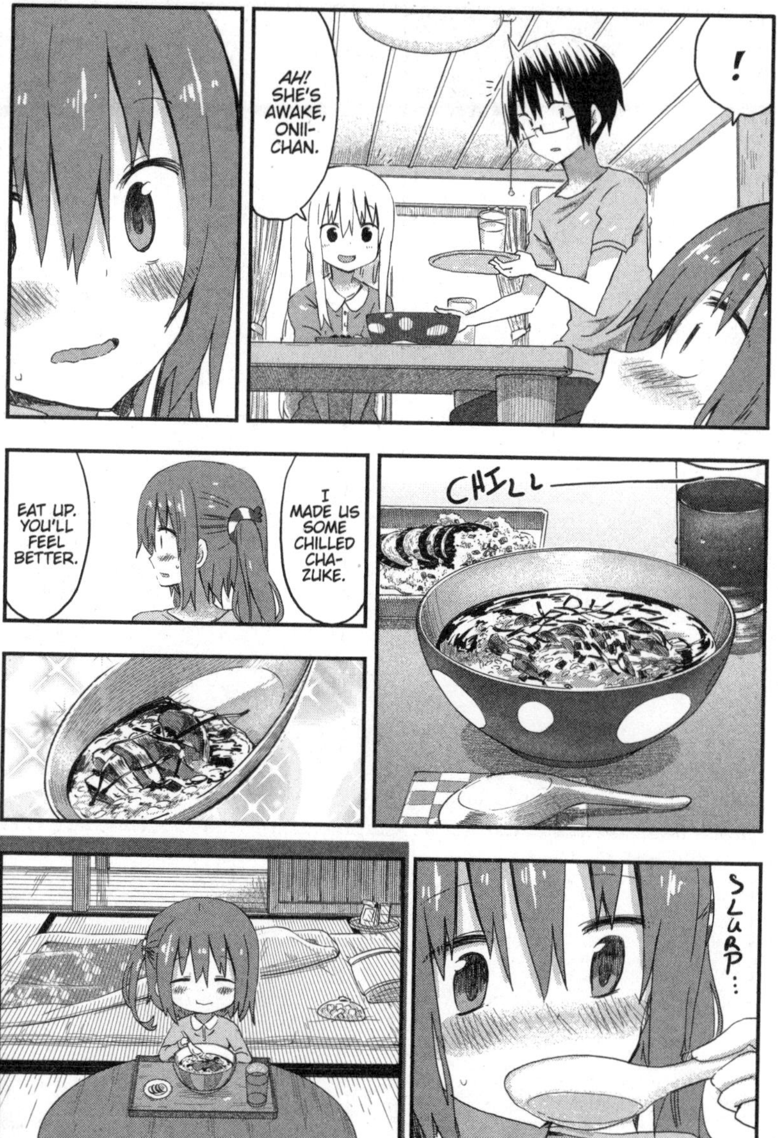
!
AH! SHE'S AWAKE, ONII-CHAN.
CHILL
I MADE US SOME CHILLED CHA-ZUKE.
EAT UP. YOU'LL FEEL BETTER.
SLURP...

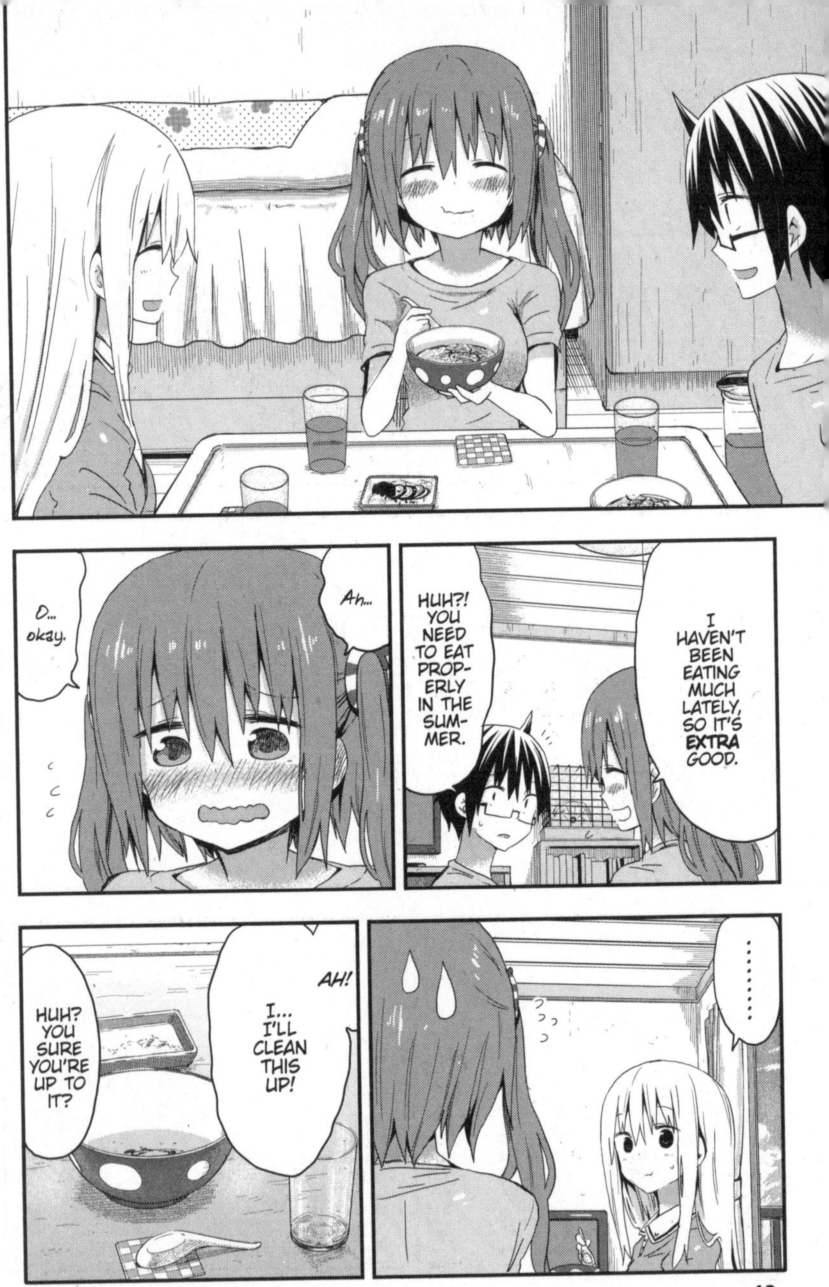
I HAVEN'T BEEN EATING MUCH LATELY, SO IT'S **EXTRA** GOOD.
HUH?! YOU NEED TO EAT PROPERLY IN THE SUMMER.
Ah...
O... okay.
....
AH!
I... I'LL CLEAN THIS UP!
HUH? YOU SURE YOU'RE UP TO IT?

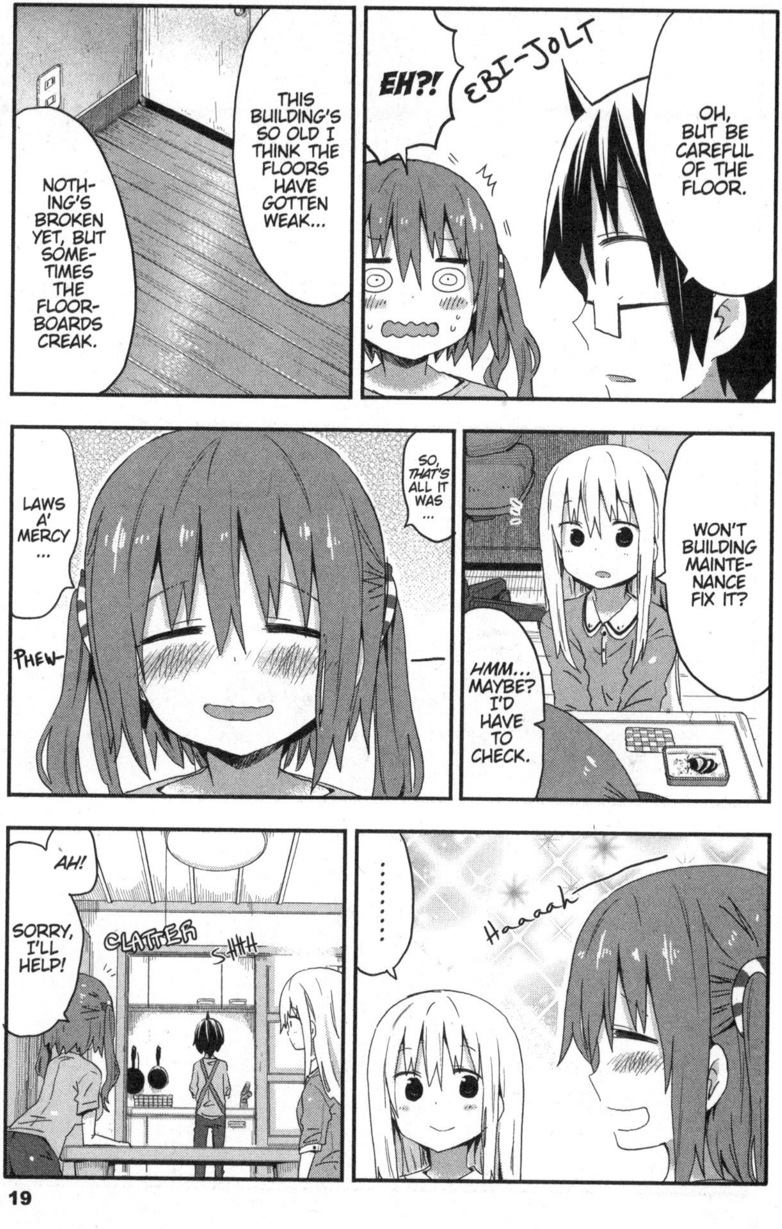
OH, BUT BE CAREFUL OF THE FLOOR.
EBI-JOLT
EH?!
THIS BUILDING'S SO OLD I THINK THE FLOORS HAVE GOTTEN WEAK...
NOTHING'S BROKEN YET, BUT SOMETIMES THE FLOORBOARDS CREAK.
WON'T BUILDING MAINTENANCE FIX IT?
HMM... MAYBE? I'D HAVE TO CHECK.
SO, THAT'S ALL IT WAS...
LAWS A' MERCY...
PHEW—
Haaaah—
......
AH!
CLATTER
SORRY, I'LL HELP!

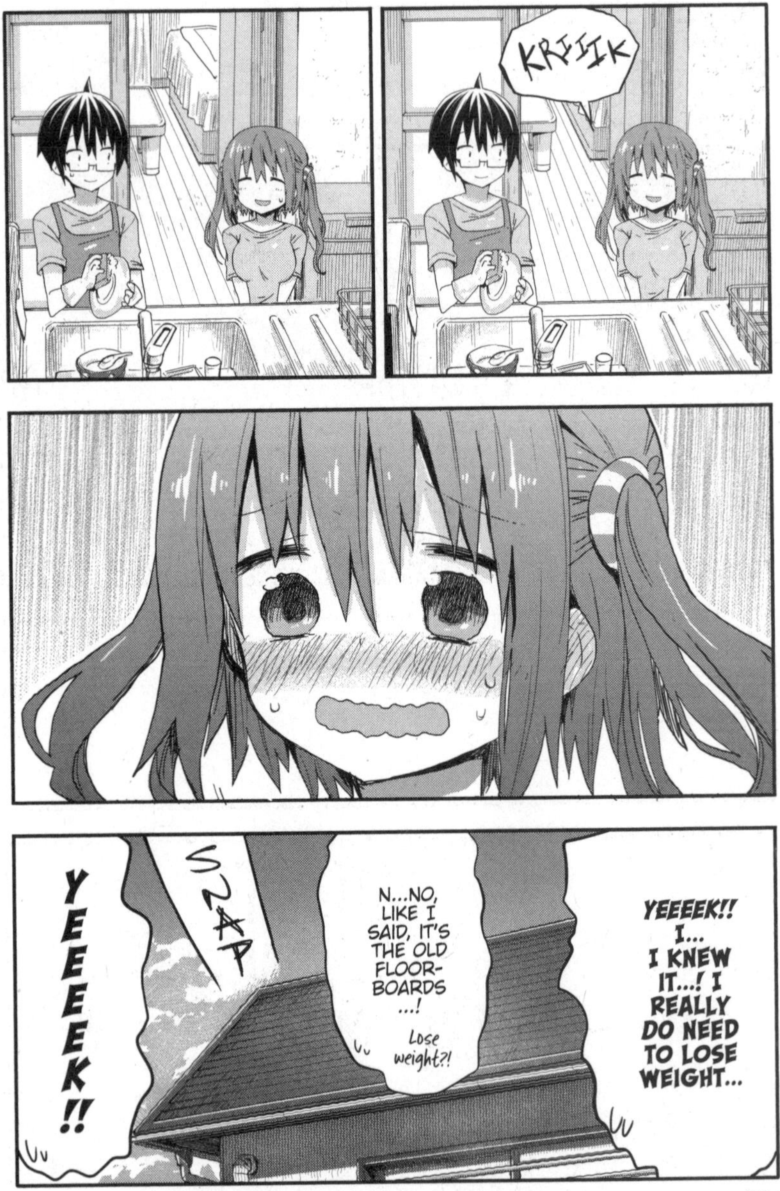
KRIIIK
YEEEEK!! I... I KNEW IT...! I REALLY DO NEED TO LOSE WEIGHT...
N...NO, LIKE I SAID, IT'S THE OLD FLOOR-BOARDS ...!
Lose weight?!
SNAP
YEEEEEK!!

No. 74 Umaru & Earpicks

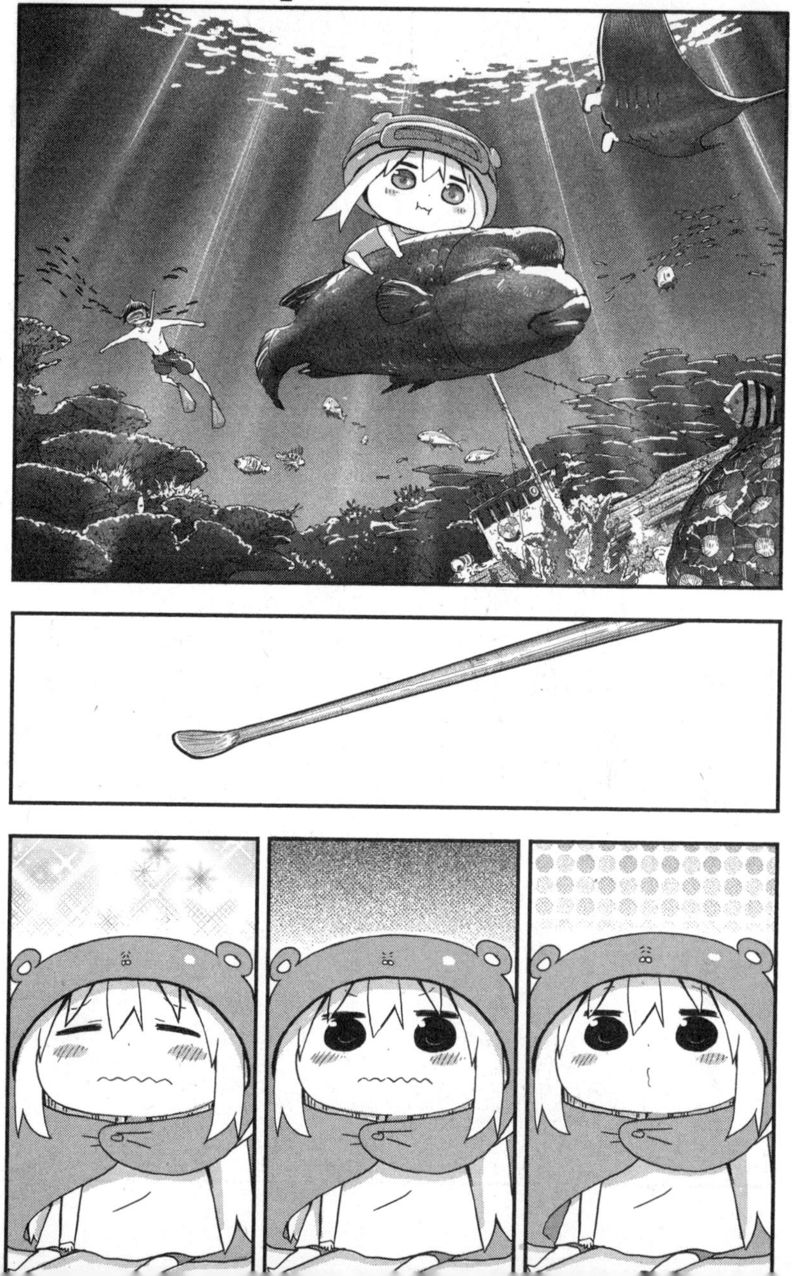

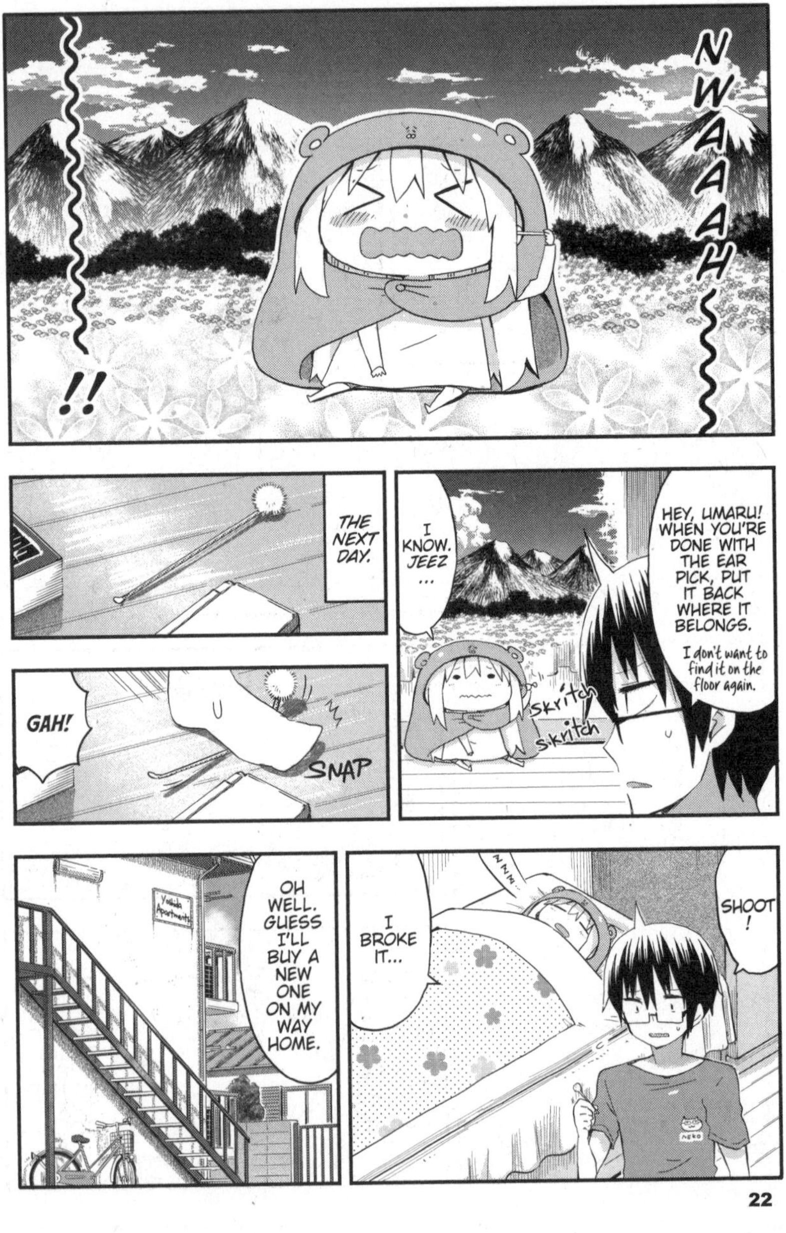

NWAAAAH~~~~
~~~~!!
HEY, UMARU! WHEN YOU'RE DONE WITH THE EAR PICK, PUT IT BACK WHERE IT BELONGS.
I don't want to find it on the floor again.
I KNOW. JEEZ...
Skritch
skritch
THE NEXT DAY.
GAH!
SNAP
SHOOT!
I BROKE IT...
OH WELL. GUESS I'LL BUY A NEW ONE ON MY WAY HOME.
Yoshida Apartments
~~~~

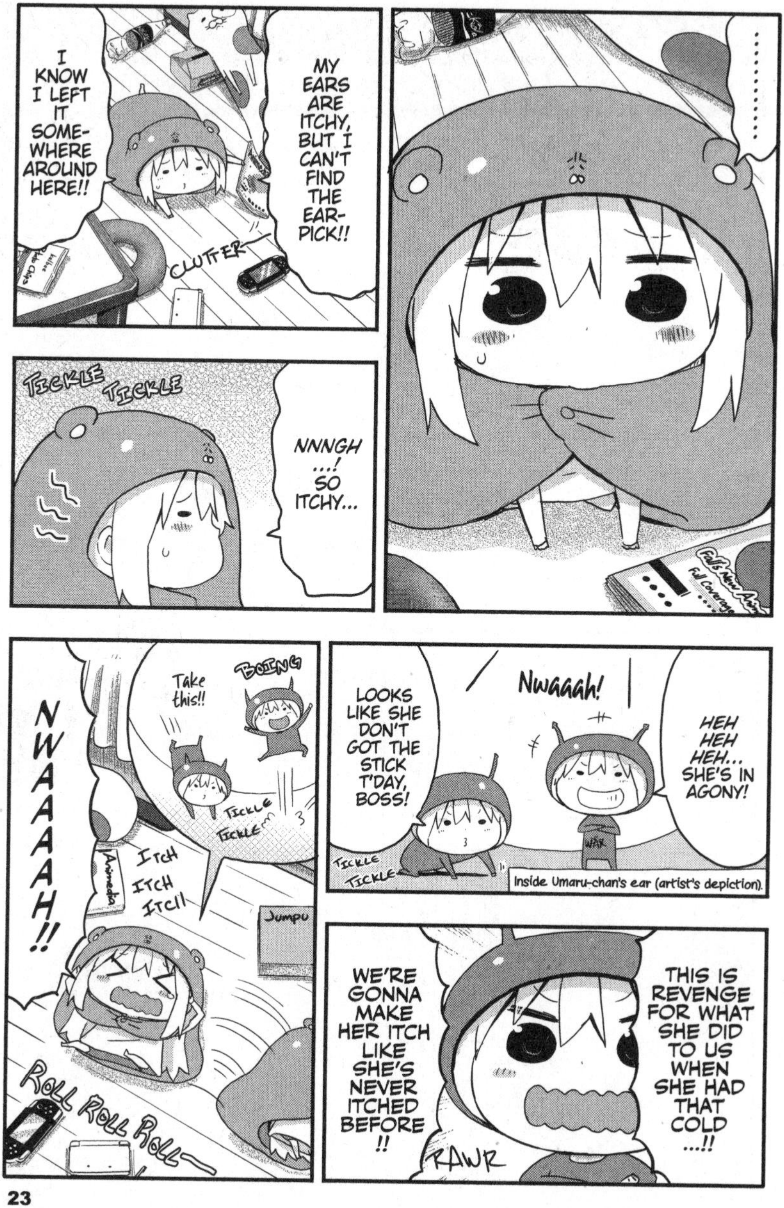
......
Fall's New Anime
Full Coverage
MY EARS ARE ITCHY, BUT I CAN'T FIND THE EAR-PICK!!
I KNOW I LEFT IT SOME-WHERE AROUND HERE!!
CLUTTER
TICKLE TICKLE
NNNGH ...! SO ITCHY...
Nwaaah!
HEH HEH HEH... SHE'S IN AGONY!
LOOKS LIKE SHE DON'T GOT THE STICK T'DAY, BOSS!
WAR
TICKLE TICKLE
Inside Umaru-chan's ear (artist's depiction).
THIS IS REVENGE FOR WHAT SHE DID TO US WHEN SHE HAD THAT COLD ...!!
WE'RE GONNA MAKE HER ITCH LIKE SHE'S NEVER ITCHED BEFORE !!
RAWR
NWAAAAAH!!
Take this!!
BOING
TICKLE TICKLE
ITCH ITCH ITCH
Animedia
Jumpu
ROLL ROLL ROLL

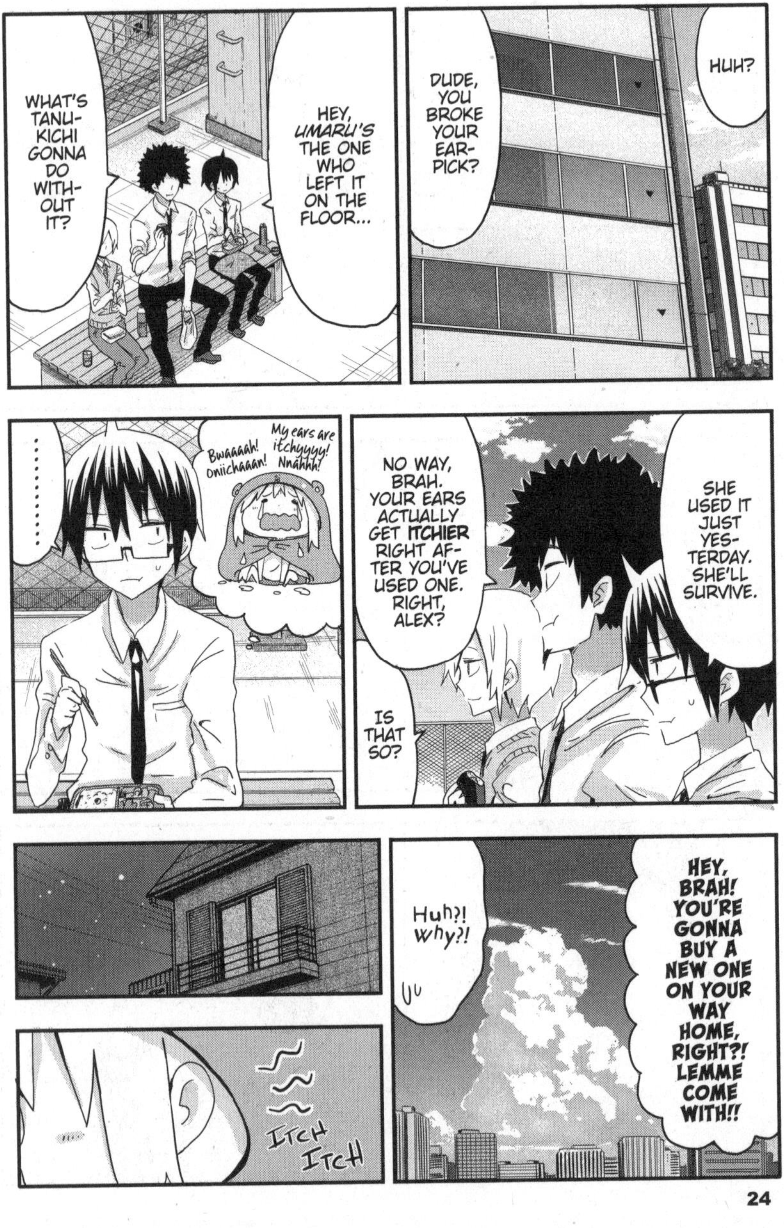
HUH?
DUDE, YOU BROKE YOUR EAR-PICK?
HEY, UMARU'S THE ONE WHO LEFT IT ON THE FLOOR...
WHAT'S TANUKICHI GONNA DO WITHOUT IT?
SHE USED IT JUST YESTERDAY. SHE'LL SURVIVE.
NO WAY, BRAH. YOUR EARS ACTUALLY GET ITCHIER RIGHT AFTER YOU'VE USED ONE. RIGHT, ALEX?
IS THAT SO?
......
My ears are itchyyyy! Nnahhh!
Bwaaaah! Oniichaaan!
HEY, BRAH! YOU'RE GONNA BUY A NEW ONE ON YOUR WAY HOME, RIGHT?! LEMME COME WITH!!
Huh?! why?!
ITCH ITCH

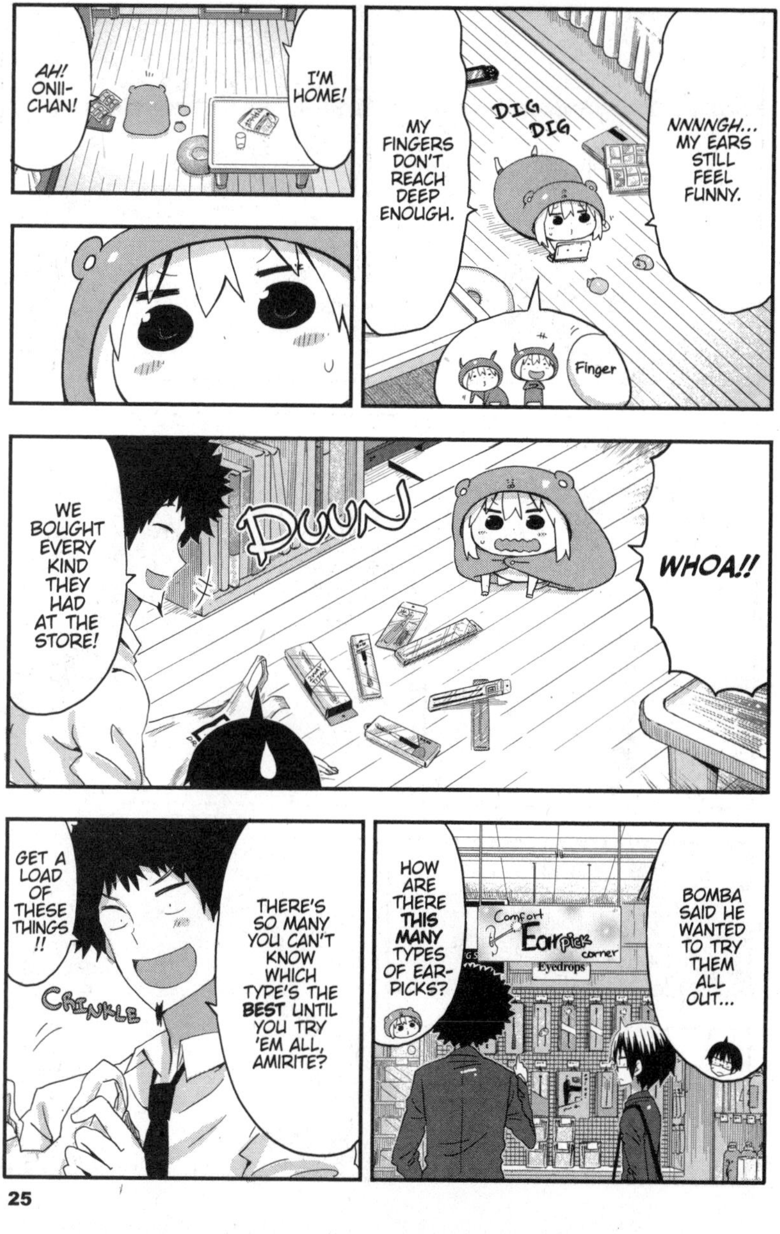
NNNNGH... MY EARS STILL FEEL FUNNY.
DIG DIG
MY FINGERS DON'T REACH DEEP ENOUGH.
Finger
I'M HOME!
AH! ONII-CHAN!
WHOA!!
DUUN
WE BOUGHT EVERY KIND THEY HAD AT THE STORE!
BOMBA SAID HE WANTED TO TRY THEM ALL OUT...
HOW ARE THERE THIS MANY TYPES OF EAR-PICKS?
Comfort Earpick corner
Eyedrops
THERE'S SO MANY YOU CAN'T KNOW WHICH TYPE'S THE BEST UNTIL YOU TRY 'EM ALL, AMIRITE?
GET A LOAD OF THESE THINGS!!
CRINKLE

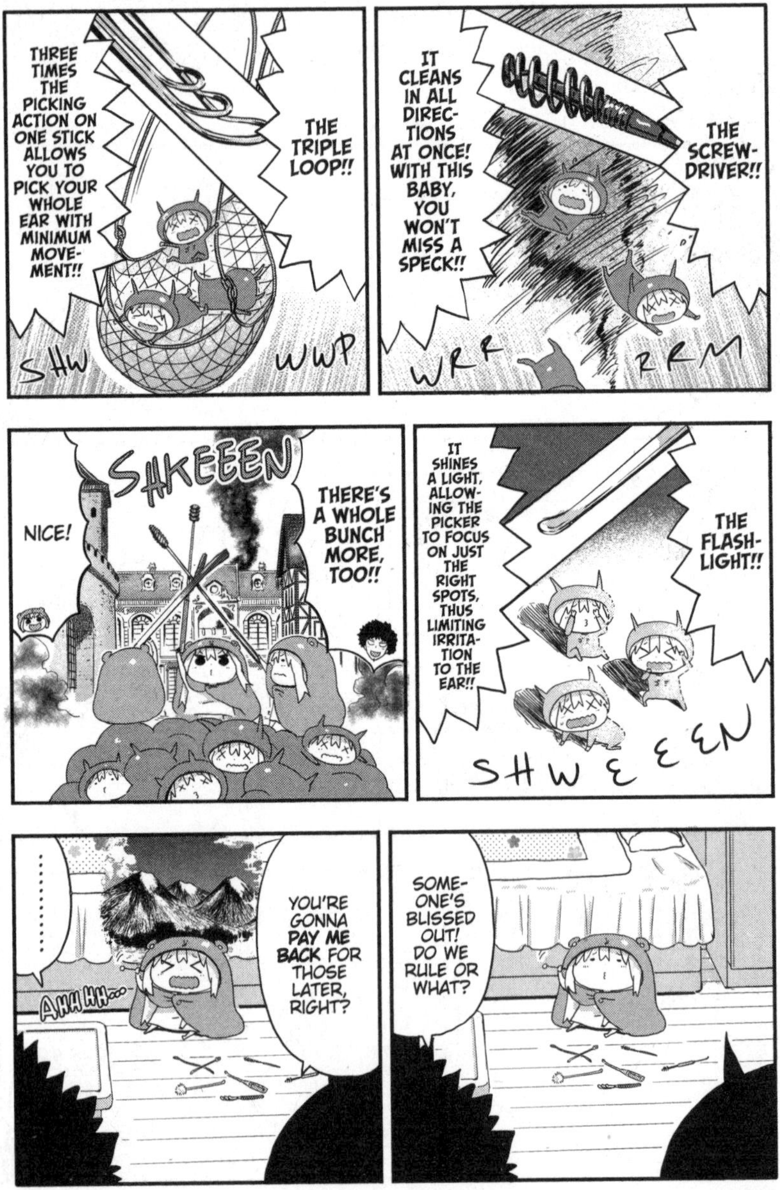
THE SCREW-DRIVER!!
IT CLEANS IN ALL DIREC-TIONS AT ONCE! WITH THIS BABY, YOU WON'T MISS A SPECK!!
WRR RRM
THE TRIPLE LOOP!!
THREE TIMES THE PICKING ACTION ON ONE STICK ALLOWS YOU TO PICK YOUR WHOLE EAR WITH MINIMUM MOVE-MENT!!
SHW WWP
THE FLASH-LIGHT!!
IT SHINES A LIGHT, ALLOW-ING THE PICKER TO FOCUS ON JUST THE RIGHT SPOTS, THUS LIMITING IRRITA-TION TO THE EAR!!
SHWEEEN
THERE'S A WHOLE BUNCH MORE, TOO!!
SHKEEEN
NICE!
SOME-ONE'S BLISSED OUT! DO WE RULE OR WHAT?
YOU'RE GONNA PAY ME BACK FOR THOSE LATER, RIGHT?
......
AHHHH...

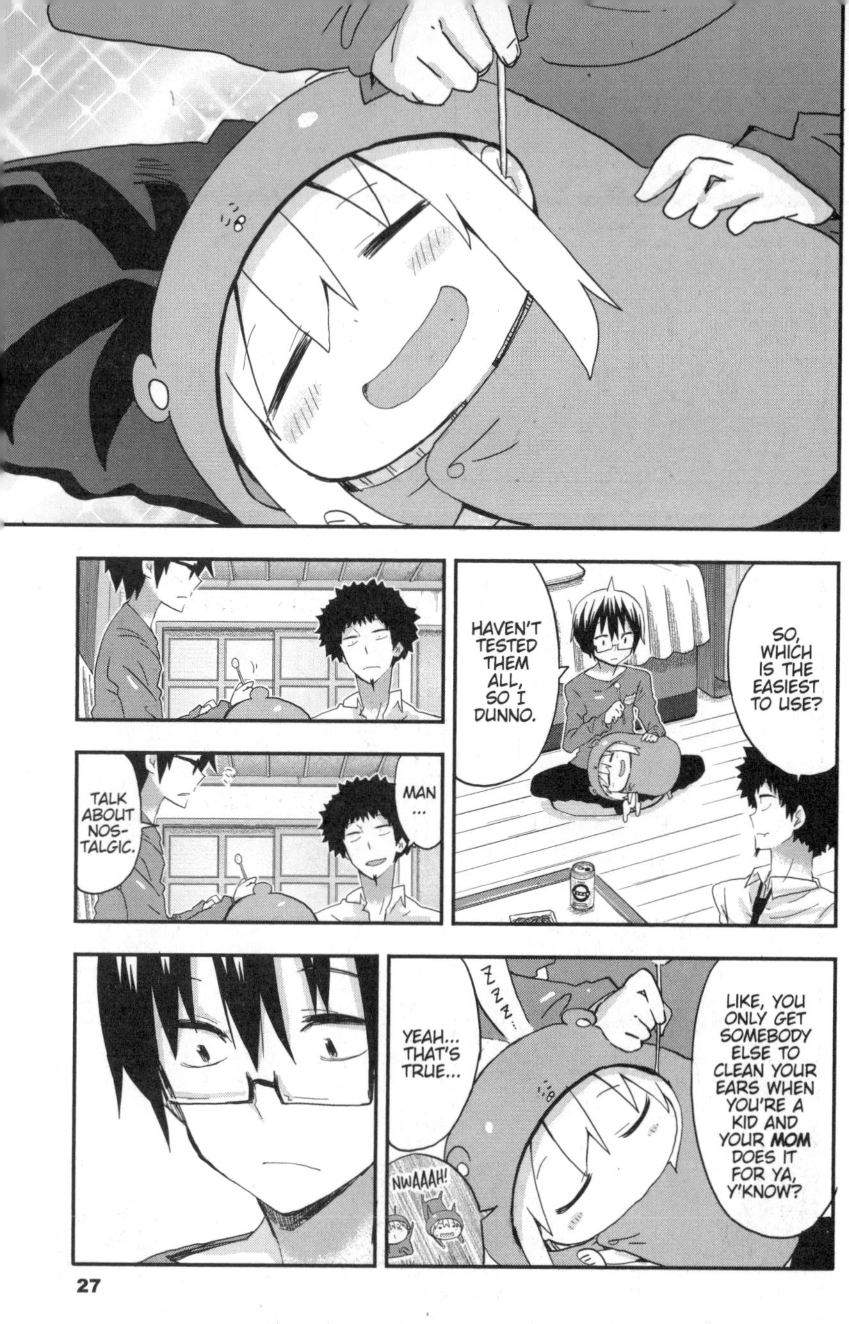
SO, WHICH IS THE EASIEST TO USE?
HAVEN'T TESTED THEM ALL, SO I DUNNO.
MAN...
TALK ABOUT NOS-TALGIC.
LIKE, YOU ONLY GET SOMEBODY ELSE TO CLEAN YOUR EARS WHEN YOU'RE A KID AND YOUR **MOM** DOES IT FOR YA, Y'KNOW?
ZZZ...
YEAH... THAT'S TRUE...
NWAAAH!

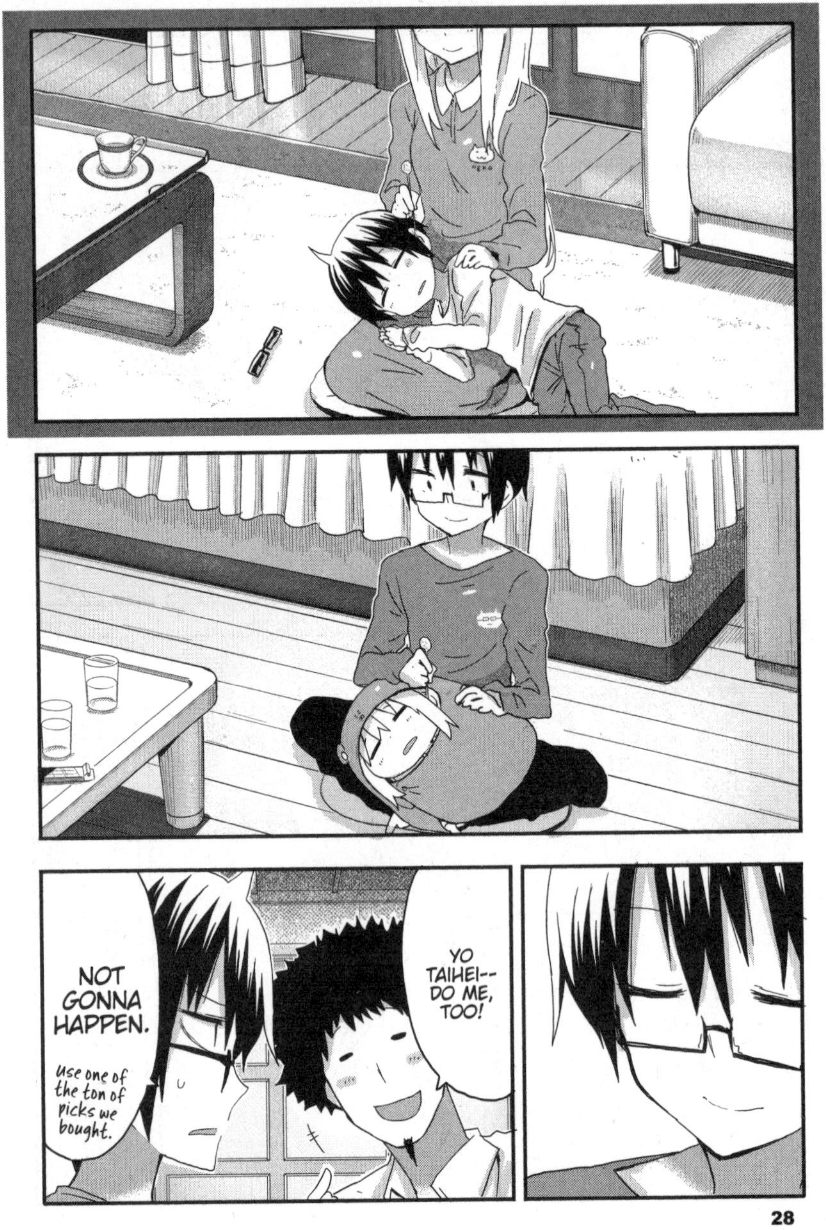
YO TAIHEI-- DO ME, TOO!
NOT GONNA HAPPEN.
Use one of the ton of picks we bought.

No. 75 **Umaru & the Dating Sim**

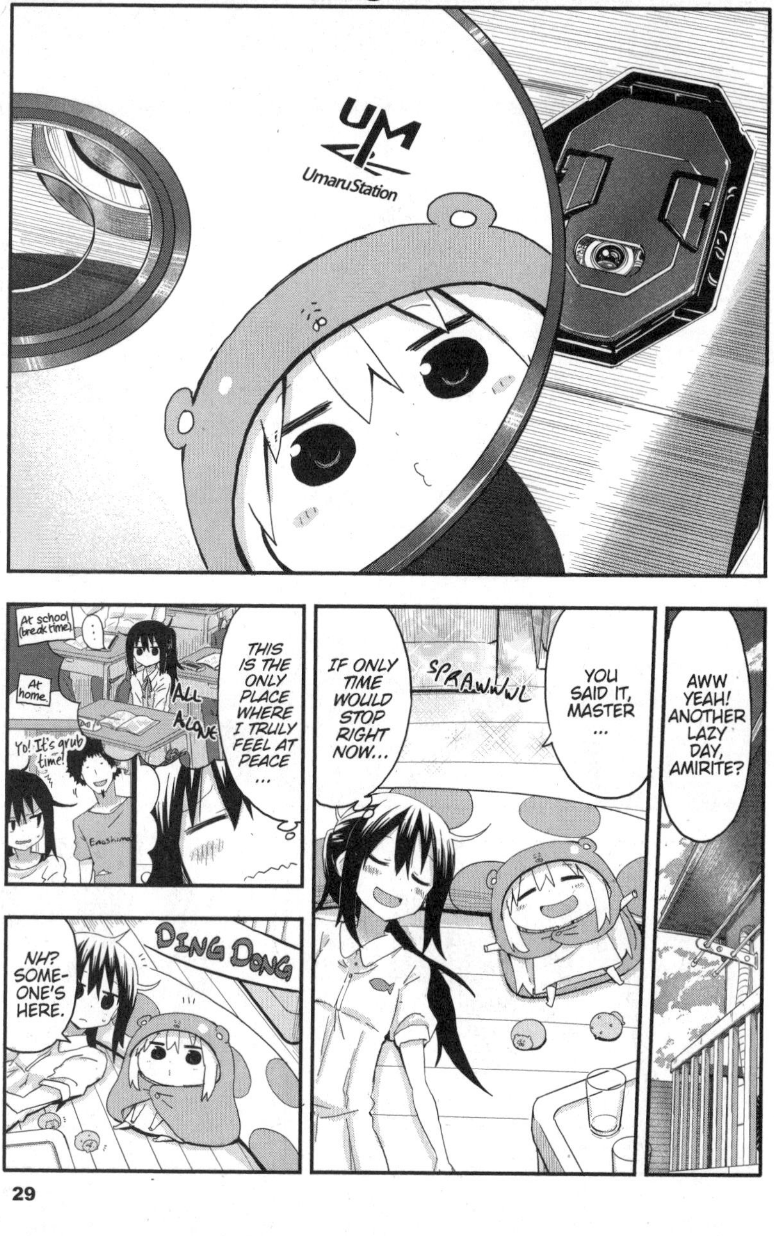
UM
UmaruStation
AWW YEAH! ANOTHER LAZY DAY, AMIRITE?
YOU SAID IT, MASTER ...
SPRAWWWL
IF ONLY TIME WOULD STOP RIGHT NOW...
THIS IS THE ONLY PLACE WHERE I TRULY FEEL AT PEACE ...
At school (break time)
ALL ALONE
At home.
Yo! It's grub time!
Ebashima
DING DONG
NH? SOME-ONE'S HERE.

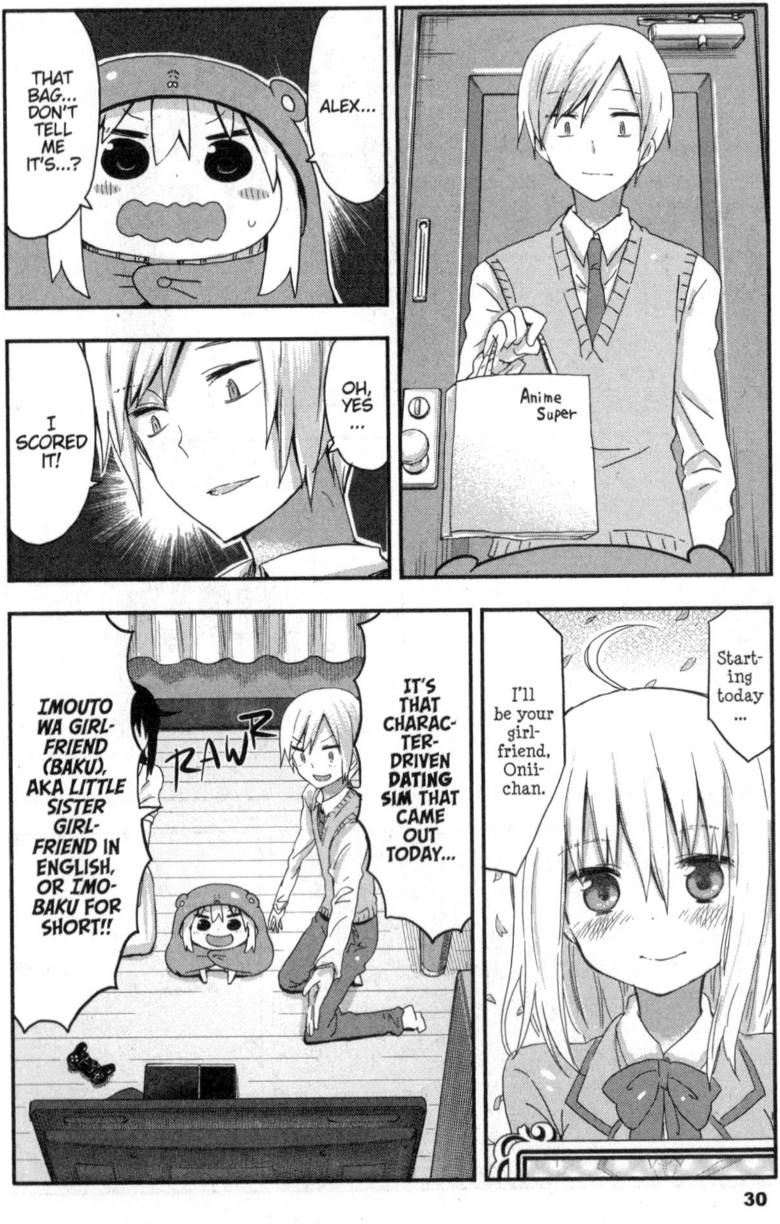
Anime Super
ALEX...
THAT BAG... DON'T TELL ME IT'S...?
OH, YES ...
I SCORED IT!
Start-ing today ...
I'll be your girl-friend, Onii-chan.
IT'S THAT CHARAC-TER-DRIVEN DATING SIM THAT CAME OUT TODAY...
RAWR
IMOUTO WA GIRL-FRIEND (BAKU), AKA LITTLE SISTER GIRL-FRIEND IN ENGLISH, OR IMO-BAKU FOR SHORT!!

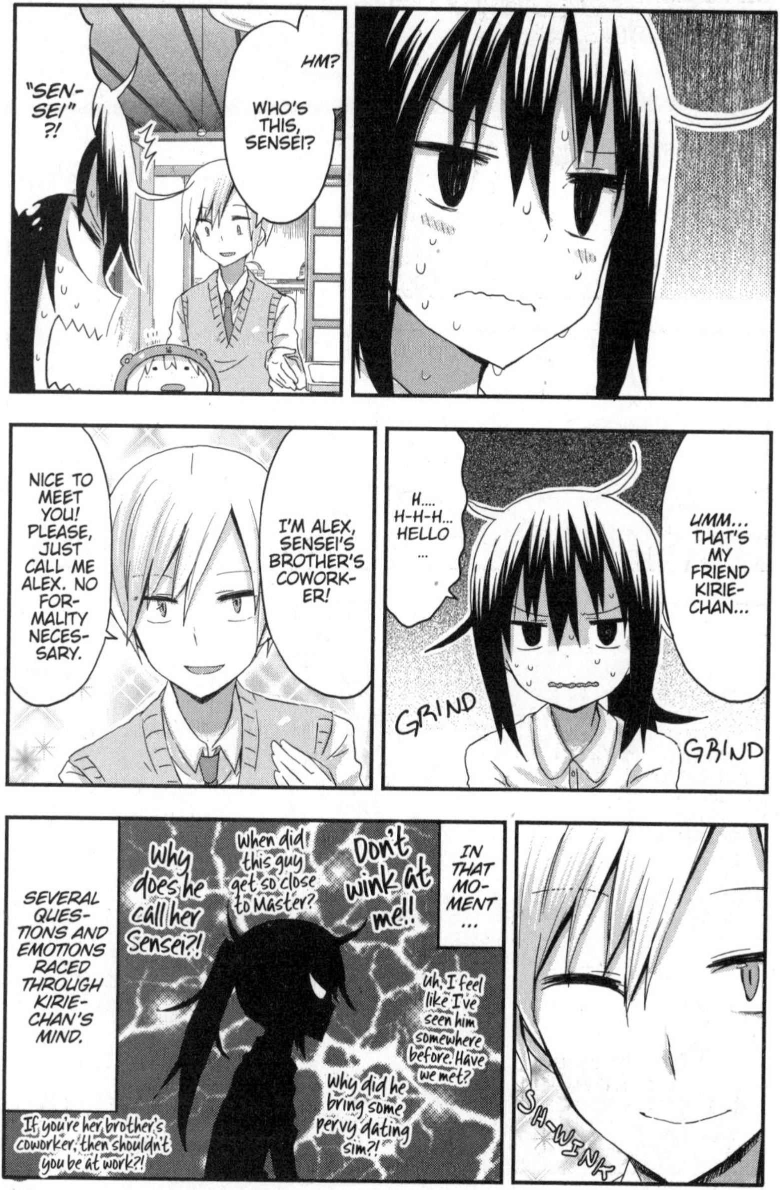
HM?
WHO'S THIS, SENSEI?
"SEN-SEI" ?!
UMM... THAT'S MY FRIEND KIRIE-CHAN...
H.... H-H-H... HELLO ...
GRIND
GRIND
I'M ALEX, SENSEI'S BROTHER'S COWORK-ER!
NICE TO MEET YOU! PLEASE, JUST CALL ME ALEX. NO FOR-MALITY NECES-SARY.
SH-WINK
IN THAT MO-MENT ...
Don't wink at me!!
when did this guy get so close to Master?
why does he call her Sensei?!
SEVERAL QUES-TIONS AND EMOTIONS RACED THROUGH KIRIE-CHAN'S MIND.
uh, I feel like I've seen him somewhere before. Have we met?
why did he bring some pervy dating sim?!
If you're her brother's coworker, then shouldn't you be at work?!

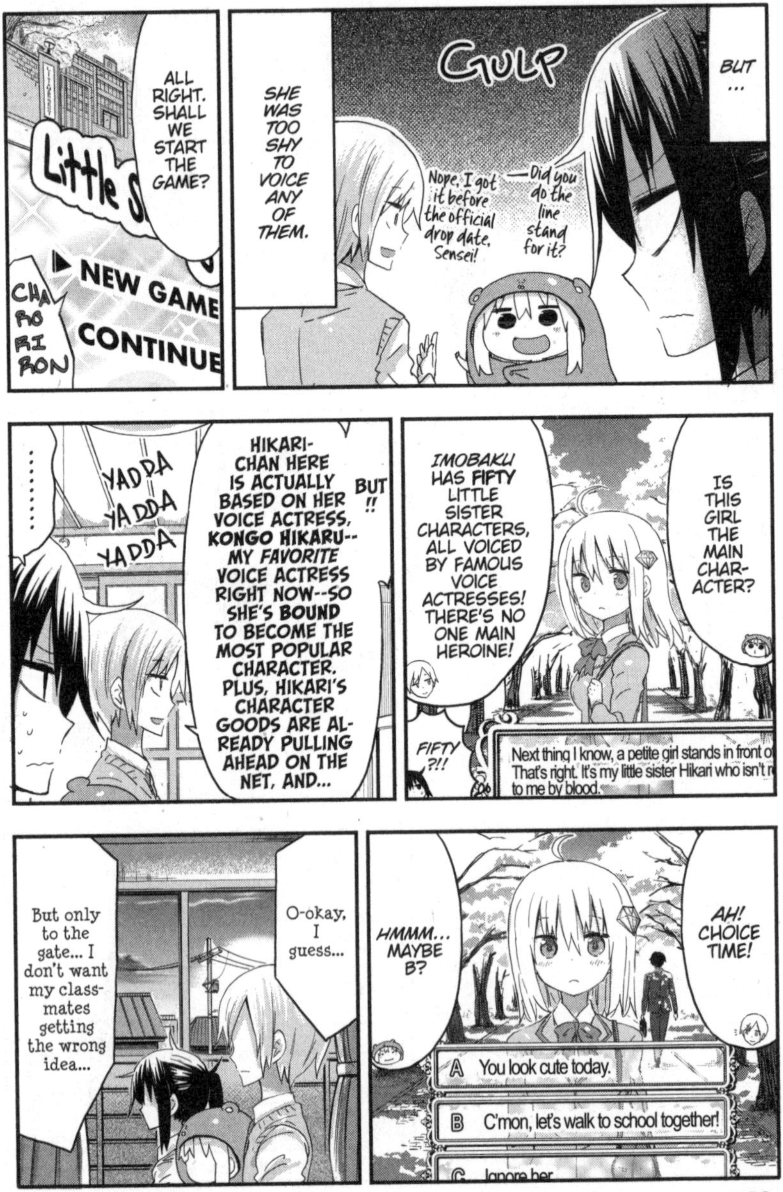
BUT...
GULP
—Did you do the line stand for it?
Nope, I got it before the official drop date, Sensei!
SHE WAS TOO SHY TO VOICE ANY OF THEM.
ALL RIGHT. SHALL WE START THE GAME?
Little S
▶ NEW GAME
CONTINUE
CHA RO RI RON
IS THIS GIRL THE MAIN CHARACTER?
IMOBAKU HAS **FIFTY** LITTLE SISTER CHARACTERS, ALL VOICED BY FAMOUS VOICE ACTRESSES! THERE'S NO ONE MAIN HEROINE!
FIFTY?!!
Next thing I know, a petite girl stands in front o
That's right. It's my little sister Hikari who isn't r
to me by blood.
BUT!!
HIKARI-CHAN HERE IS ACTUALLY BASED ON HER VOICE ACTRESS, **KONGO HIKARU**--MY *FAVORITE* VOICE ACTRESS RIGHT NOW--SO SHE'S **BOUND** TO BECOME THE MOST POPULAR CHARACTER. PLUS, HIKARI'S CHARACTER GOODS ARE ALREADY PULLING AHEAD ON THE NET, AND...
YADDA YADDA YADDA
......
AH! CHOICE TIME!
HMMM... MAYBE B?
A You look cute today.
B C'mon, let's walk to school together!
O-okay, I guess...
But only to the gate... I don't want my classmates getting the wrong idea...

WHAT SHOULD I DO? IT'S LIKE I DON'T KNOW THEIR LANGUAGE...!!

...

OHH, I LIKE HOW SHE'S -DERE, BUT NOT TOO -DERE!

GREAT VOICE ACTING, RIGHT?! SHE'S IMPROVED SINCE HER WORK ON OREOMO!!

I CAN'T MAKE MASTER FEEL LIKE SHE HAS TO GO OUT OF HER WAY TO INCLUDE ME!!

SHAKY GRIN

?

OH NO...!! I'M TOTALLY A THIRD WHEEL HERE...!!

GACK!!

...

KIRIE-CHAN?

SHE PROBABLY DOESN'T WANT TO BE TALKED TO AT SCHOOL.

MAYBE C WOULD BE BEST? THIS TYPE OF CHARACTER IS SHY AROUND OTHER PEOPLE.

HMMM... THIS IS A TOUGH ONE...

OH! WE RAN INTO HER IN THE HALLWAY!

A	Talk to her.
B	Leave her alone.
C	Pretend you didn't even see her.

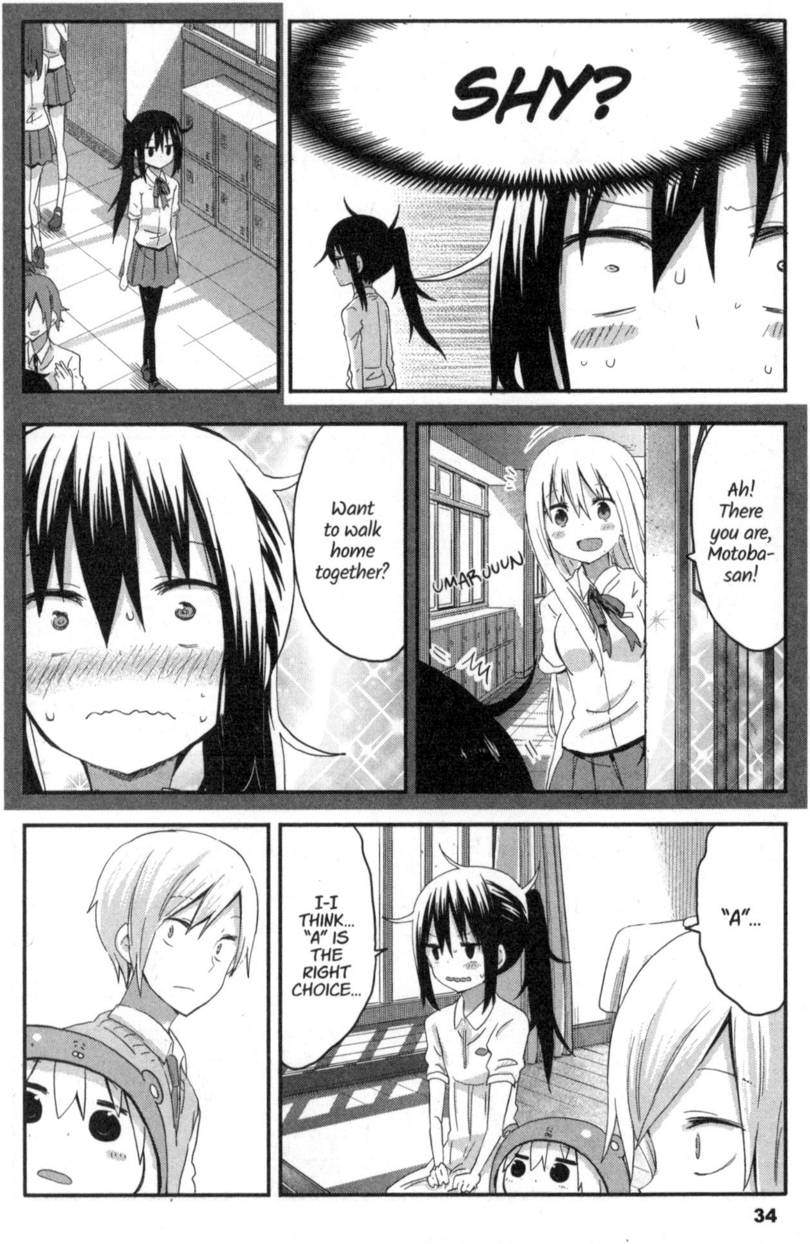
SHY?
Ah! There you are, Motoba-san!
UMARUUUN
Want to walk home together?
"A"...
I-I THINK... "A" IS THE RIGHT CHOICE...

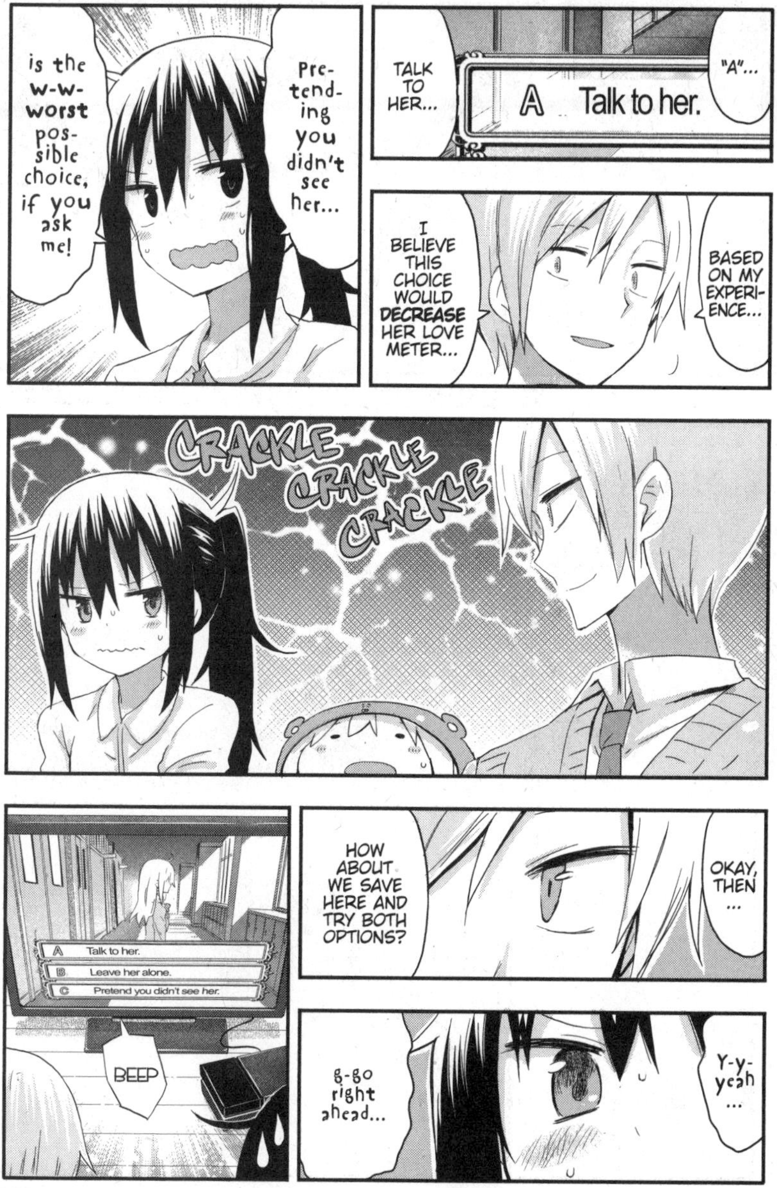
"A"...
A Talk to her.
TALK TO HER...
BASED ON MY EXPERIENCE...
I BELIEVE THIS CHOICE WOULD **DECREASE** HER LOVE METER...
Pretending you didn't see her...
is the w-w-**worst** possible choice, if you ask me!
CRACKLE CRACKLE CRACKLE
OKAY, THEN ...
HOW ABOUT WE SAVE HERE AND TRY BOTH OPTIONS?
Y-y-yeah ...
g-go right ahead...
A Talk to her.
B Leave her alone.
C Pretend you didn't see her.
BEEP

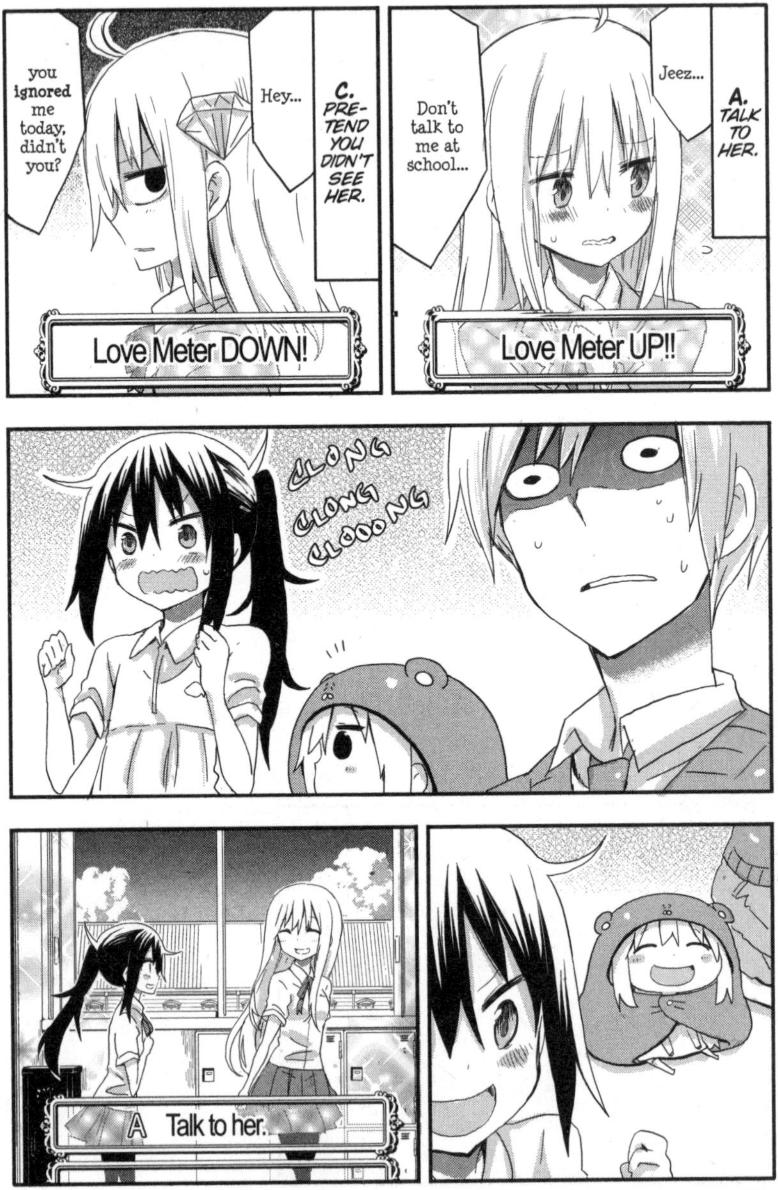
A. TALK TO HER.
Jeez...
Don't talk to me at school...
Love Meter UP!!
C. PRE-TEND YOU DIDN'T SEE HER.
Hey...
you ignored me today, didn't you?
Love Meter DOWN!
CLONG CLONG CLOOONG
A Talk to her.

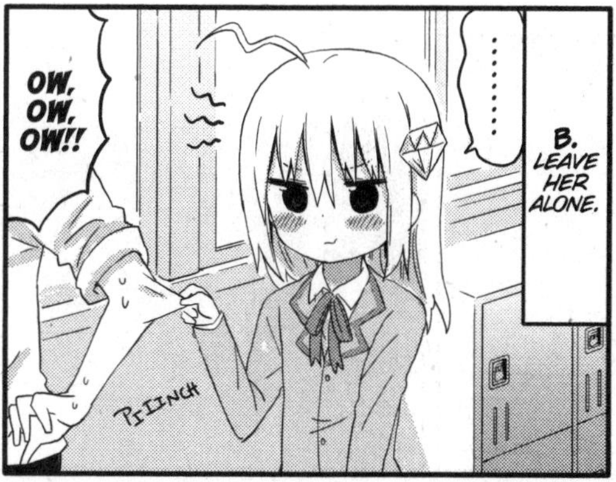
B. LEAVE HER ALONE.
....
OW, OW, OW!!
PIIINCH

HIMOUTO! UMARU-CHAN

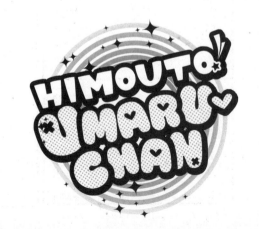

No. 76 Umaru Skips School

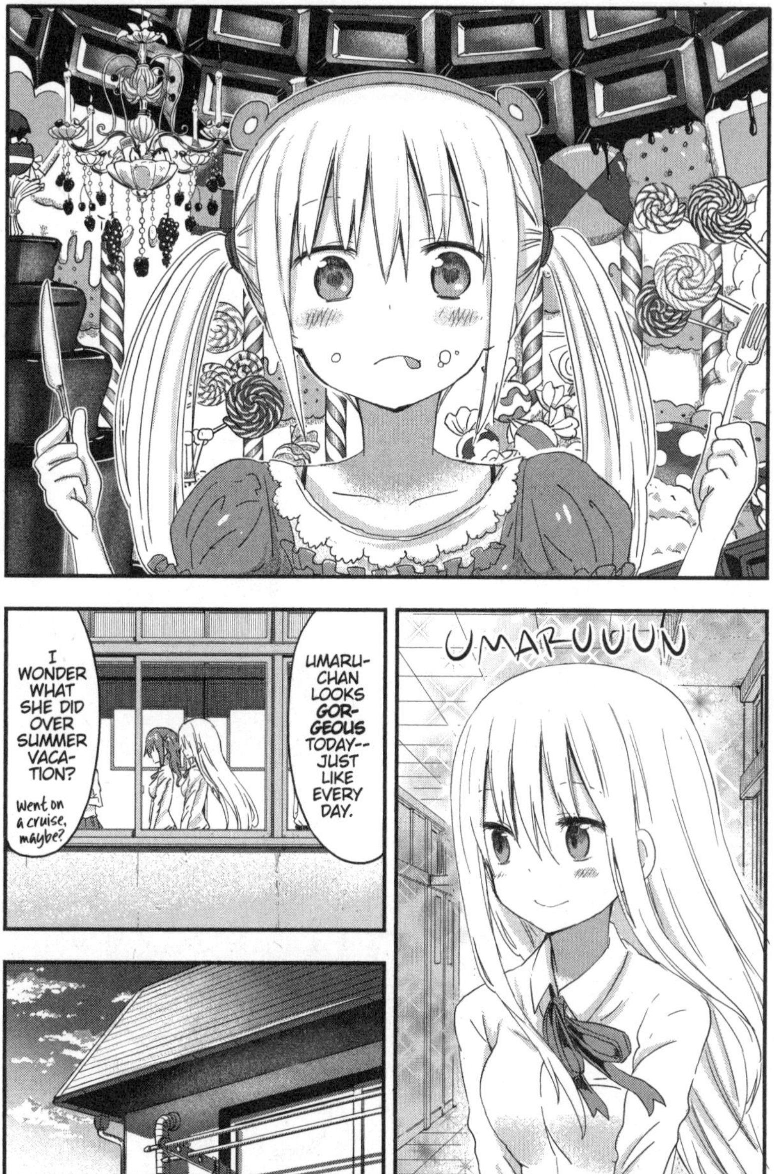
UMARUUUN
UMARU-CHAN LOOKS GORGEOUS TODAY--JUST LIKE EVERY DAY.
I WONDER WHAT SHE DID OVER SUMMER VACATION?
Went on a cruise, maybe?

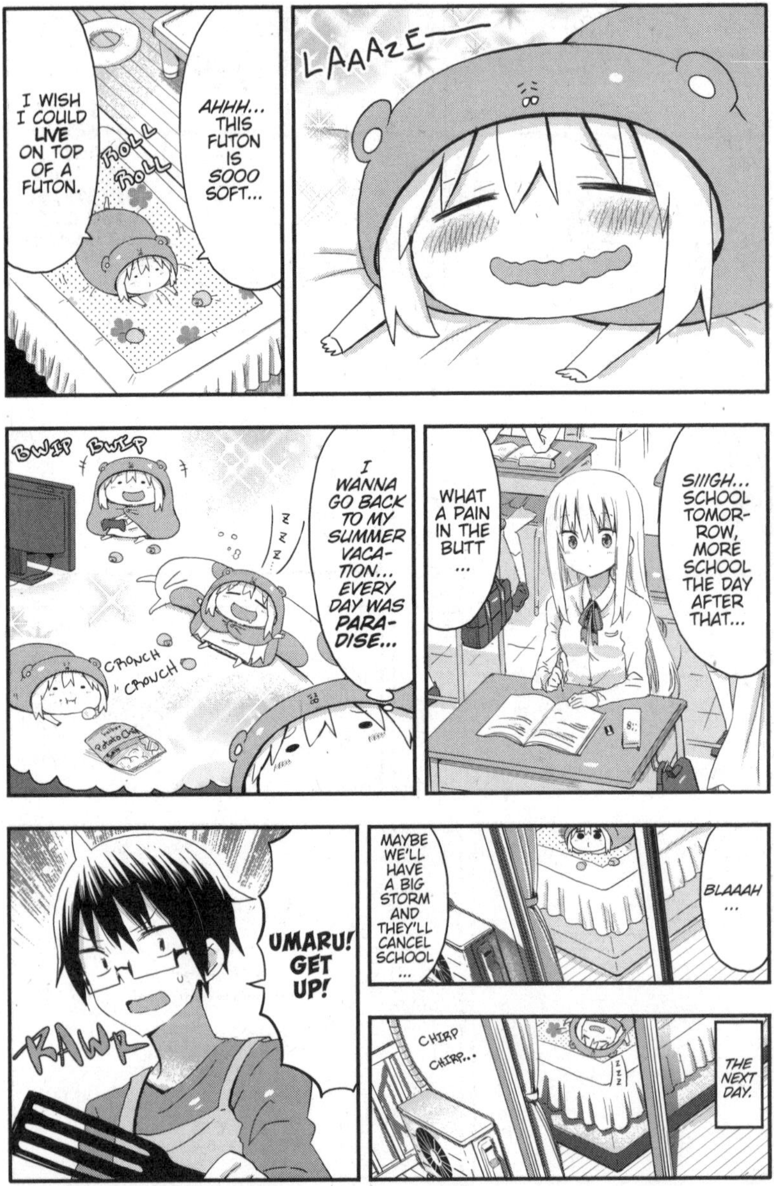

LAAAZE——
AHHH... THIS FUTON IS SOOO SOFT...
ROLL ROLL
I WISH I COULD LIVE ON TOP OF A FUTON.
SIIIGH... SCHOOL TOMORROW, MORE SCHOOL THE DAY AFTER THAT...
WHAT A PAIN IN THE BUTT...
I WANNA GO BACK TO MY SUMMER VACATION... EVERY DAY WAS PARADISE...
BWIP BWIP
Z Z Z
CRONCH CRONCH
BLAAAH...
MAYBE WE'LL HAVE A BIG STORM AND THEY'LL CANCEL SCHOOL...
THE NEXT DAY.
CHIRP CHIRP...
Z Z Z
UMARU! GET UP!
RAWR

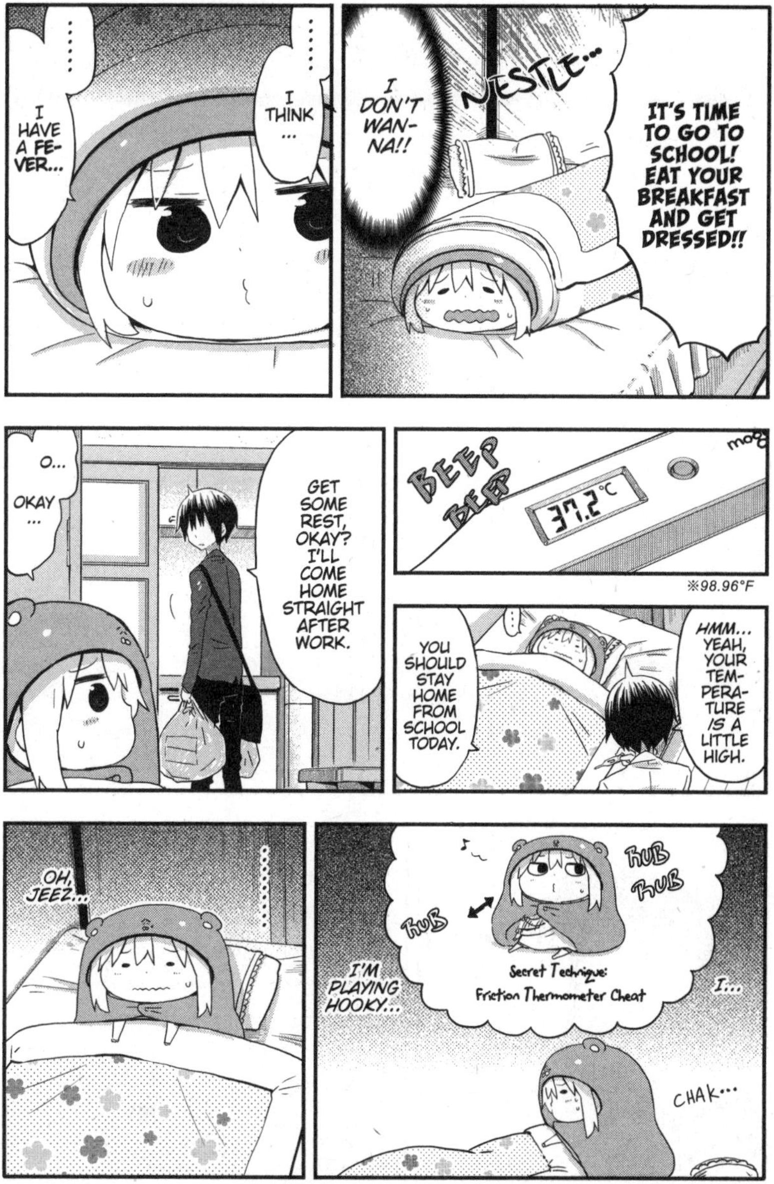
IT'S TIME TO GO TO SCHOOL! EAT YOUR BREAKFAST AND GET DRESSED!!
NESTLE...
I DON'T WANNA!!
......
I THINK ...
......
I HAVE A FEVER...
BEEP BEEP
37.2°C
mog
※98.96°F
HMM... YEAH, YOUR TEMPERATURE IS A LITTLE HIGH.
...
YOU SHOULD STAY HOME FROM SCHOOL TODAY.
GET SOME REST, OKAY? I'LL COME HOME STRAIGHT AFTER WORK.
O... OKAY ...
I...
RUB RUB
RUB
Secret Technique: Friction Thermometer Cheat
I'M PLAYING HOOKY...
CHAK...
......
OH, JEEZ...

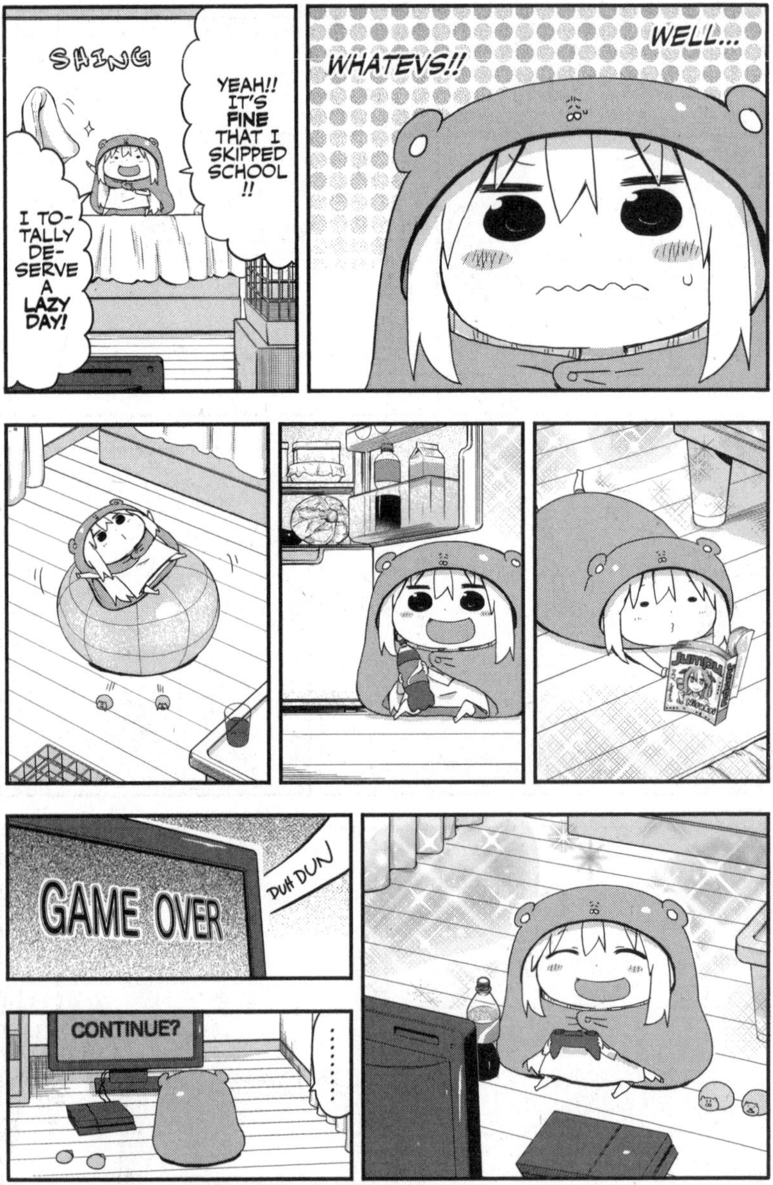

WELL...
WHATEVS!!
YEAH!! IT'S FINE THAT I SKIPPED SCHOOL!!
SHING
I TO-TALLY DE-SERVE A LAZY DAY!
GAME OVER
DUH DUN
CONTINUE?
......

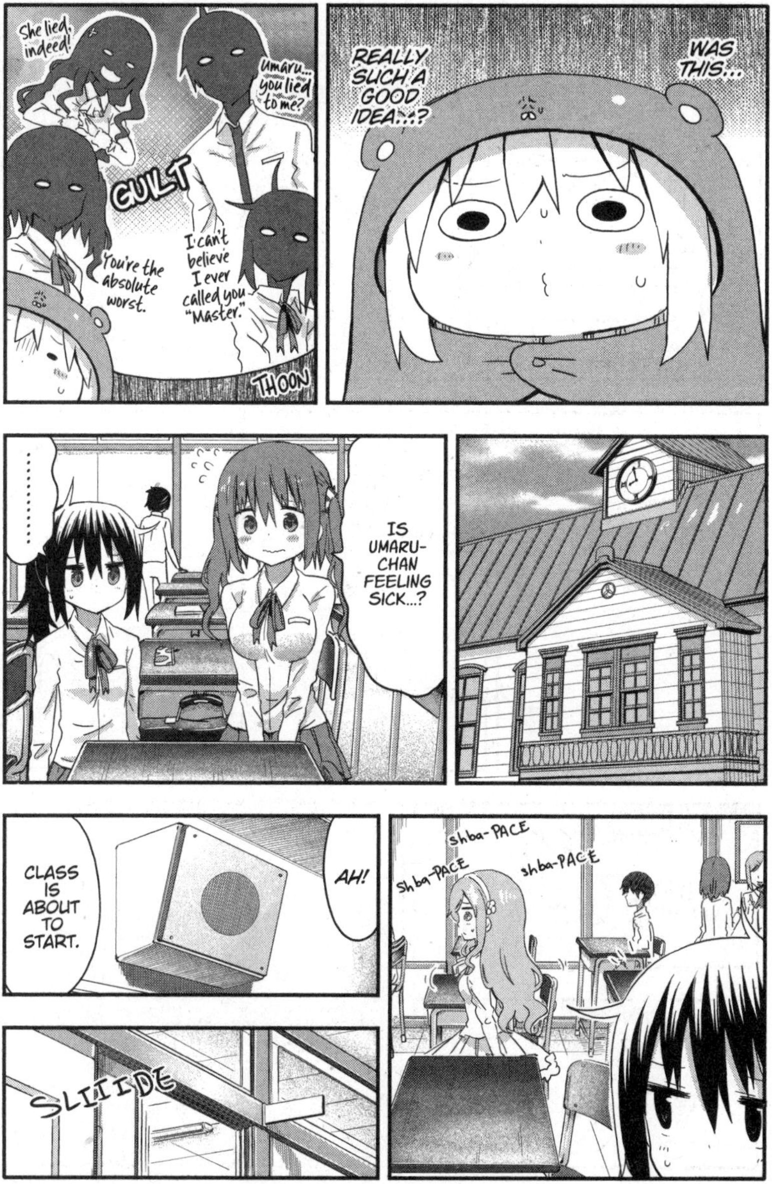
WAS THIS...
REALLY SUCH A GOOD IDEA...?
Umaru... you lied to me?
She lied, indeed!
GULT
I can't believe I ever called you "Master."
You're the absolute worst.
THOON
IS UMARU-CHAN FEELING SICK...?
......
shba-PACE
shba-PACE
Shba-PACE
AH!
CLASS IS ABOUT TO START.
SLIIIDE

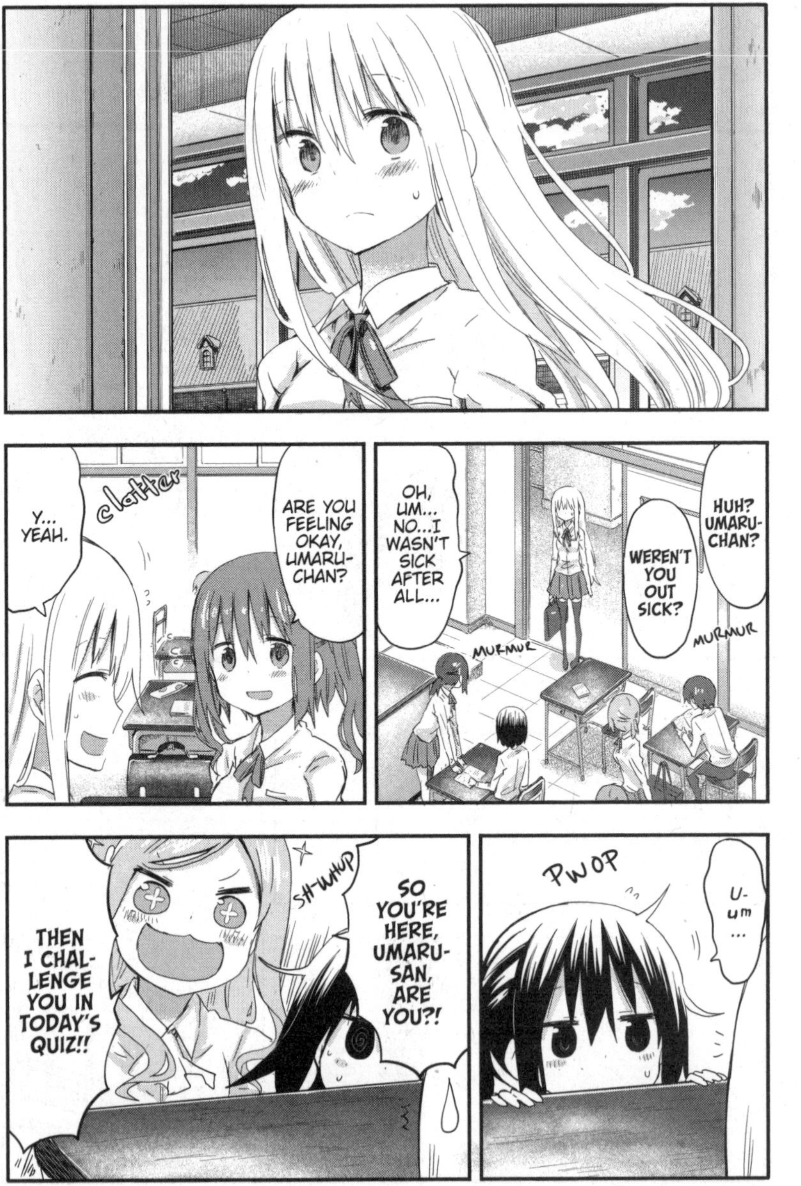
HUH? UMARU-CHAN?
WEREN'T YOU OUT SICK?
MURMUR
MURMUR
OH, UM... NO...I WASN'T SICK AFTER ALL...
ARE YOU FEELING OKAY, UMARU-CHAN?
clatter
Y... YEAH.
PWOP
U-um ...
SO YOU'RE HERE, UMARU-SAN, ARE YOU?!
SH-WHUP
THEN I CHAL-LENGE YOU IN TODAY'S QUIZ!!

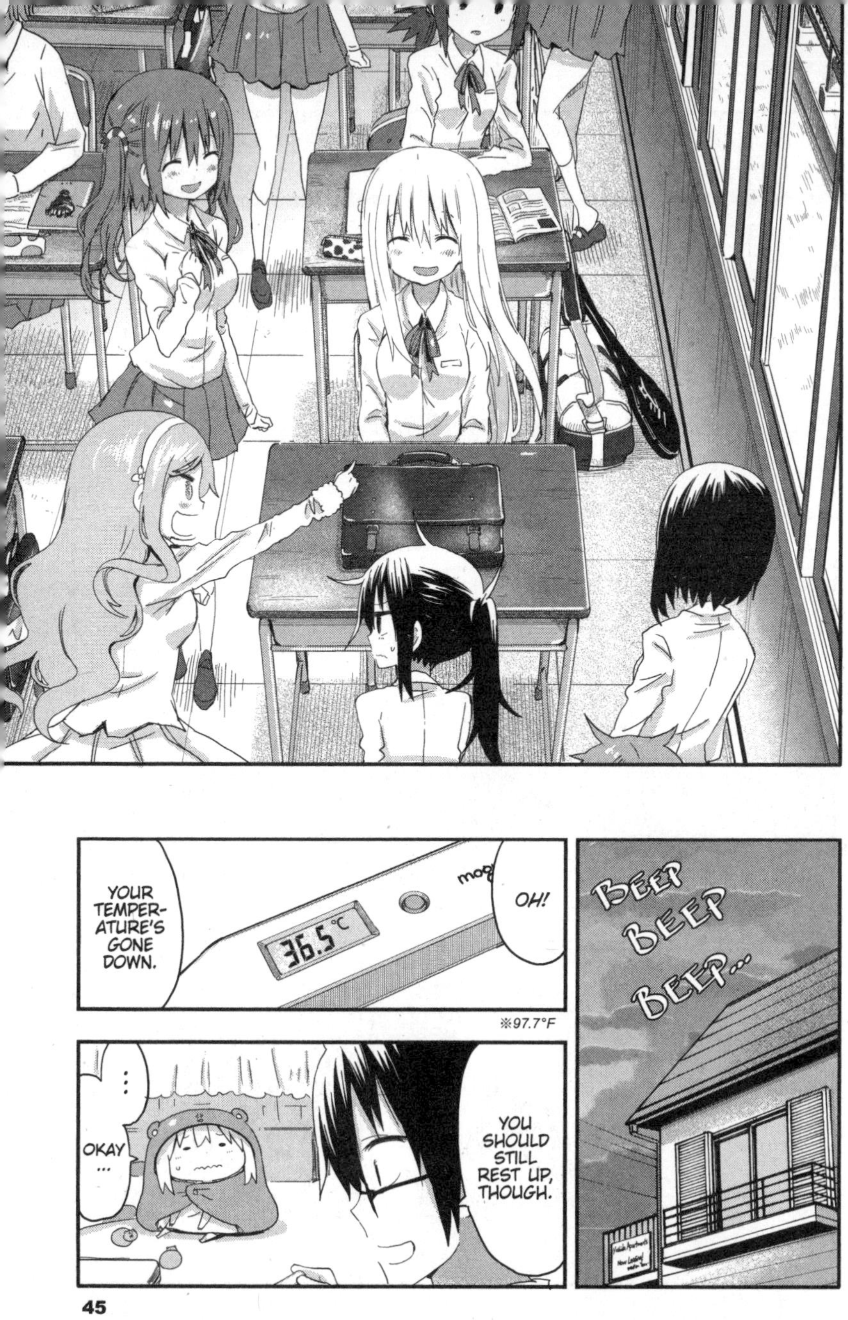
BEEP BEEP BEEP...
mog
OH!
36.5°C
YOUR TEMPER-ATURE'S GONE DOWN.
※97.7°F
YOU SHOULD STILL REST UP, THOUGH.
...
OKAY ...

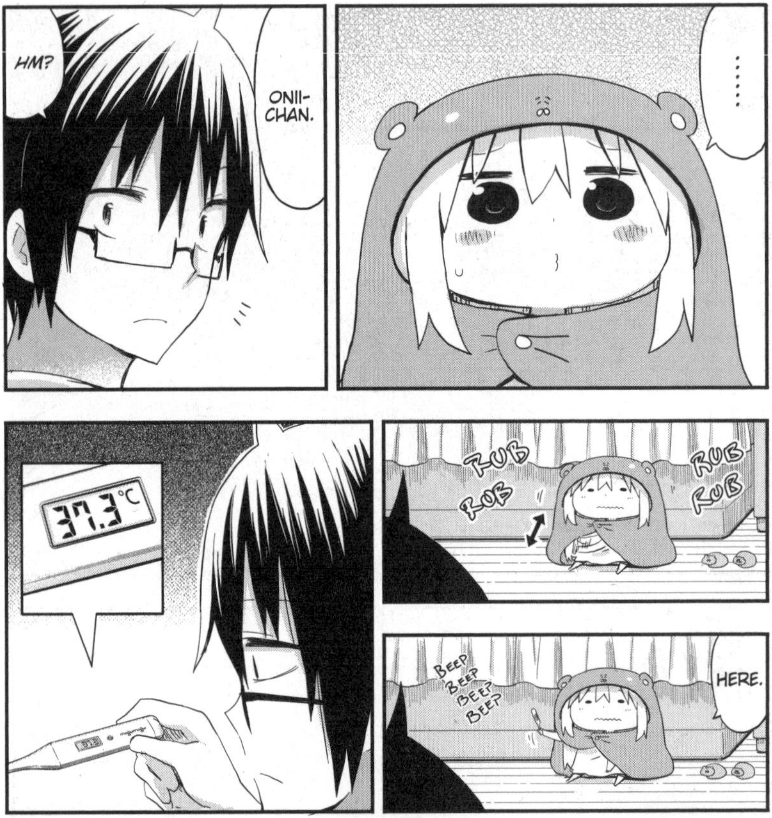
......
ONII-CHAN.
HM?
RUB RUB
RUB RUB
BEEP BEEP BEEP BEEP
HERE.
37.3°C

※99.14°F.

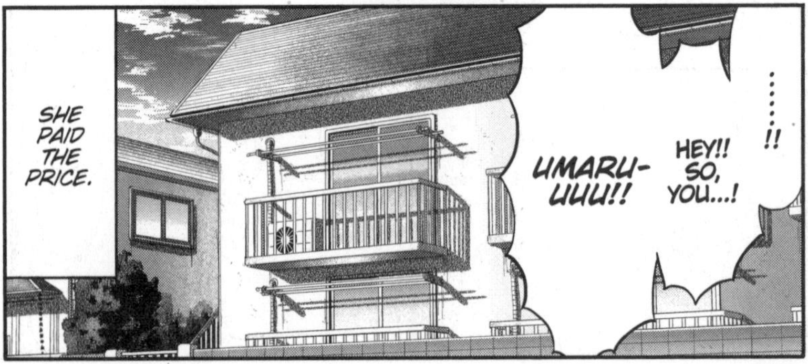
......!!
HEY!! SO, YOU...!
UMARU-UUU!!
SHE PAID THE PRICE.

No. 77 Umaru & Gossip

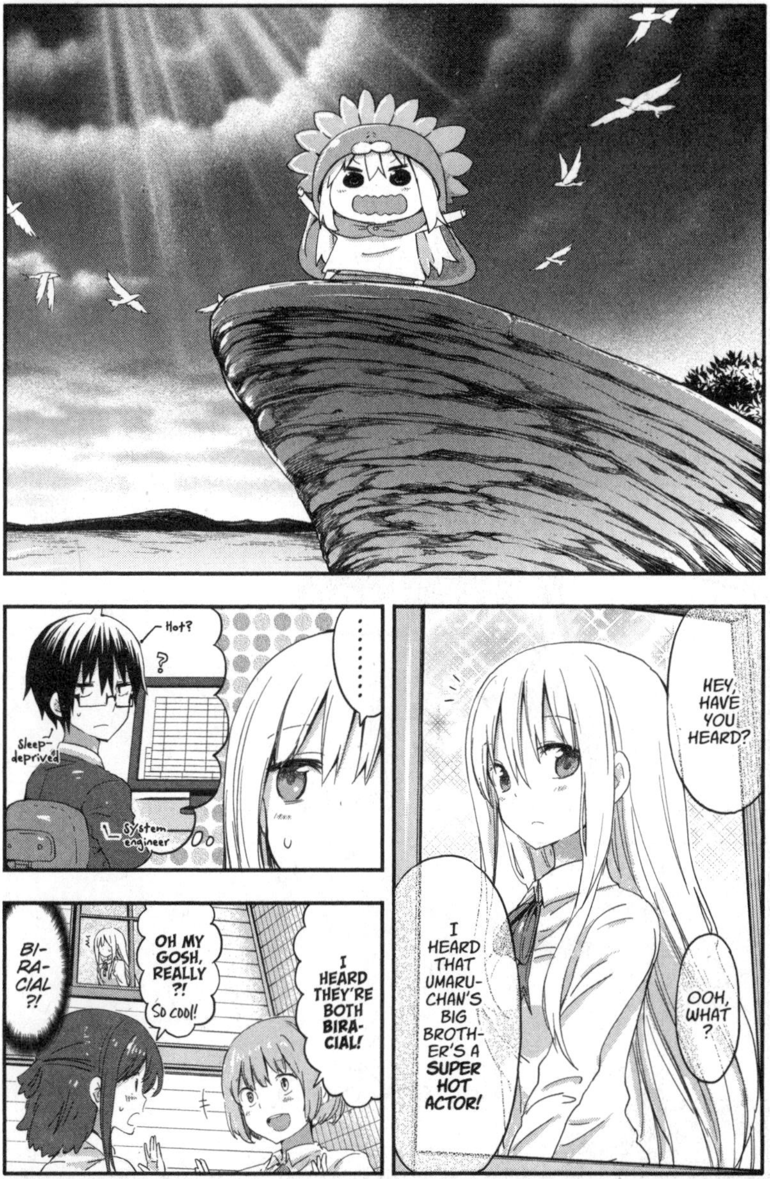
HEY, HAVE YOU HEARD?
OOH, WHAT?
I HEARD THAT UMARU-CHAN'S BIG BROTHER'S A SUPER HOT ACTOR!
......
Hot?
?
Sleep-deprived
System engineer
I HEARD THEY'RE BOTH BIRACIAL!
OH MY GOSH, REALLY?!
So cool!
BI-RA-CIAL?!

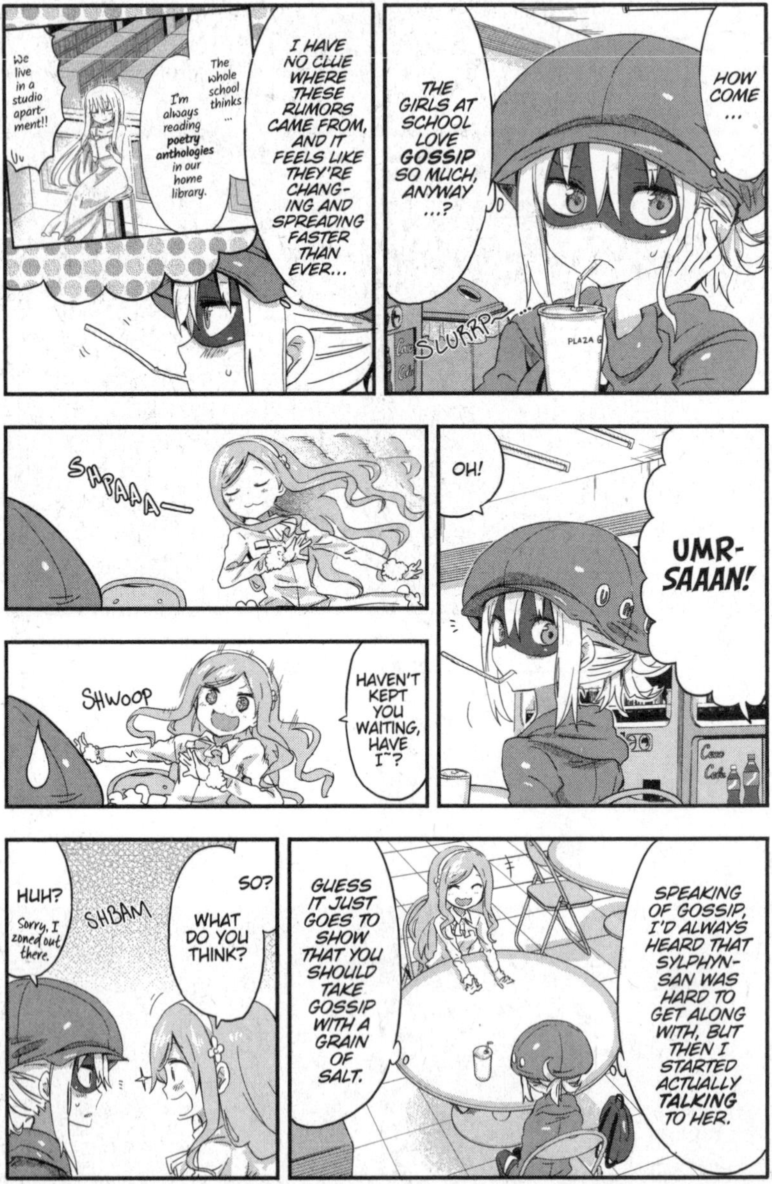
HOW COME ...
THE GIRLS AT SCHOOL LOVE GOSSIP SO MUCH, ANYWAY ...?
SLURRP—...
I HAVE NO CLUE WHERE THESE RUMORS CAME FROM, AND IT FEELS LIKE THEY'RE CHANGING AND SPREADING FASTER THAN EVER...
The whole school thinks ...
I'm always reading poetry anthologies in our home library.
We live in a studio apartment!!
OH!
UMR-SAAAN!
SHPAAAA—
HAVEN'T KEPT YOU WAITING, HAVE I~?
SHWOOP
SPEAKING OF GOSSIP, I'D ALWAYS HEARD THAT SYLPHYN-SAN WAS HARD TO GET ALONG WITH, BUT THEN I STARTED ACTUALLY TALKING TO HER.
GUESS IT JUST GOES TO SHOW THAT YOU SHOULD TAKE GOSSIP WITH A GRAIN OF SALT.
SO?
WHAT DO YOU THINK?
SHBAM
HUH?
Sorry, I zoned out there.

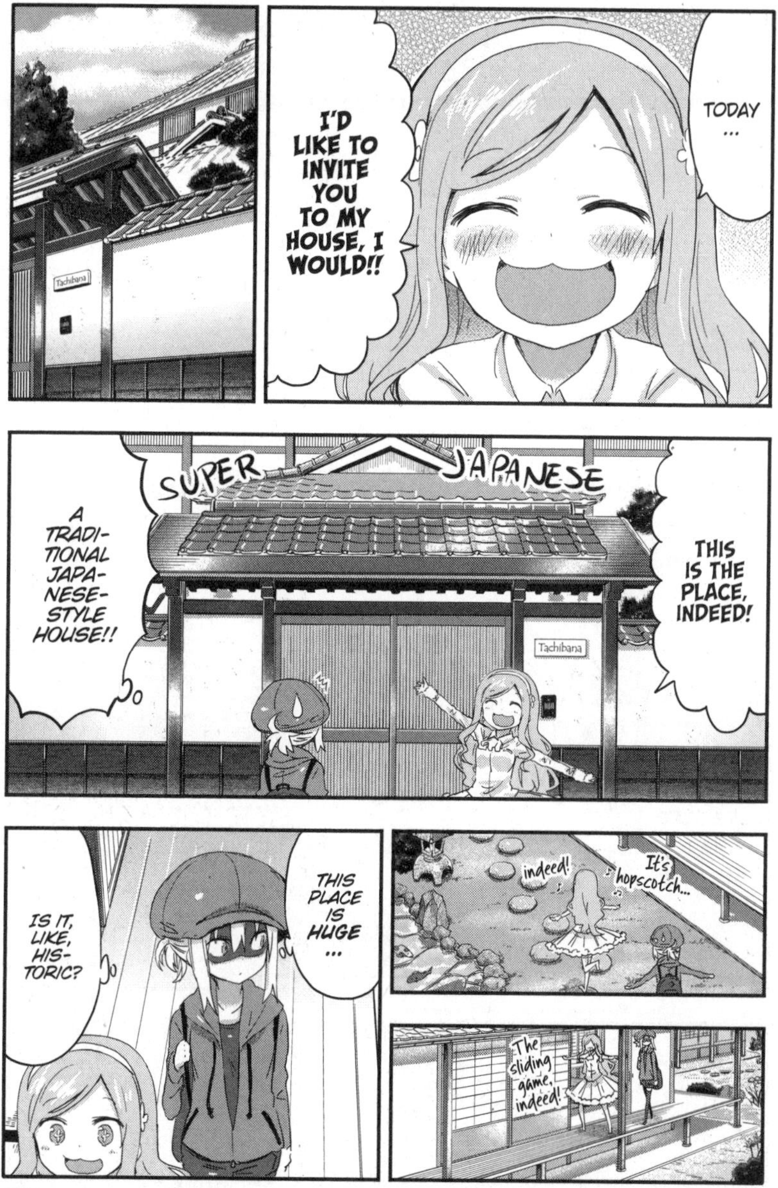

TODAY ...
I'D LIKE TO INVITE YOU TO MY HOUSE, I WOULD!!
Tachibana
THIS IS THE PLACE, INDEED!
SUPER JAPANESE
A TRADI-TIONAL JAPA-NESE-STYLE HOUSE!!
Tachibana
It's hopscotch...
indeed!
The sliding game, indeed!
THIS PLACE IS HUGE ...
IS IT, LIKE, HIS-TORIC?

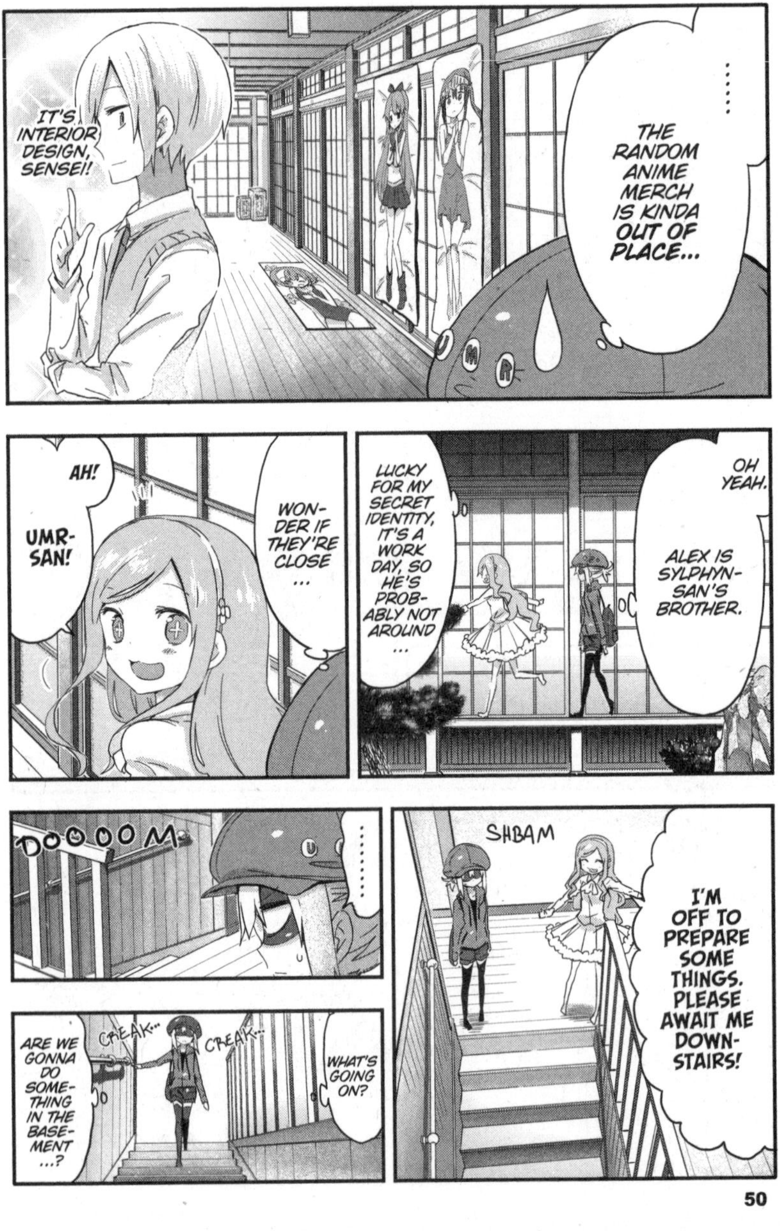
......
THE RANDOM ANIME MERCH IS KINDA OUT OF PLACE...
IT'S INTERIOR DESIGN, SENSEI!
OH YEAH.
ALEX IS SYLPHYN-SAN'S BROTHER.
LUCKY FOR MY SECRET IDENTITY, IT'S A WORK DAY, SO HE'S PROBABLY NOT AROUND...
WONDER IF THEY'RE CLOSE...
AH!
UMR-SAN!
I'M OFF TO PREPARE SOME THINGS. PLEASE AWAIT ME DOWNSTAIRS!
SHBAM
......
DOOOOOM
WHAT'S GOING ON?
CREAK...
CREAK...
ARE WE GONNA DO SOMETHING IN THE BASEMENT...?

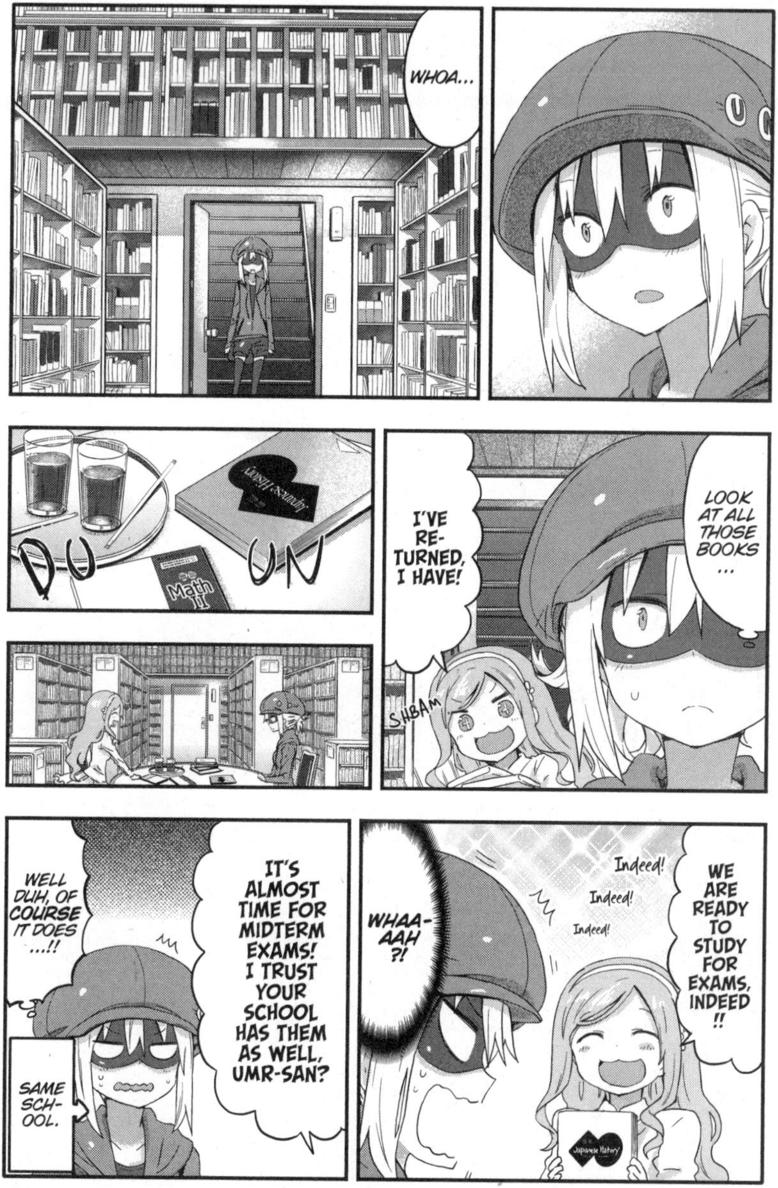
WHOA...
LOOK AT ALL THOSE BOOKS ...
I'VE RE-TURNED, I HAVE!
SHBAM
Japanese History
DU UN
Math II
WE ARE READY TO STUDY FOR EXAMS, INDEED!!
Indeed!
Indeed!
Indeed!
WHAA-AAH?!
Japanese History
IT'S ALMOST TIME FOR MIDTERM EXAMS! I TRUST YOUR SCHOOL HAS THEM AS WELL, UMR-SAN?
WELL DUH, OF COURSE IT DOES ...!!
SAME SCH-OOL.

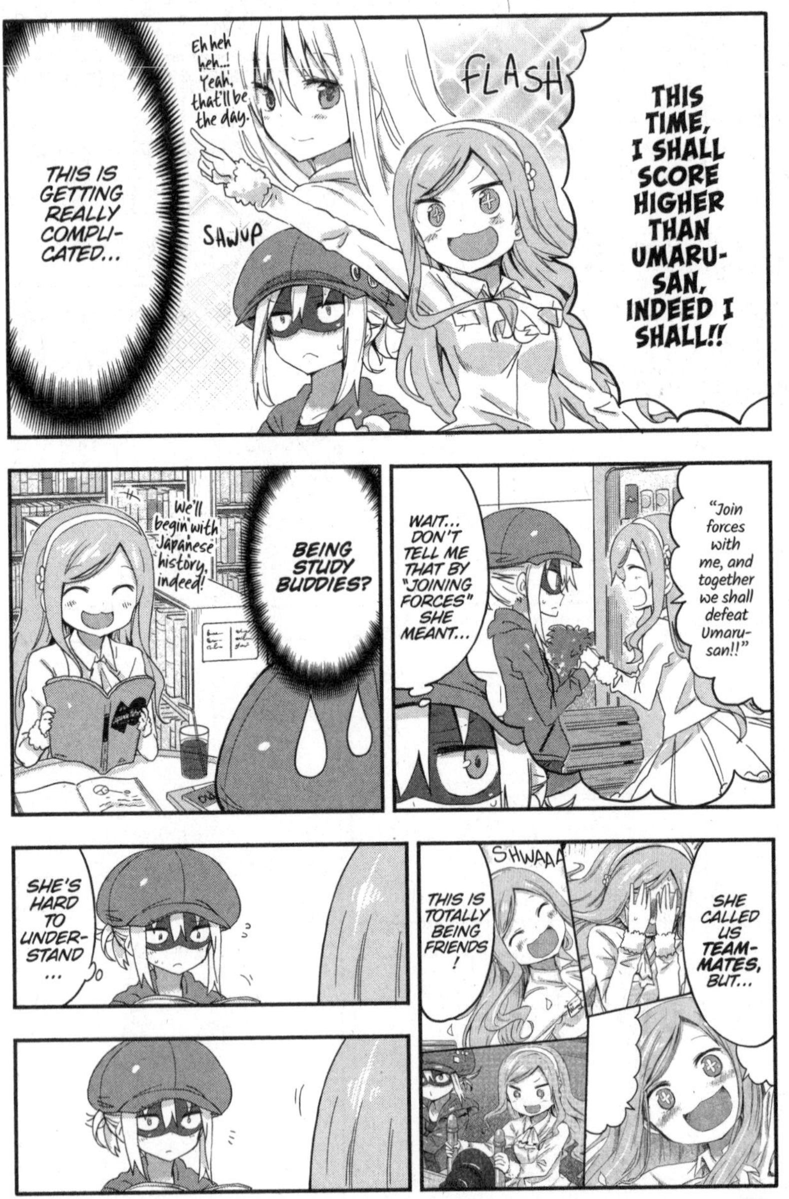
THIS TIME, I SHALL SCORE HIGHER THAN UMARU-SAN, INDEED I SHALL!!
FLASH
Eh heh heh...! Yeah, that'll be the day.
SAWUP
THIS IS GETTING REALLY COMPLICATED...
"Join forces with me, and together we shall defeat Umaru-san!!"
WAIT... DON'T TELL ME THAT BY "JOINING FORCES" SHE MEANT...
BEING STUDY BUDDIES?
We'll begin with Japanese history, indeed!
SHE CALLED US TEAMMATES, BUT...
SHWAAA
THIS IS TOTALLY BEING FRIENDS!
SHE'S HARD TO UNDERSTAND...

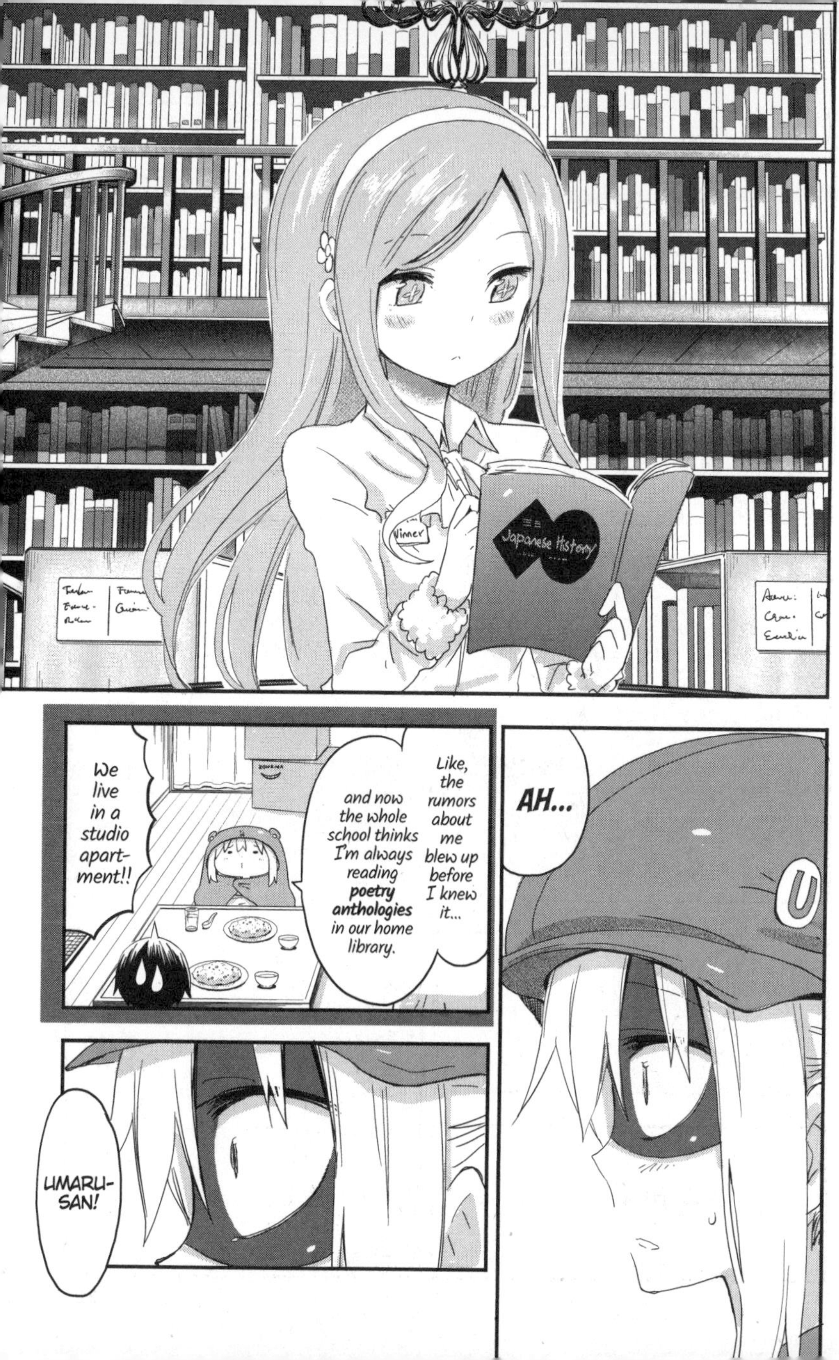
Winner
Japanese History
AH...
Like, the rumors about me blew up before I knew it...
and now the whole school thinks I'm always reading **poetry anthologies** in our home library.
We live in a studio apartment!!
UMARU-SAN!

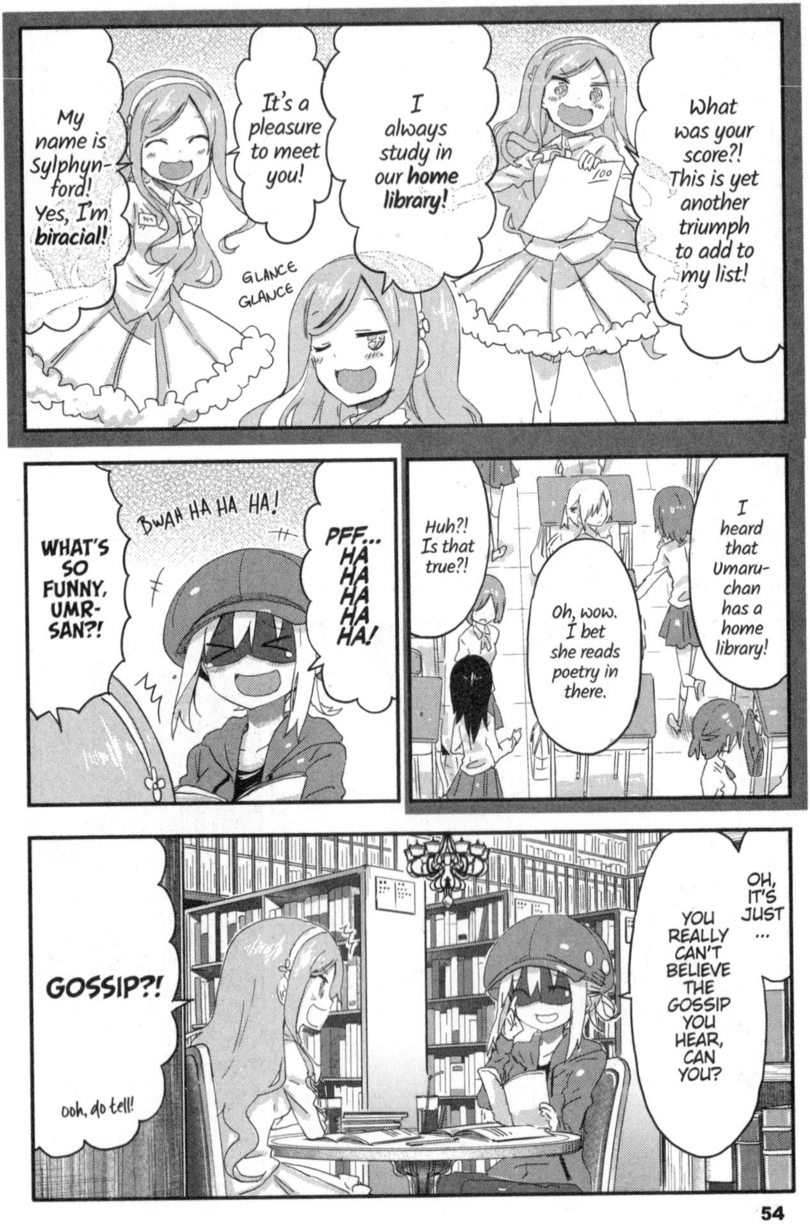
What was your score?! This is yet another triumph to add to my list!
I always study in our **home library**!
It's a pleasure to meet you!
My name is Sylphynford! Yes, I'm **biracial**!
GLANCE GLANCE
I heard that Umaru-chan has a home library!
Huh?! Is that true?!
Oh, wow. I bet she reads poetry in there.
PFF... HA HA HA HA HA HA!
BWAH HA HA HA!
WHAT'S SO FUNNY, UMR-SAN?!
OH, IT'S JUST ...
YOU REALLY CAN'T BELIEVE THE GOSSIP YOU HEAR, CAN YOU?
GOSSIP?!
ooh, do tell!

No. 78 Umaru & Halloween

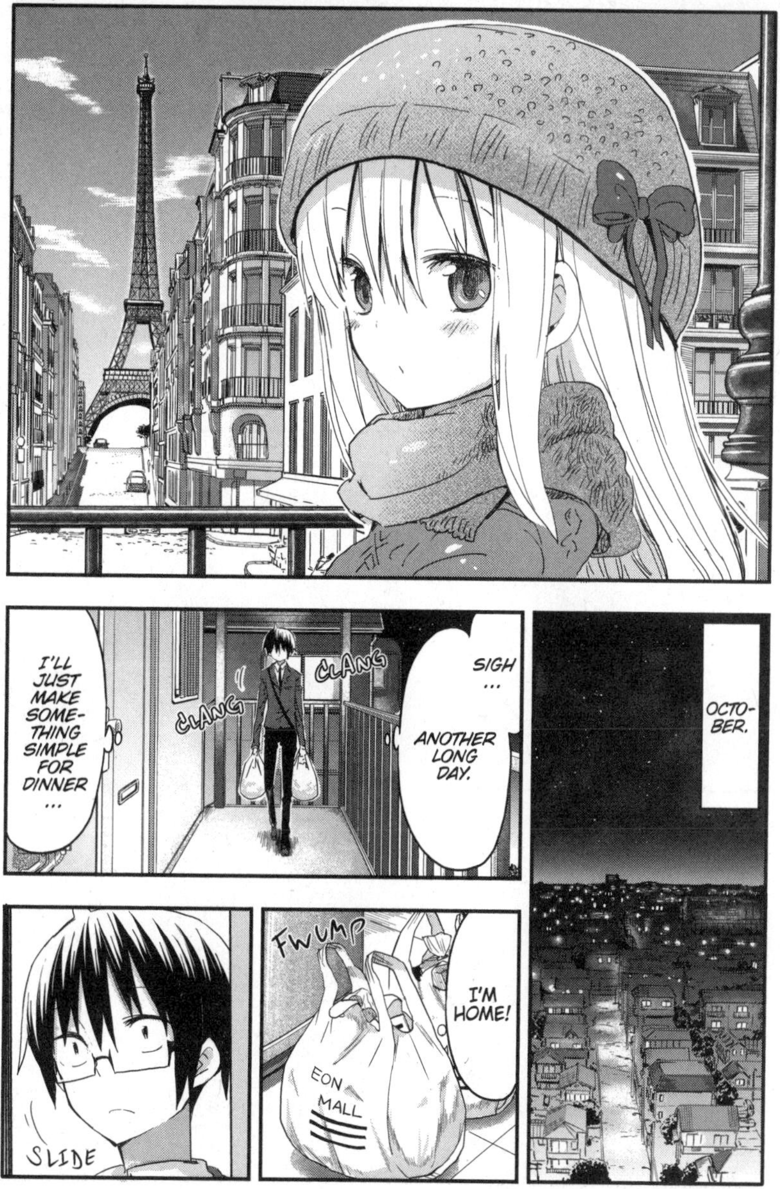

OCTOBER.
SIGH ...
ANOTHER LONG DAY.
CLANG
CLANG
I'LL JUST MAKE SOMETHING SIMPLE FOR DINNER ...
I'M HOME!
FWUMP
EON MALL
SLIDE

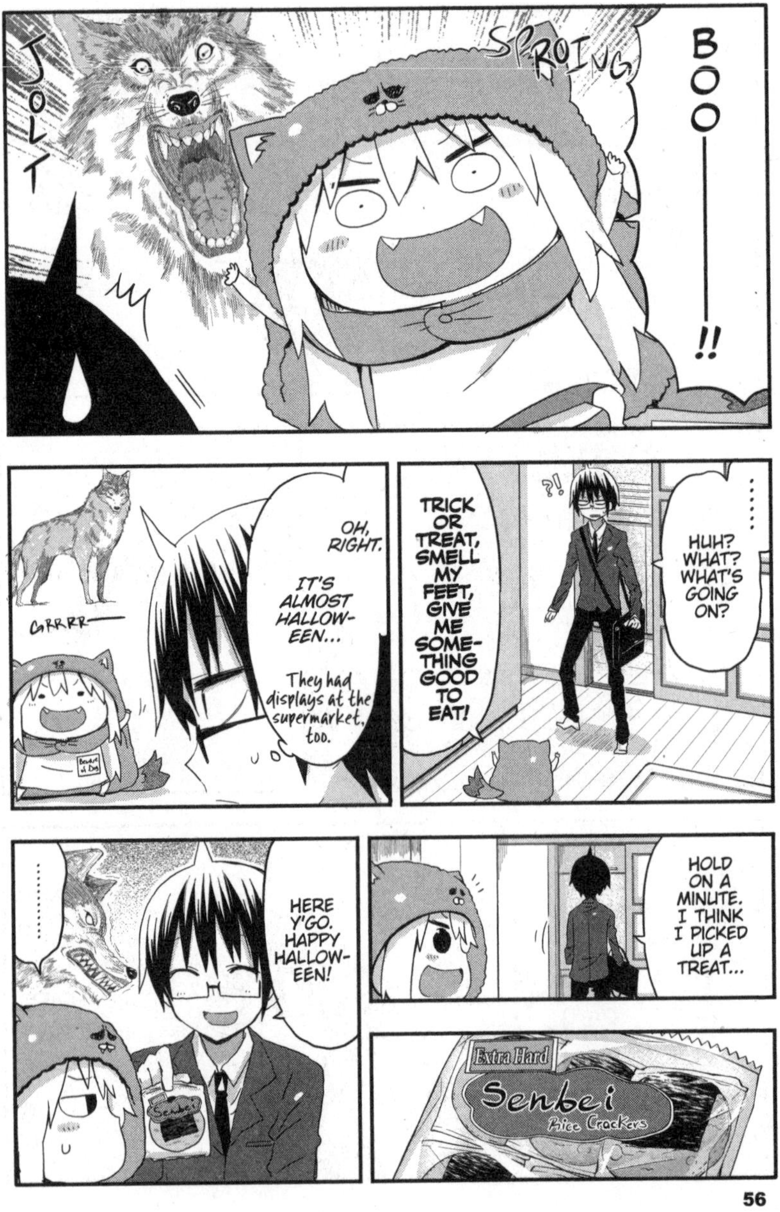
BOO—!!
SPROING
JOLT
......
HUH? WHAT? WHAT'S GOING ON?
?!
TRICK OR TREAT, SMELL MY FEET, GIVE ME SOMETHING GOOD TO EAT!
OH, RIGHT.
IT'S ALMOST HALLOWEEN...
They had displays at the supermarket, too.
GRRRR—
Beware of Dog
HOLD ON A MINUTE. I THINK I PICKED UP A TREAT...
Extra Hard
Senbei
Rice Crackers
HERE Y'GO. HAPPY HALLOWEEN!
......
Senbei

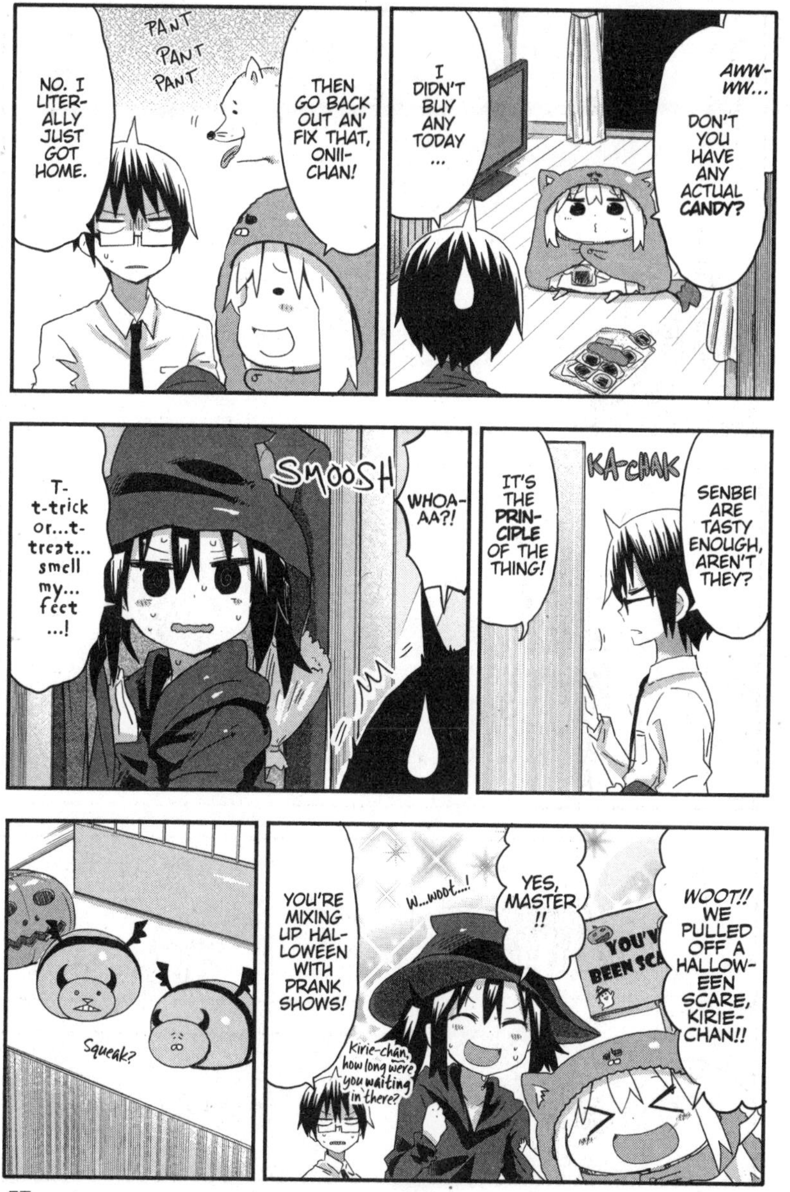
AWW-WW...
DON'T YOU HAVE ANY ACTUAL CANDY?
I DIDN'T BUY ANY TODAY ...
THEN GO BACK OUT AN' FIX THAT, ONII-CHAN!
PANT PANT PANT
NO. I LITER-ALLY JUST GOT HOME.
SENBEI ARE TASTY ENOUGH, AREN'T THEY?
KA-CHAK
IT'S THE PRIN-CIPLE OF THE THING!
WHOA-AA?!
SMOOSH
T-t-trick or...t-treat... smell my... feet ...!
WOOT!! WE PULLED OFF A HALLOW-EEN SCARE, KIRIE-CHAN!!
YOU'V BEEN SCA
YES, MASTER !!
w...woot...!
YOU'RE MIXING UP HAL-LOWEEN WITH PRANK SHOWS!
Kirie-chan, how long were you waiting in there?
Squeak?

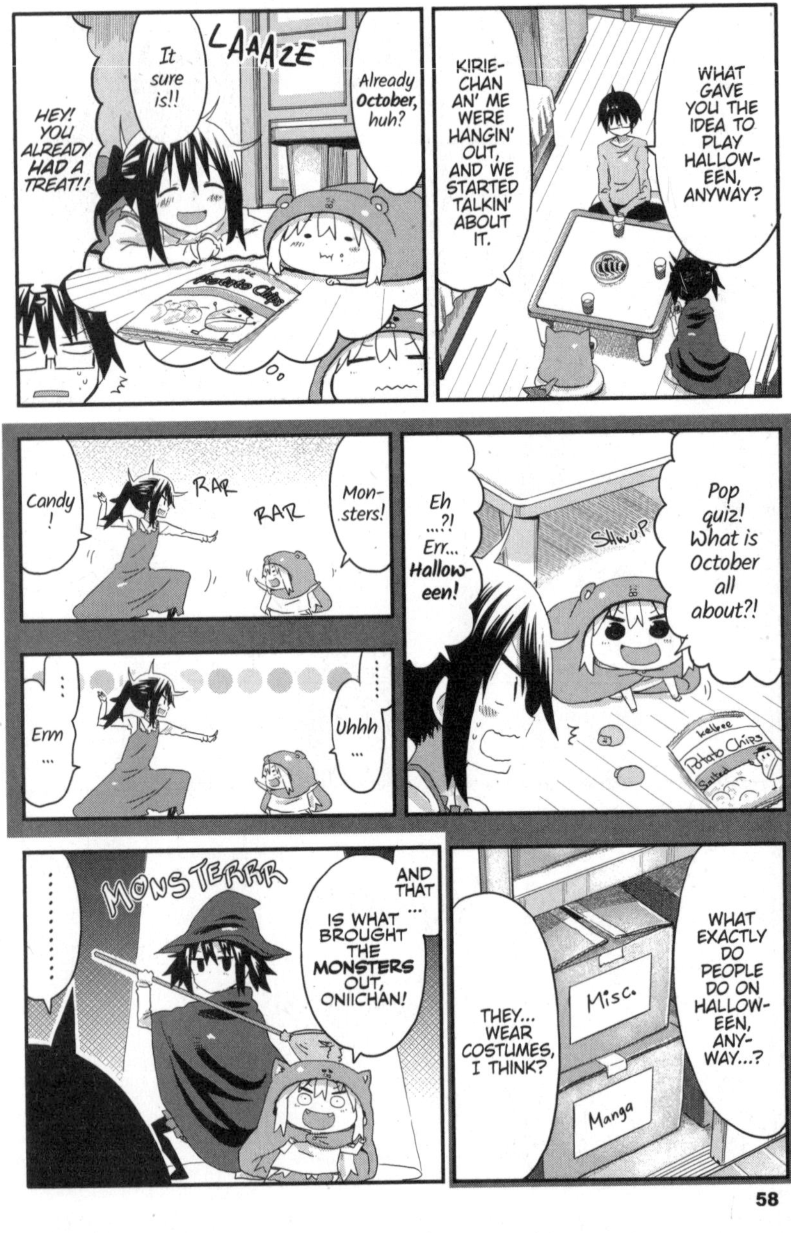

WHAT GAVE YOU THE IDEA TO PLAY HALLOWEEN, ANYWAY?
KIRIE-CHAN AN' ME WERE HANGIN' OUT, AND WE STARTED TALKIN' ABOUT IT.
Already October, huh?
LAAAZE
It sure is!!
HEY! YOU ALREADY HAD A TREAT!!
Pop quiz! What is October all about?!
SHWUP
Eh ...?! Err... Halloween!
kelbee Potato Chips
Monsters!
RAR
RAR
Candy!
......
Uhhh ...
... Erm ...
WHAT EXACTLY DO PEOPLE DO ON HALLOWEEN, ANYWAY...?
THEY... WEAR COSTUMES, I THINK?
Misc.
Manga
AND THAT ... IS WHAT BROUGHT THE MONSTERS OUT, ONIICHAN!
MONSTERRR
....

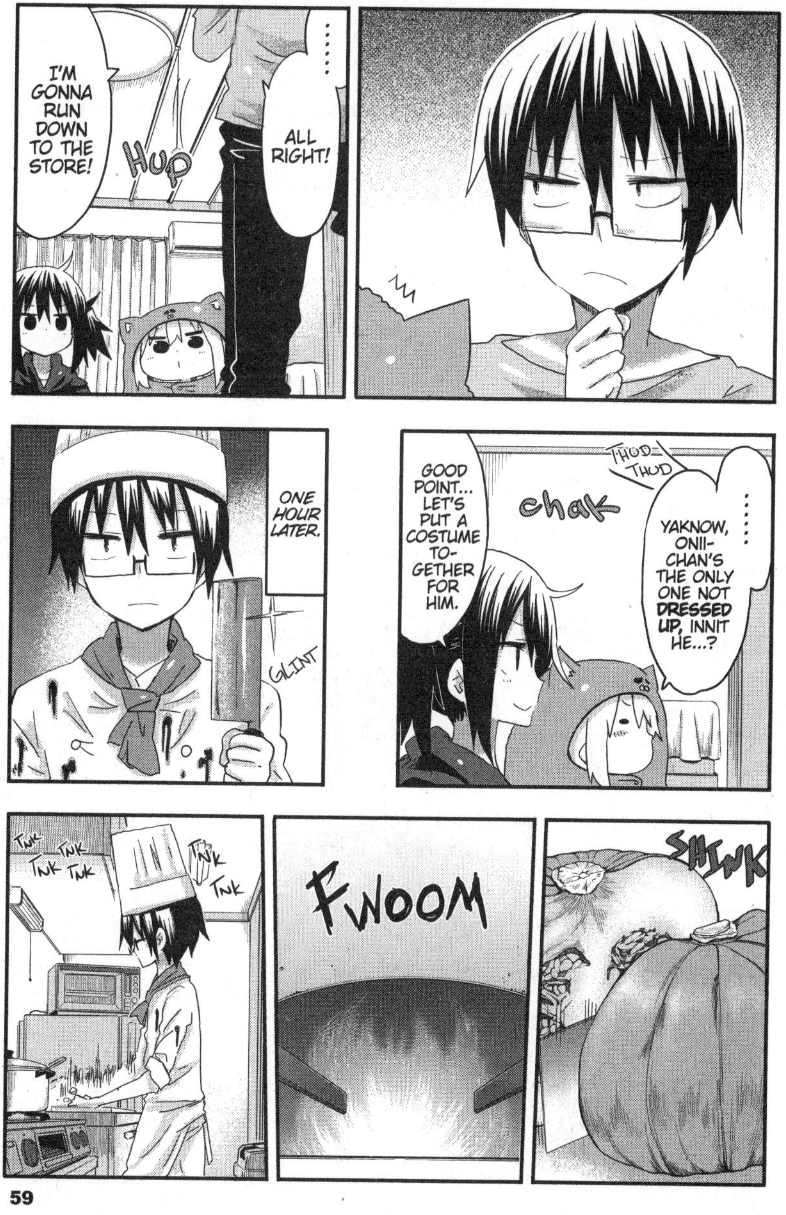

......
ALL RIGHT!
I'M GONNA RUN DOWN TO THE STORE!
HUP
THUD THUD
...... YAKNOW, ONII-CHAN'S THE ONLY ONE NOT **DRESSED UP**, INNIT HE...?
chak
GOOD POINT... LET'S PUT A COSTUME TO-GETHER FOR HIM.
ONE HOUR LATER.
GLINT
SHINK
FWOOM
TNK TNK
TNK TNK
TNK TNK

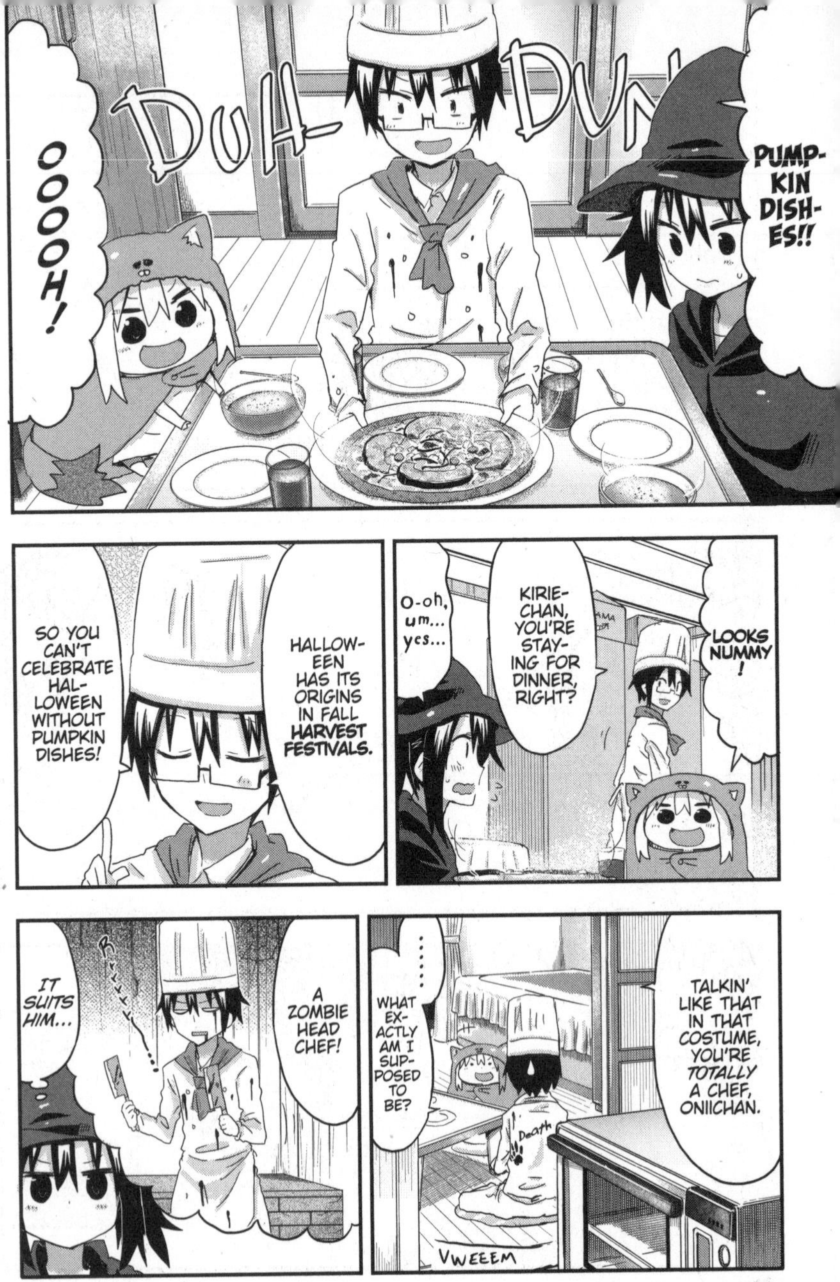
PUMP-KIN DISH-ES!!
DUH-DUN!
OOOOOH!
LOOKS NUMMY!
KIRIE-CHAN, YOU'RE STAY-ING FOR DINNER, RIGHT?
O-oh, um... yes...
HALLOW-EEN HAS ITS ORIGINS IN FALL **HARVEST FESTIVALS.**
SO YOU CAN'T CELEBRATE HAL-LOWEEN WITHOUT PUMPKIN DISHES!
TALKIN' LIKE THAT IN THAT COSTUME, YOU'RE *TOTALLY* A CHEF, ONIICHAN.
......
WHAT EX-ACTLY AM I SUP-POSED TO BE?
Death
VWEEEM
A ZOMBIE HEAD CHEF!
IT SUITS HIM...

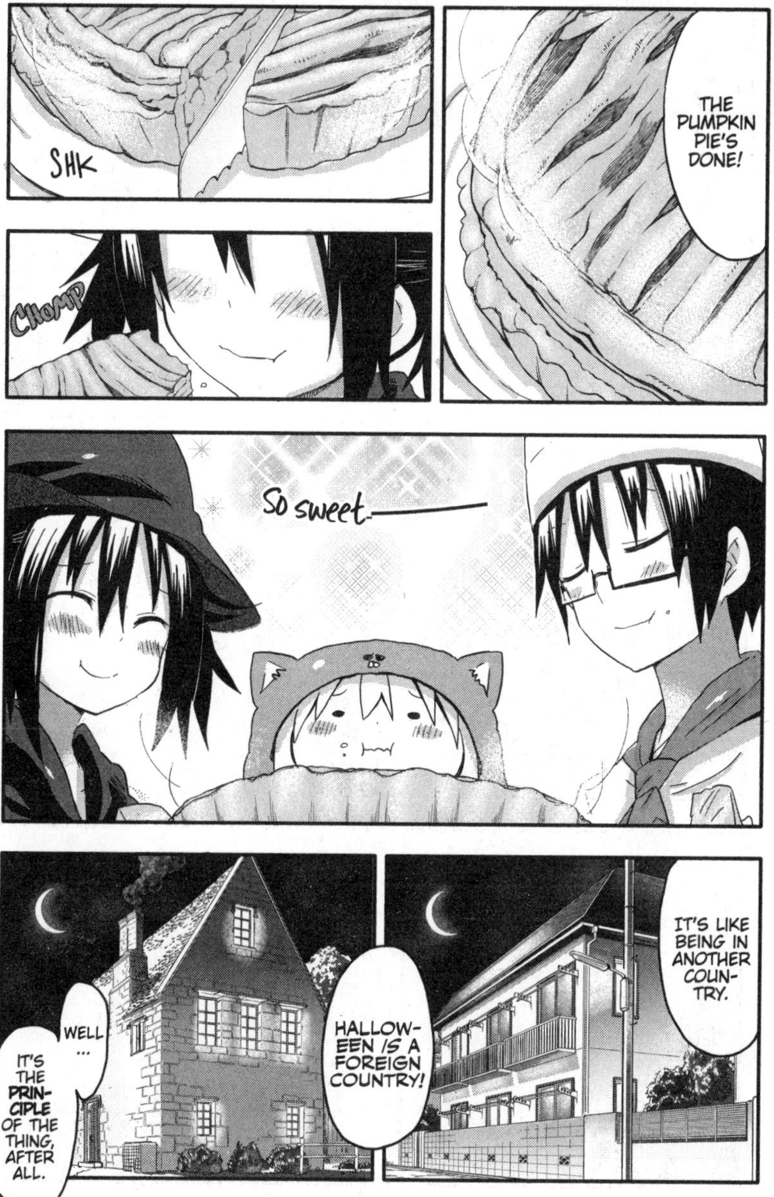
THE PUMPKIN PIE'S DONE!
SHK
CHOMP
So sweet—
IT'S LIKE BEING IN ANOTHER COUN-TRY.
HALLOW-EEN *IS* A FOREIGN COUNTRY!
WELL...
IT'S THE **PRIN-CIPLE** OF THE THING, AFTER ALL.

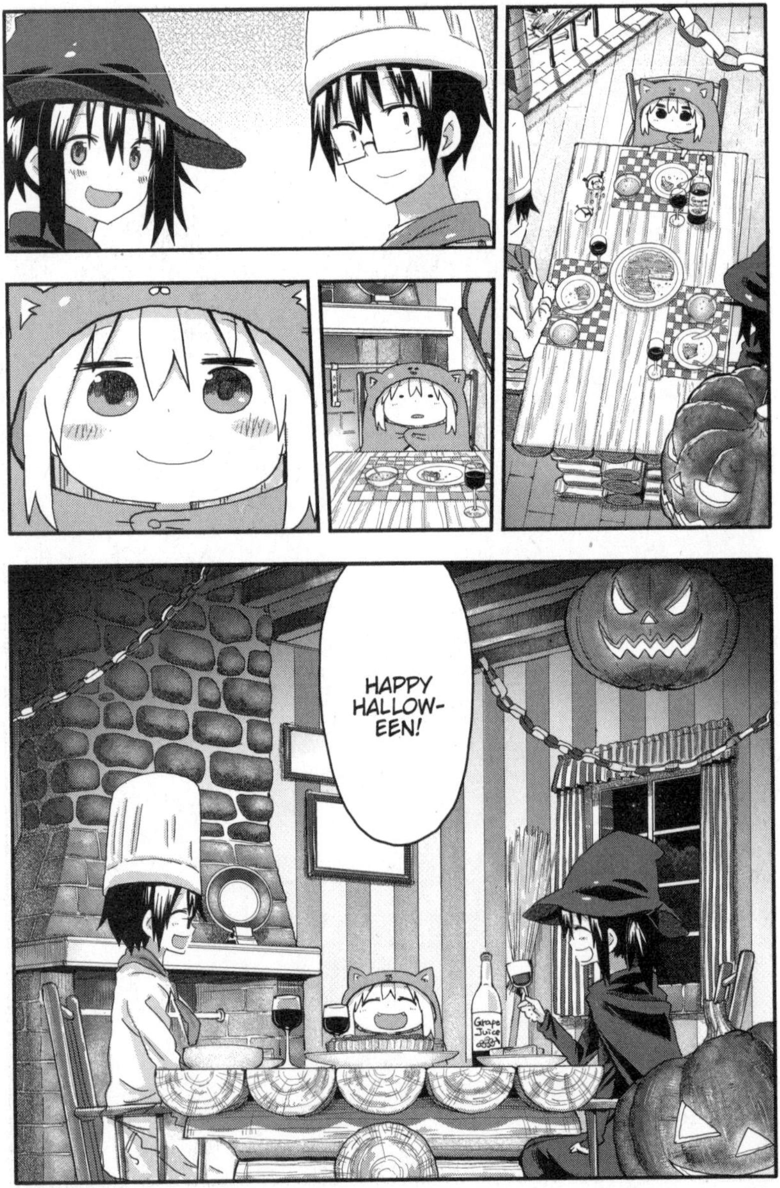
HAPPY HALLOW-EEN!
Grape Juice

No. 79 Umaru & Cleaning

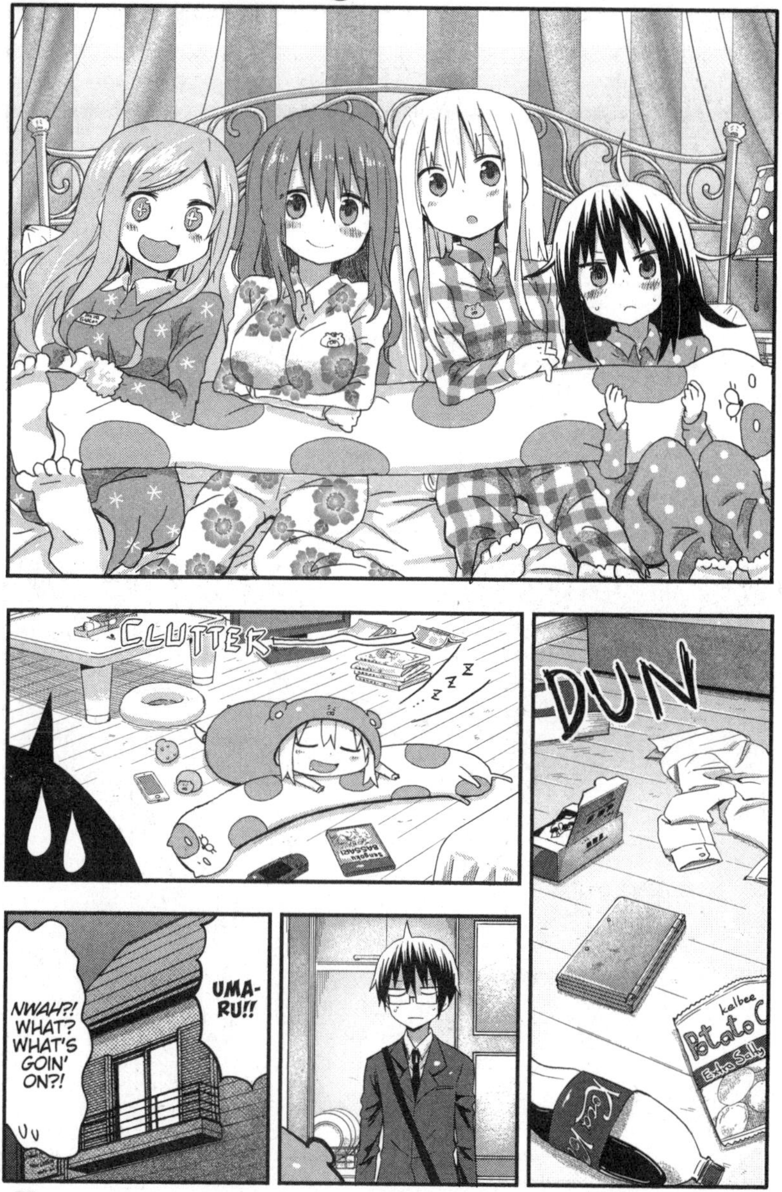
DUN
kelbee
CLUTTER
ZZZ
UMA-RU!!
NWAH?! WHAT? WHAT'S GOIN' ON?!

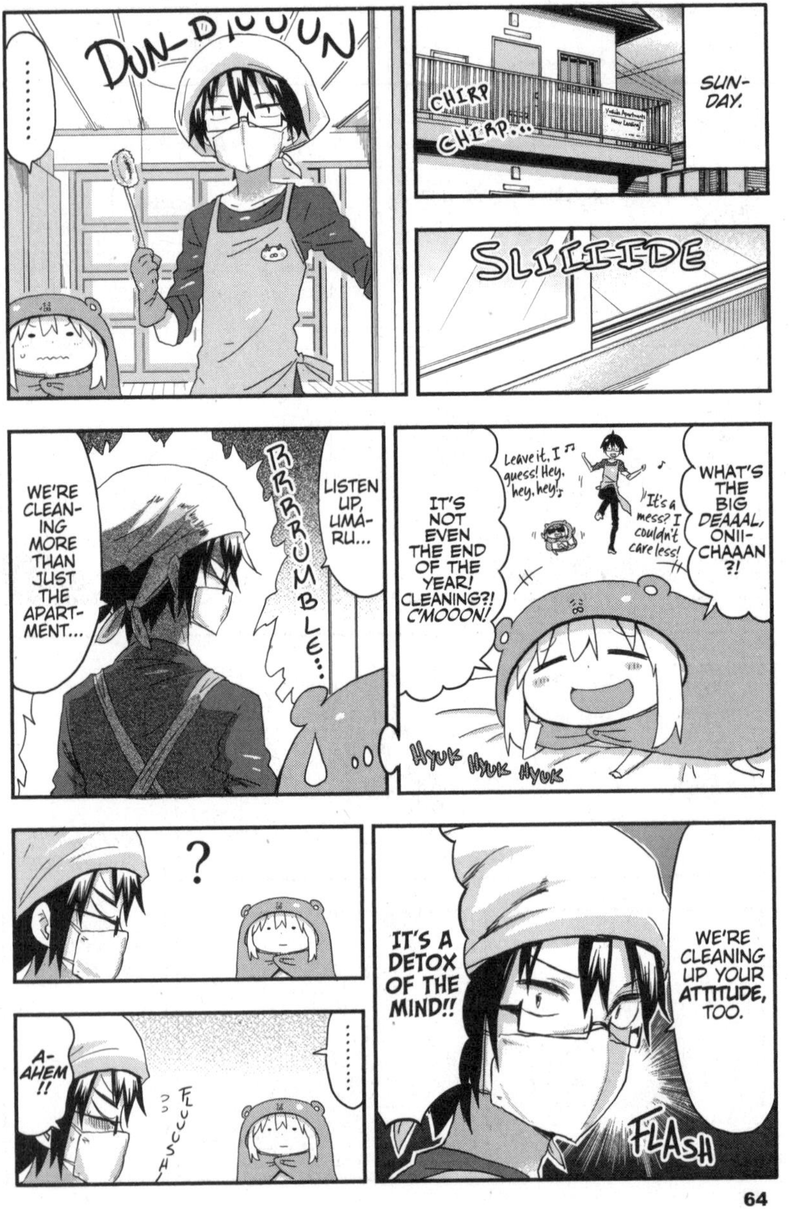
SUN-DAY.
CHIRP CHIRP...
SLIIIIDE
DUN-DUUUUN
......
WHAT'S THE BIG DEAAAL, ONII-CHAAAN?!
It's a mess? I couldn't care less!
Leave it, I guess! Hey, hey, hey!
IT'S NOT EVEN THE END OF THE YEAR! CLEANING?! C'MOOON!
HYUK HYUK HYUK
LISTEN UP, UMARU...
RRRUMBLE...
WE'RE CLEANING MORE THAN JUST THE APARTMENT...
WE'RE CLEANING UP YOUR ATTITUDE, TOO.
IT'S A DETOX OF THE MIND!!
FLASH
?
......
FLUUUSH
A-AHEM!!

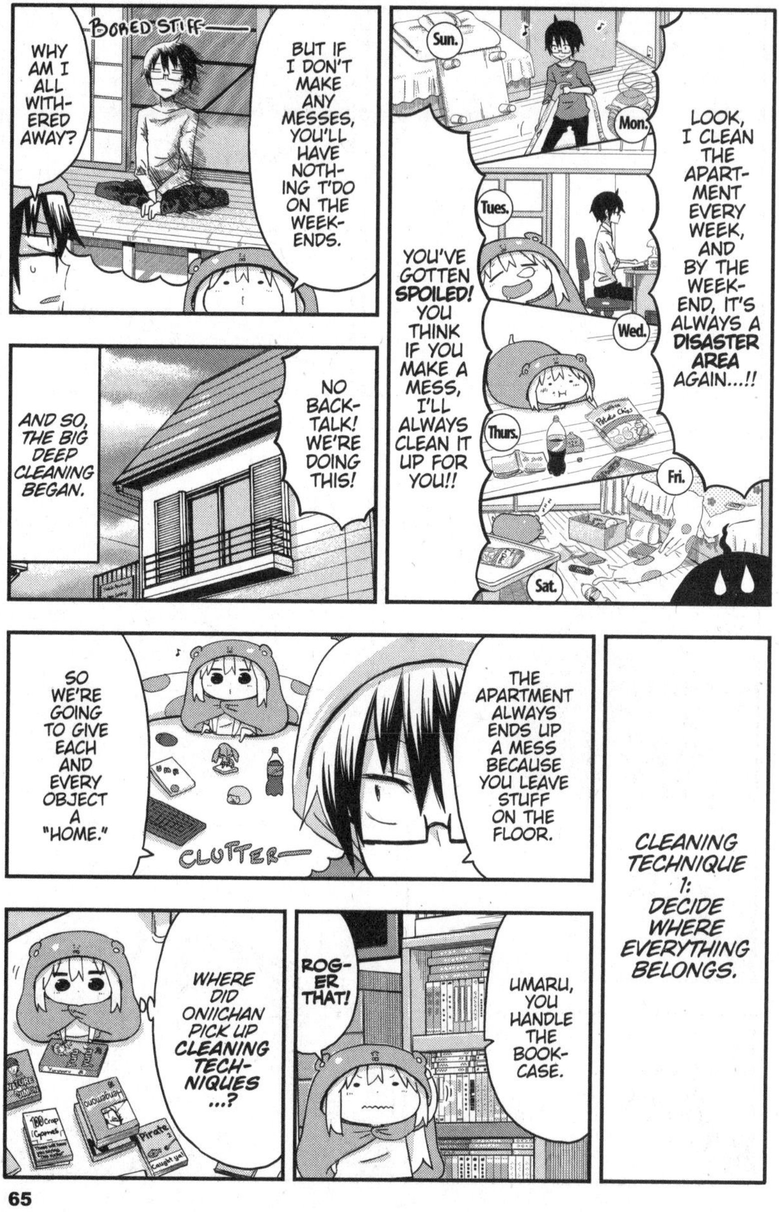

LOOK, I CLEAN THE APARTMENT EVERY WEEK, AND BY THE WEEKEND, IT'S ALWAYS A **DISASTER AREA** AGAIN...!!
Sun.
Mon.
Tues.
Wed.
Thurs.
Fri.
Sat.
YOU'VE GOTTEN **SPOILED!** YOU THINK IF YOU MAKE A MESS, I'LL ALWAYS CLEAN IT UP FOR YOU!!
BUT IF I DON'T MAKE ANY MESSES, YOU'LL HAVE NOTHING T'DO ON THE WEEKENDS.
BORED STIFF——
WHY AM I ALL WITHERED AWAY?
NO BACK-TALK! WE'RE DOING THIS!
AND SO, THE BIG DEEP CLEANING BEGAN.
CLEANING TECHNIQUE 1: DECIDE WHERE EVERYTHING BELONGS.
THE APARTMENT ALWAYS ENDS UP A MESS BECAUSE YOU LEAVE STUFF ON THE FLOOR.
SO WE'RE GOING TO GIVE EACH AND EVERY OBJECT A "HOME."
CLUTTER——
UMARU, YOU HANDLE THE BOOKCASE.
ROGER THAT!
WHERE DID ONIICHAN PICK UP **CLEANING TECHNIQUES**...?

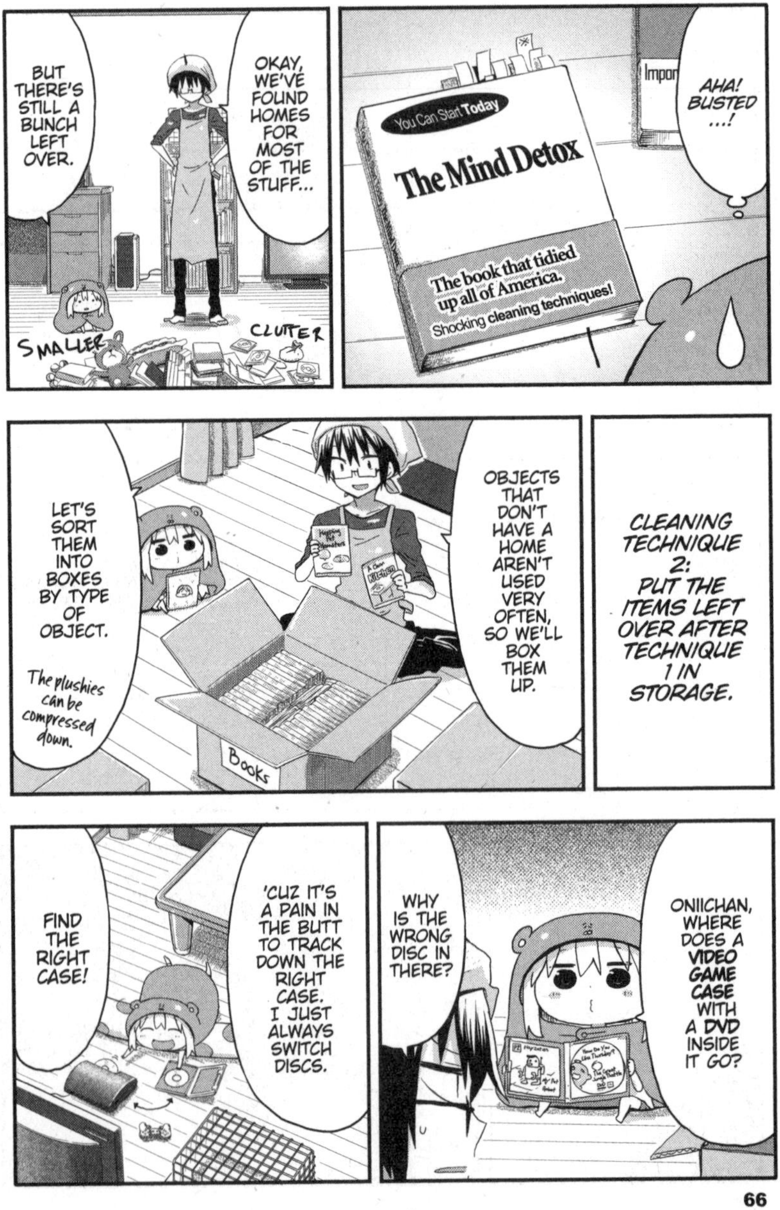
Impor
AHA! BUSTED ...!
You Can Start Today
The Mind Detox
The book that tidied up all of America.
Shocking cleaning techniques!
OKAY, WE'VE FOUND HOMES FOR MOST OF THE STUFF...
BUT THERE'S STILL A BUNCH LEFT OVER.
CLUTTER
SMALLER
CLEANING TECHNIQUE 2: PUT THE ITEMS LEFT OVER AFTER TECHNIQUE 1 IN STORAGE.
OBJECTS THAT DON'T HAVE A HOME AREN'T USED VERY OFTEN, SO WE'LL BOX THEM UP.
LET'S SORT THEM INTO BOXES BY TYPE OF OBJECT.
The plushies can be compressed down.
Books
ONIICHAN, WHERE DOES A **VIDEO GAME CASE** WITH A **DVD** INSIDE IT GO?
WHY IS THE WRONG DISC IN THERE?
'CUZ IT'S A PAIN IN THE BUTT TO TRACK DOWN THE RIGHT CASE. I JUST ALWAYS SWITCH DISCS.
FIND THE RIGHT CASE!

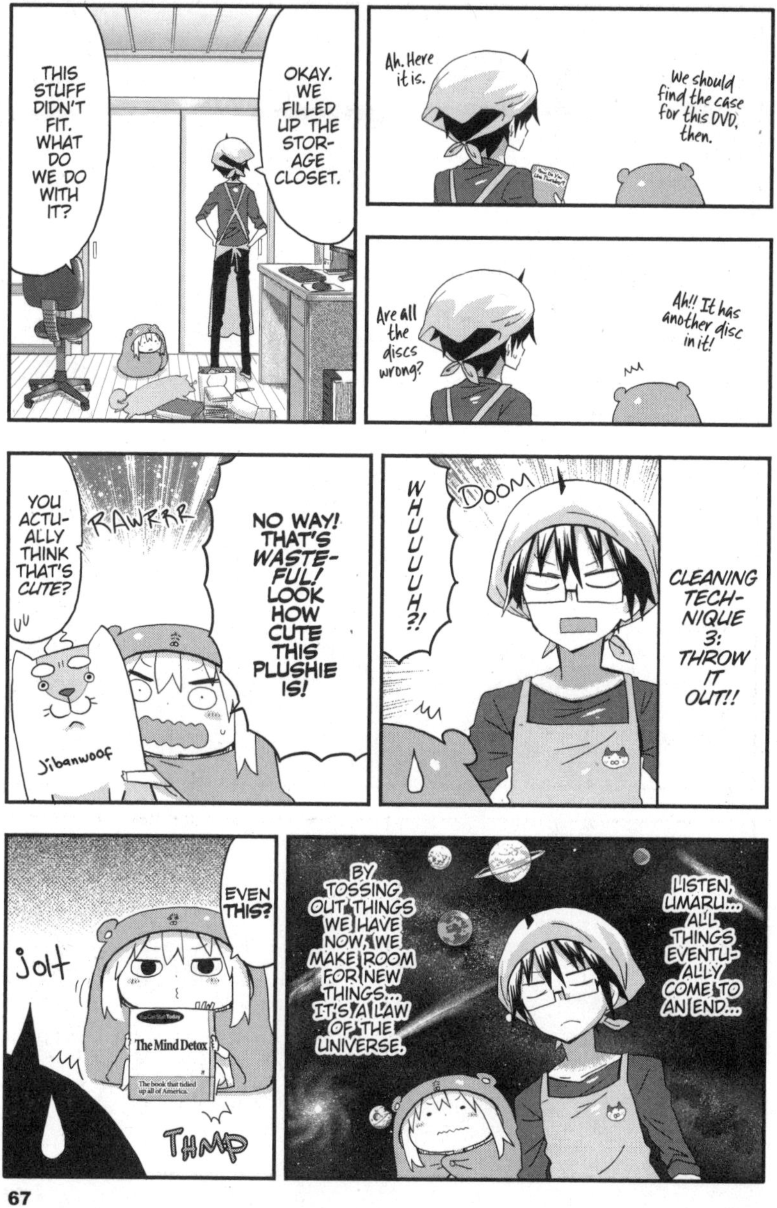
We should find the case for this DVD, then.
Ah. Here it is.
Ah!! It has another disc in it!
Are all the discs wrong?
OKAY. WE FILLED UP THE STORAGE CLOSET.
THIS STUFF DIDN'T FIT. WHAT DO WE DO WITH IT?
CLEANING TECHNIQUE 3: THROW IT OUT!!
DOOM
WHUUUUH?!
NO WAY! THAT'S WASTEFUL! LOOK HOW CUTE THIS PLUSHIE IS!
RAWRRR
YOU ACTUALLY THINK THAT'S CUTE?
Jibanwoof
LISTEN, UMARU... ALL THINGS EVENTUALLY COME TO AN END...
BY TOSSING OUT THINGS WE HAVE NOW, WE MAKE ROOM FOR NEW THINGS... IT'S A LAW OF THE UNIVERSE.
EVEN THIS?
jolt
The Mind Detox
The book that tidied up all of America.
THMP

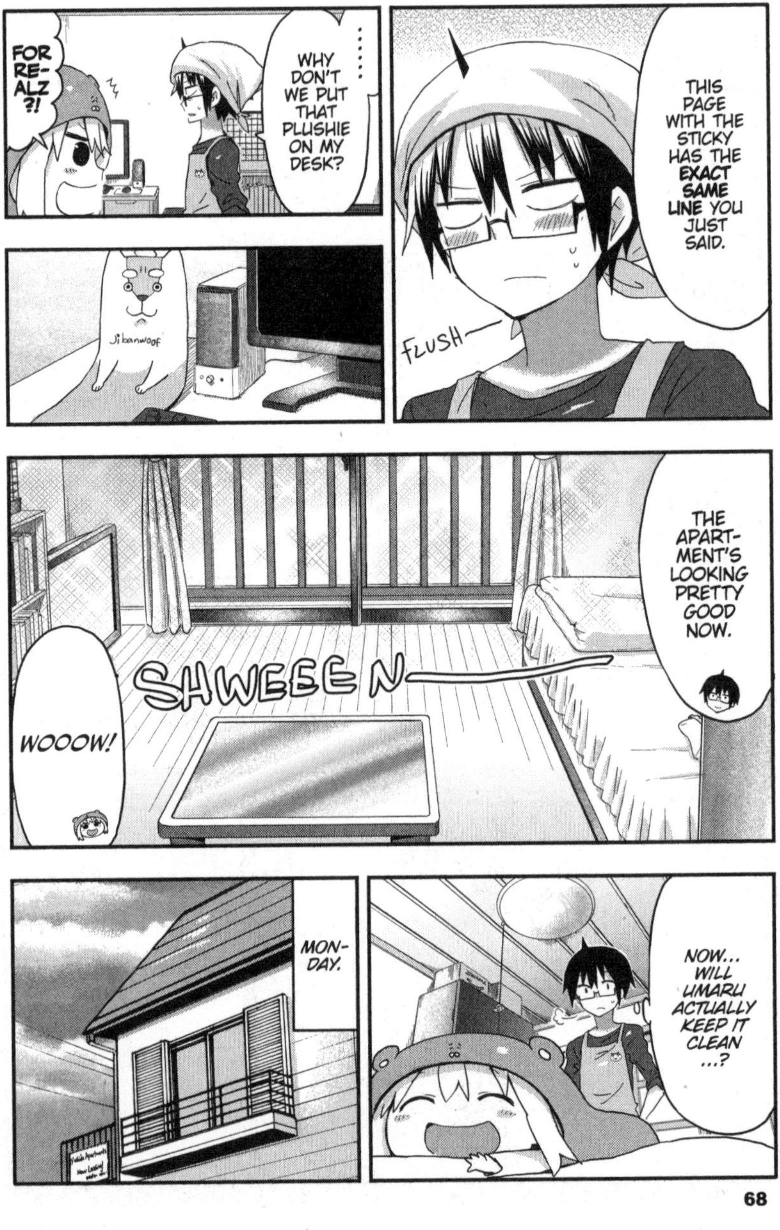

THIS PAGE WITH THE STICKY HAS THE **EXACT SAME LINE** YOU JUST SAID.
FLUSH
......
WHY DON'T WE PUT THAT PLUSHIE ON MY DESK?
FOR RE-ALZ?!
Jibanwoof
THE APART-MENT'S LOOKING PRETTY GOOD NOW.
SHWEEEN
WOOOW!
NOW... WILL UMARU ACTUALLY KEEP IT CLEAN ...?
MON-DAY.

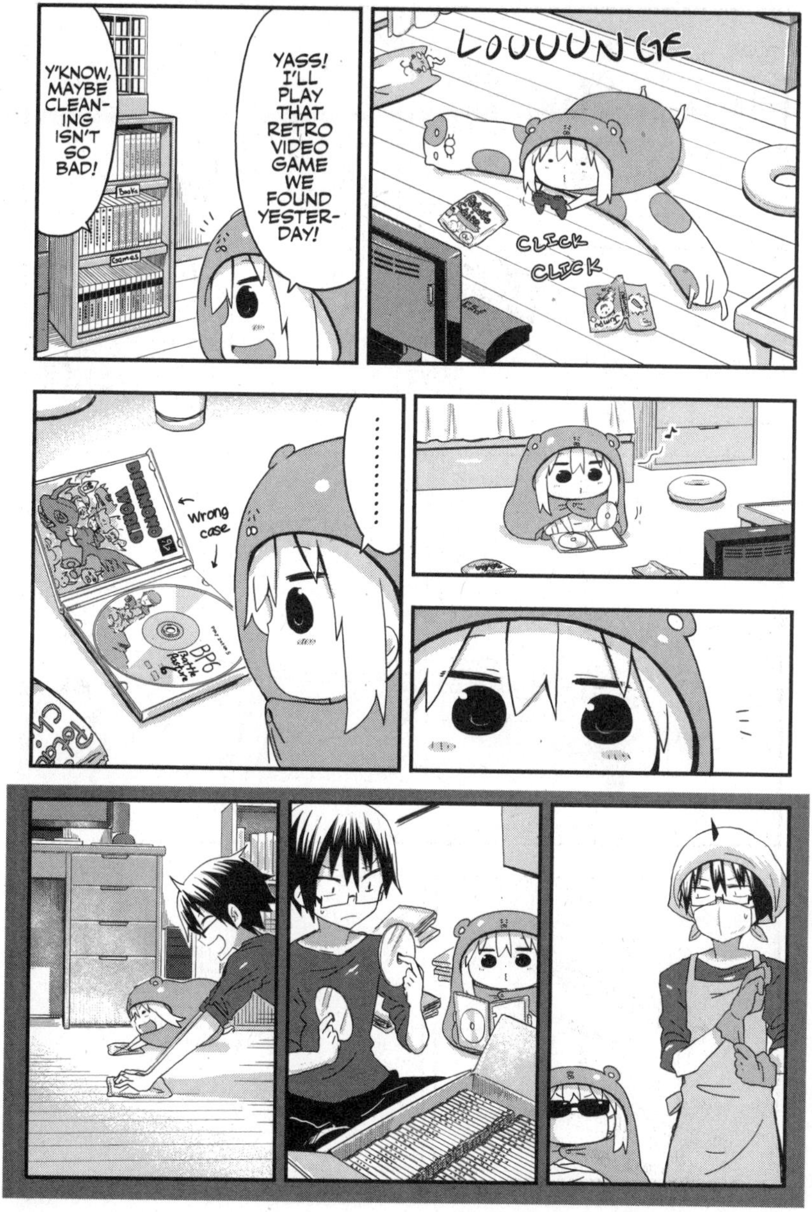
LOUUUNGE
CLICK
CLICK
YASS! I'LL PLAY THAT RETRO VIDEO GAME WE FOUND YESTER-DAY!
Y'KNOW, MAYBE CLEAN-ING ISN'T SO BAD!
Books
Games
......
Wrong case
BP6 Battle Pasture 6

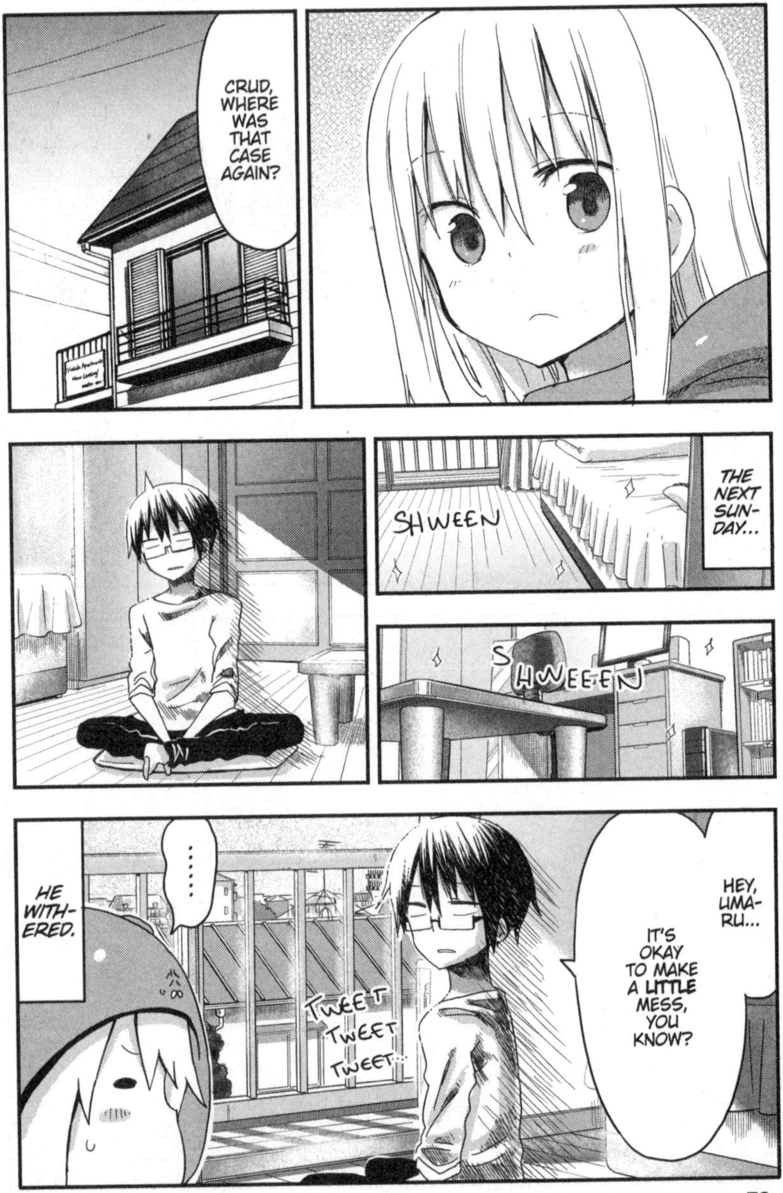
CRUD, WHERE WAS THAT CASE AGAIN?
THE NEXT SUN-DAY...
SHWEEN
SHWEEEN
HEY, UMA-RU...
IT'S OKAY TO MAKE A LITTLE MESS, YOU KNOW?
TWEET TWEET TWEET...
......
HE WITH-ERED.

No. 80 Umaru & the Soccer Tourney: Part 1

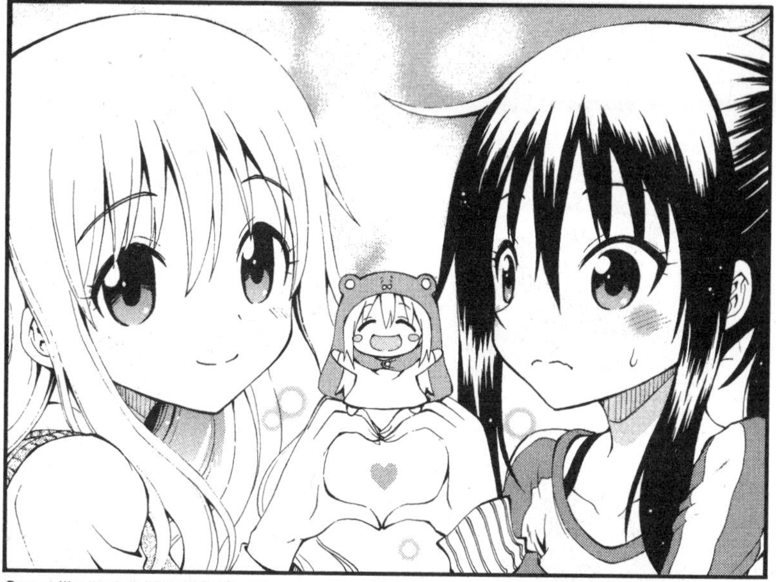

Guest Illustrator: Yuichi Hayashi

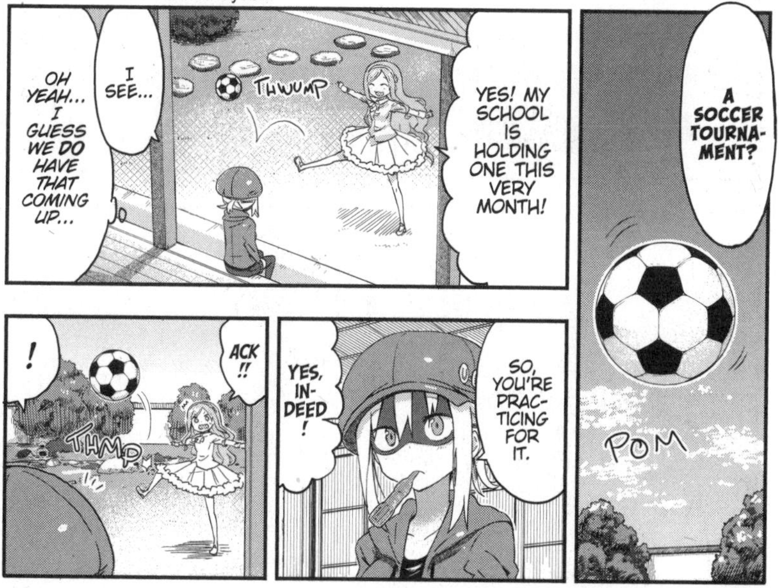
A SOCCER TOURNAMENT?
POM
YES! MY SCHOOL IS HOLDING ONE THIS VERY MONTH!
THWUMP
I SEE...
OH YEAH... I GUESS WE DO HAVE THAT COMING UP...
SO, YOU'RE PRACTICING FOR IT.
YES, INDEED!
ACK!!
!
THMP

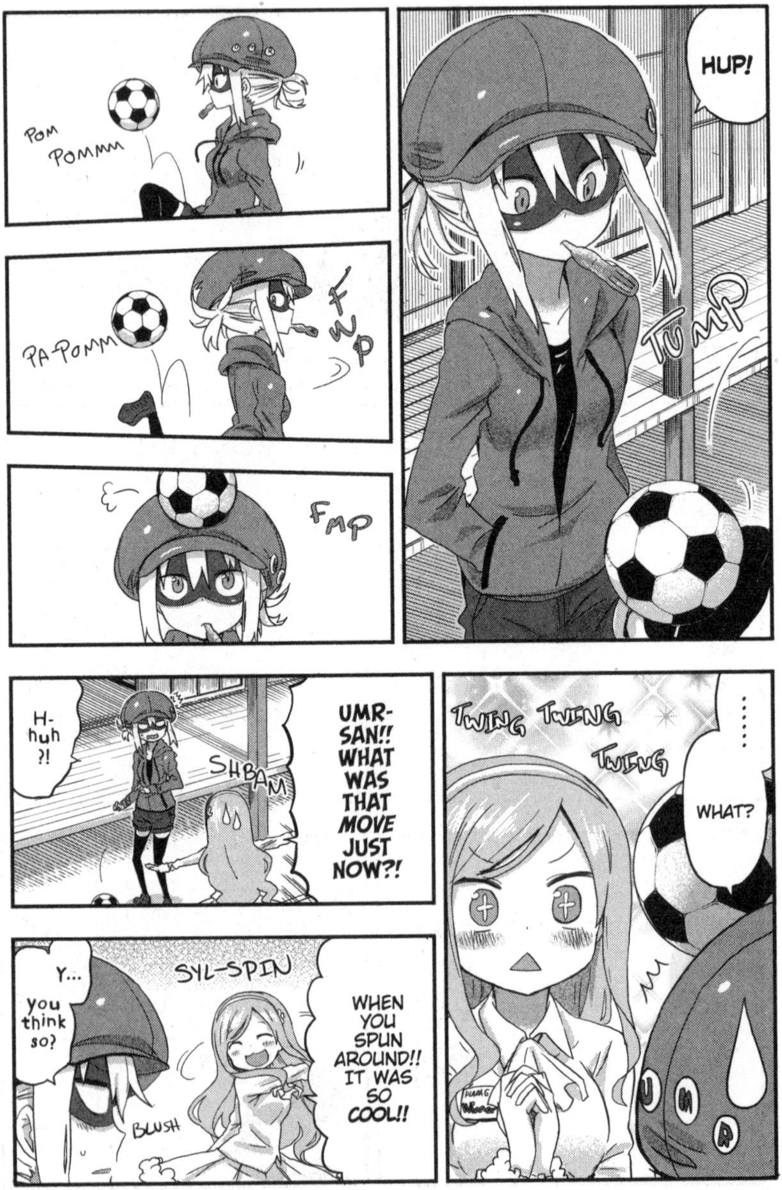

POM POMMM
PA-POMM
FWP
FMP
HUP!
TUMP
UMR-SAN!! WHAT WAS THAT MOVE JUST NOW?!
SHBAM
H-huh?!
WHEN YOU SPUN AROUND!! IT WAS SO COOL!!
SYL-SPIN
Y... you think so?
BLUSH
TWING TWING TWING
......
WHAT?

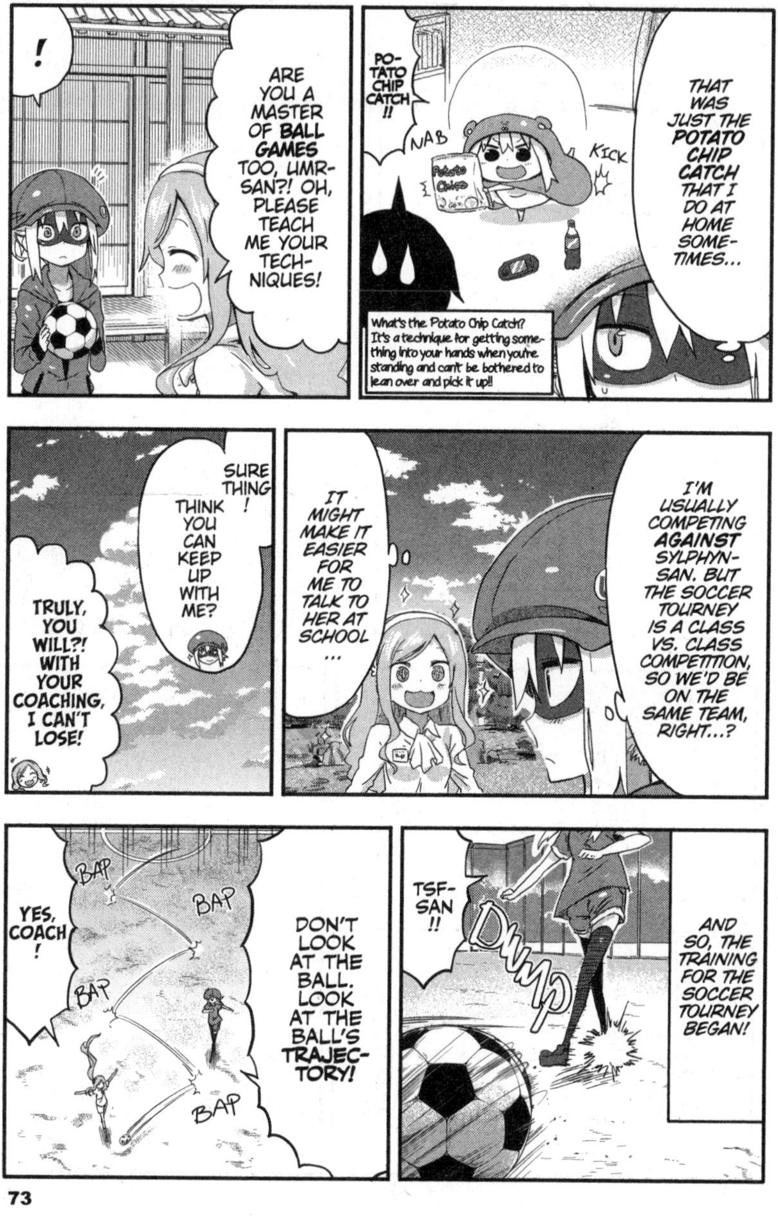
THAT WAS JUST THE POTATO CHIP CATCH THAT I DO AT HOME SOMETIMES...
KICK
PO-TATO CHIP CATCH!!
NAB
Potato Chips
What's the Potato Chip Catch? It's a technique for getting something into your hands when you're standing and can't be bothered to lean over and pick it up!!
ARE YOU A MASTER OF BALL GAMES TOO, UMR-SAN?! OH, PLEASE TEACH ME YOUR TECH-NIQUES!
!
I'M USUALLY COMPETING AGAINST SYLPHYN-SAN. BUT THE SOCCER TOURNEY IS A CLASS VS. CLASS COMPETITION, SO WE'D BE ON THE SAME TEAM, RIGHT...?
IT MIGHT MAKE IT EASIER FOR ME TO TALK TO HER AT SCHOOL...
SURE THING!
THINK YOU CAN KEEP UP WITH ME?
TRULY, YOU WILL?! WITH YOUR COACHING, I CAN'T LOSE!
AND SO, THE TRAINING FOR THE SOCCER TOURNEY BEGAN!
TSF-SAN!!
DUMP
DON'T LOOK AT THE BALL. LOOK AT THE BALL'S TRAJEC-TORY!
BAP
BAP
BAP
BAP
YES, COACH!

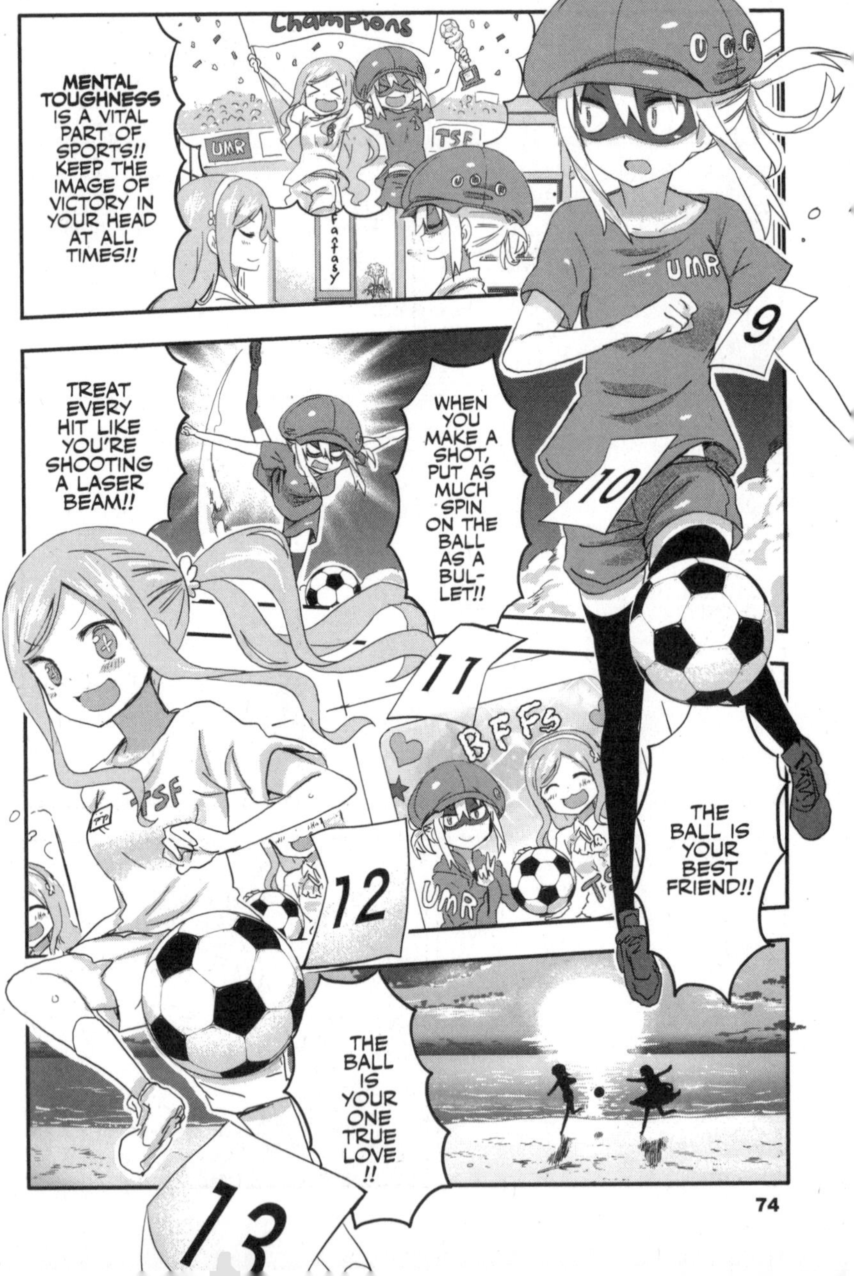
Champions
UMR
TSF
Fantasy
MENTAL TOUGHNESS IS A VITAL PART OF SPORTS!! KEEP THE IMAGE OF VICTORY IN YOUR HEAD AT ALL TIMES!!
UMR
9
10
WHEN YOU MAKE A SHOT, PUT AS MUCH SPIN ON THE BALL AS A BUL-LET!!
TREAT EVERY HIT LIKE YOU'RE SHOOTING A LASER BEAM!!
11
BFFs
UMR
THE BALL IS YOUR BEST FRIEND!!
TSF
12
THE BALL IS YOUR ONE TRUE LOVE!!
13

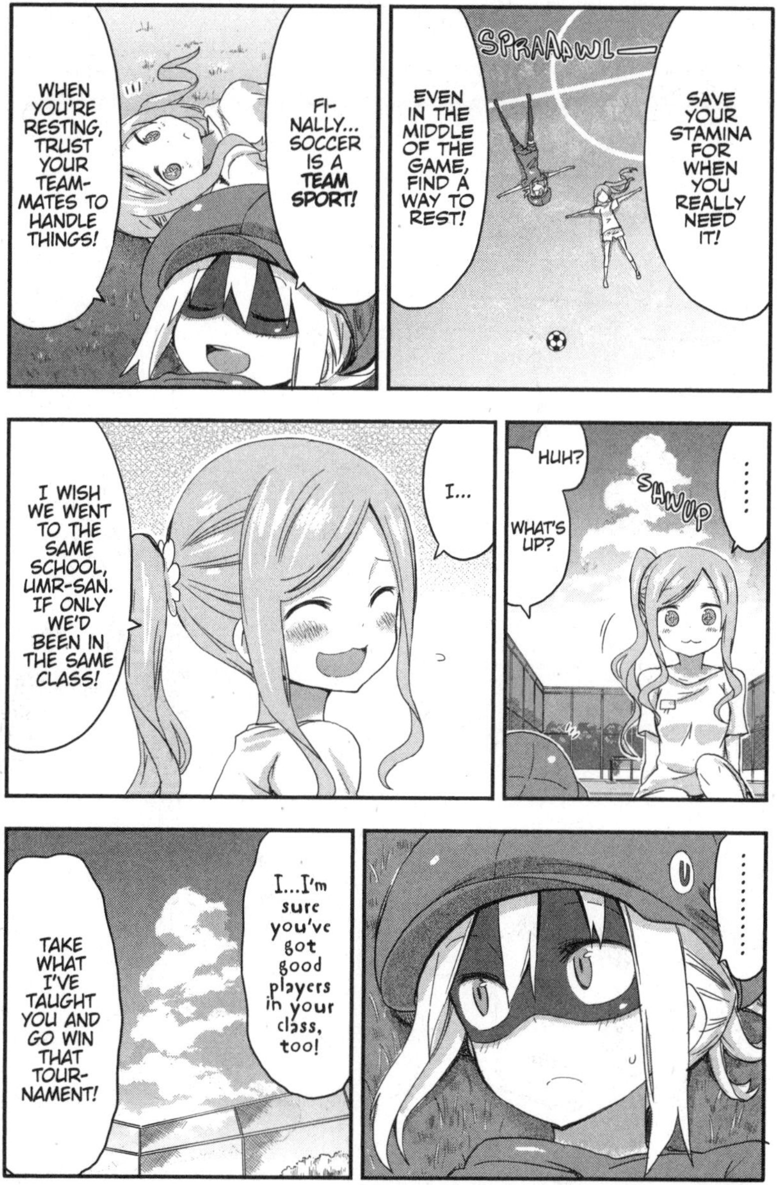

SPRAAAWL—
SAVE YOUR STAMINA FOR WHEN YOU REALLY NEED IT!
EVEN IN THE MIDDLE OF THE GAME, FIND A WAY TO REST!
FI-NALLY... SOCCER IS A **TEAM SPORT!**
WHEN YOU'RE RESTING, TRUST YOUR TEAM-MATES TO HANDLE THINGS!
......
SHWUP
HUH?
WHAT'S UP?
I...
I WISH WE WENT TO THE SAME SCHOOL, UMR-SAN. IF ONLY WE'D BEEN IN THE SAME CLASS!
....
I...I'm sure you've got good players in your class, too!
TAKE WHAT I'VE TAUGHT YOU AND GO WIN THAT TOUR-NAMENT!

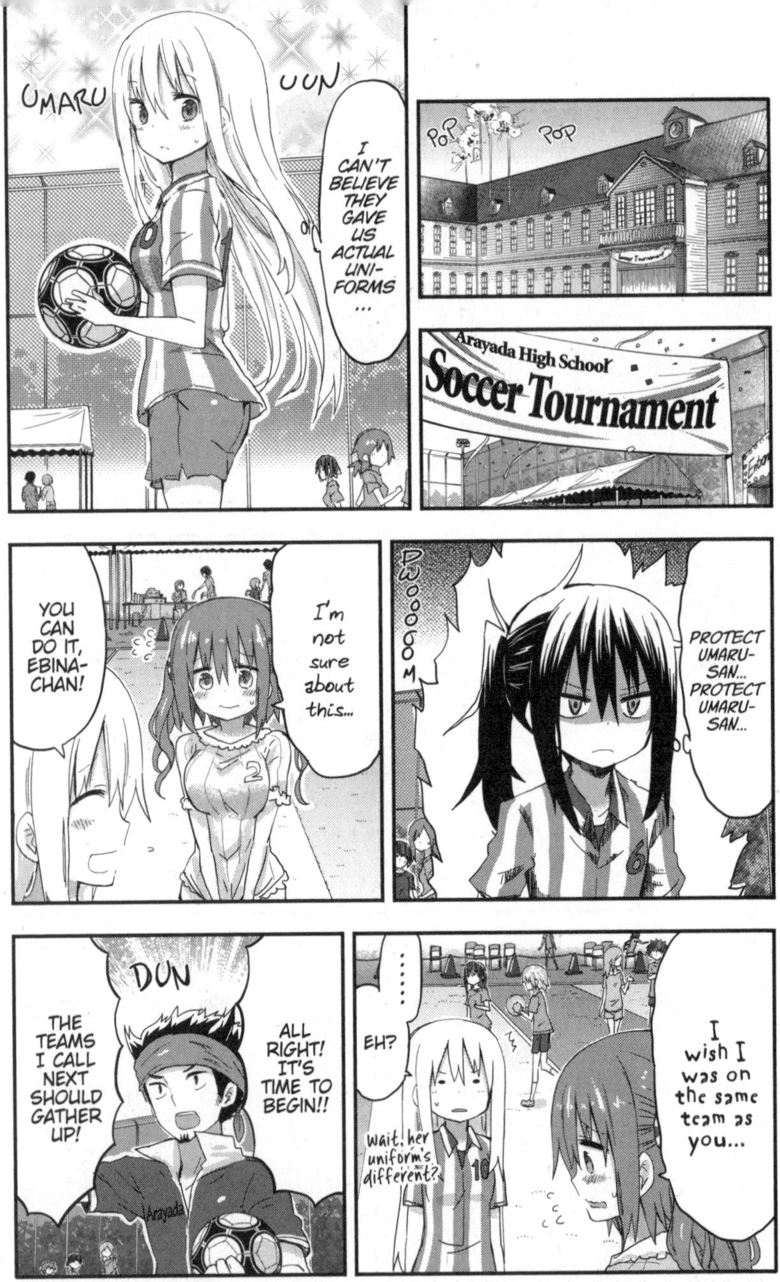
POP
POP
Arayada High School
Soccer Tournament
UMARU
UUN
I CAN'T BELIEVE THEY GAVE US ACTUAL UNI-FORMS...
PWOOOOOOM
PROTECT UMARU-SAN... PROTECT UMARU-SAN...
I'm not sure about this...
YOU CAN DO IT, EBINA-CHAN!
I wish I was on the same team as you...
......
EH?
Wait, her uniform's different?
DUN
ALL RIGHT! IT'S TIME TO BEGIN!!
THE TEAMS I CALL NEXT SHOULD GATHER UP!
Arayada

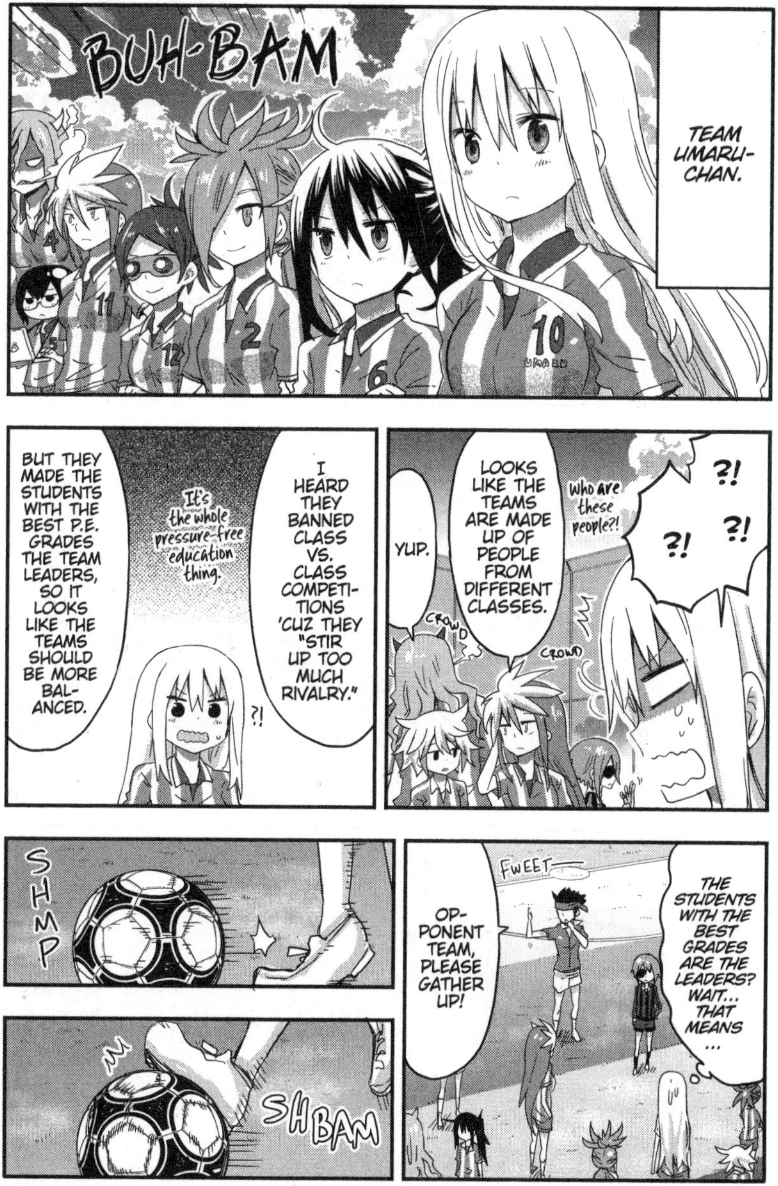
TEAM UMARU-CHAN.
BUH-BAM
?!
?!
?!
Who are these people?!
LOOKS LIKE THE TEAMS ARE MADE UP OF PEOPLE FROM DIFFERENT CLASSES.
YUP.
CROWD
CROWD
I HEARD THEY BANNED CLASS VS. CLASS COMPETITIONS 'CUZ THEY "STIR UP TOO MUCH RIVALRY."
It's the whole pressure-free education thing.
BUT THEY MADE THE STUDENTS WITH THE BEST P.E. GRADES THE TEAM LEADERS, SO IT LOOKS LIKE THE TEAMS SHOULD BE MORE BALANCED.
?!
THE STUDENTS WITH THE BEST GRADES ARE THE LEADERS? WAIT... THAT MEANS...
FWEET
OPPONENT TEAM, PLEASE GATHER UP!
SHMP
SHBAM

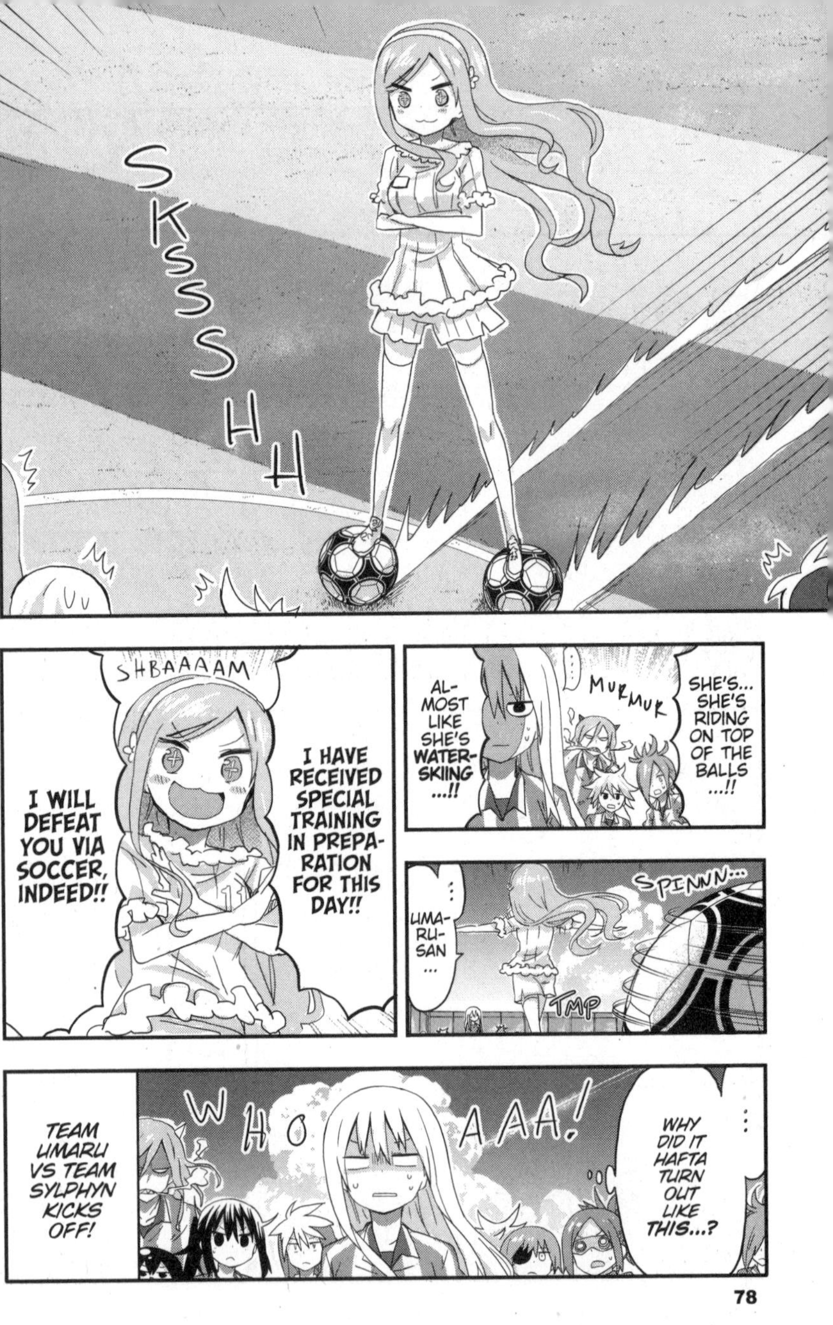
SKSSSHH
SHE'S... SHE'S RIDING ON TOP OF THE BALLS ...!!
MURMUR
AL-MOST LIKE SHE'S WATER-SKIING ...!!
...
SPINNN...
... UMA-RU-SAN ...
TMP
SHBAAAAM
I HAVE RECEIVED SPECIAL TRAINING IN PREPA-RATION FOR THIS DAY!!
I WILL DEFEAT YOU VIA SOCCER, INDEED!!
...
WHY DID IT HAFTA TURN OUT LIKE THIS...?
WHOAAA!
TEAM UMARU VS TEAM SYLPHYN KICKS OFF!

No. 81

Umaru & the Soccer Tourney: Part 2

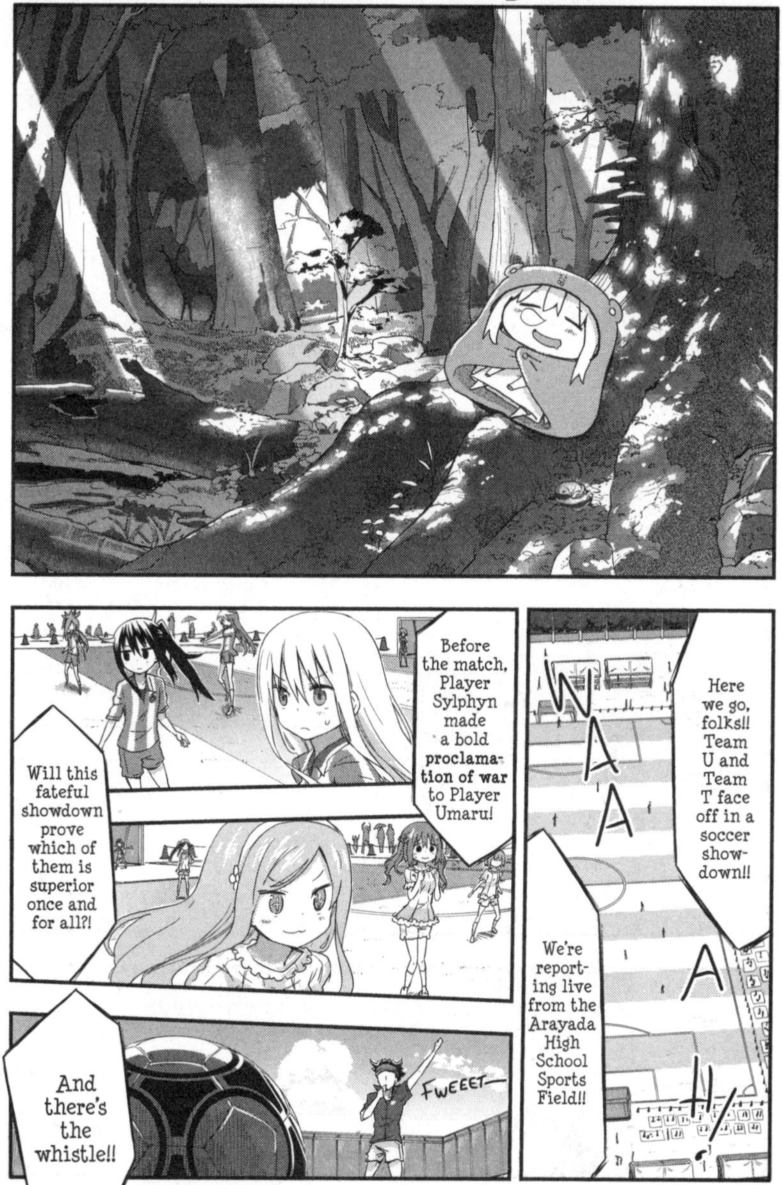

Here we go, folks!! Team U and Team T face off in a soccer showdown!!
WAAAH!
We're reporting live from the Arayada High School Sports Field!!
Before the match, Player Sylphyn made a bold **proclamation of war** to Player Umaru!
Will this fateful showdown prove which of them is superior once and for all?!
FWEEET—
And there's the whistle!!

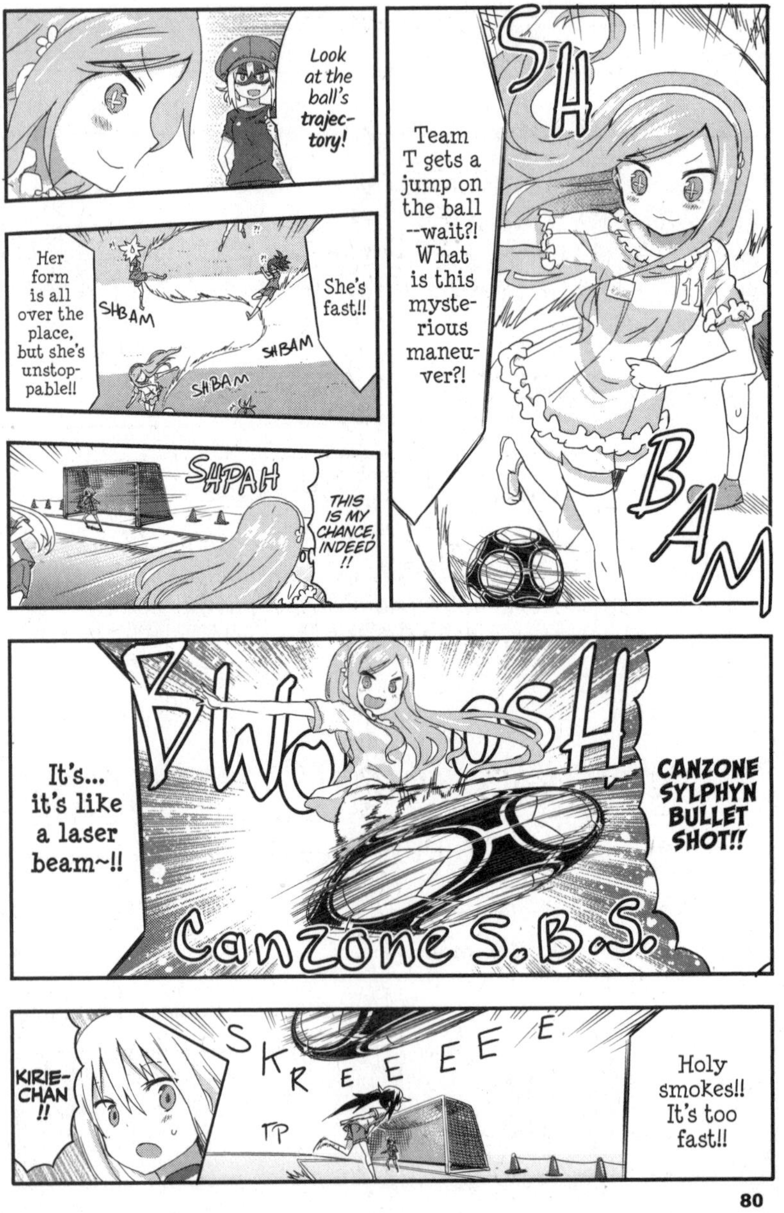
SH
Team T gets a jump on the ball --wait?! What is this mysterious maneuver?!
BAM
Look at the ball's trajectory!
She's fast!!
SHBAM
SHBAM
SHBAM
Her form is all over the place, but she's unstoppable!!
SHPAH
THIS IS MY CHANCE, INDEED!!
CANZONE SYLPHYN BULLET SHOT!!
It's... it's like a laser beam~!!
Canzone S.B.S.
Holy smokes!! It's too fast!!
SKREEEEE
TP
KIRIE-CHAN!!

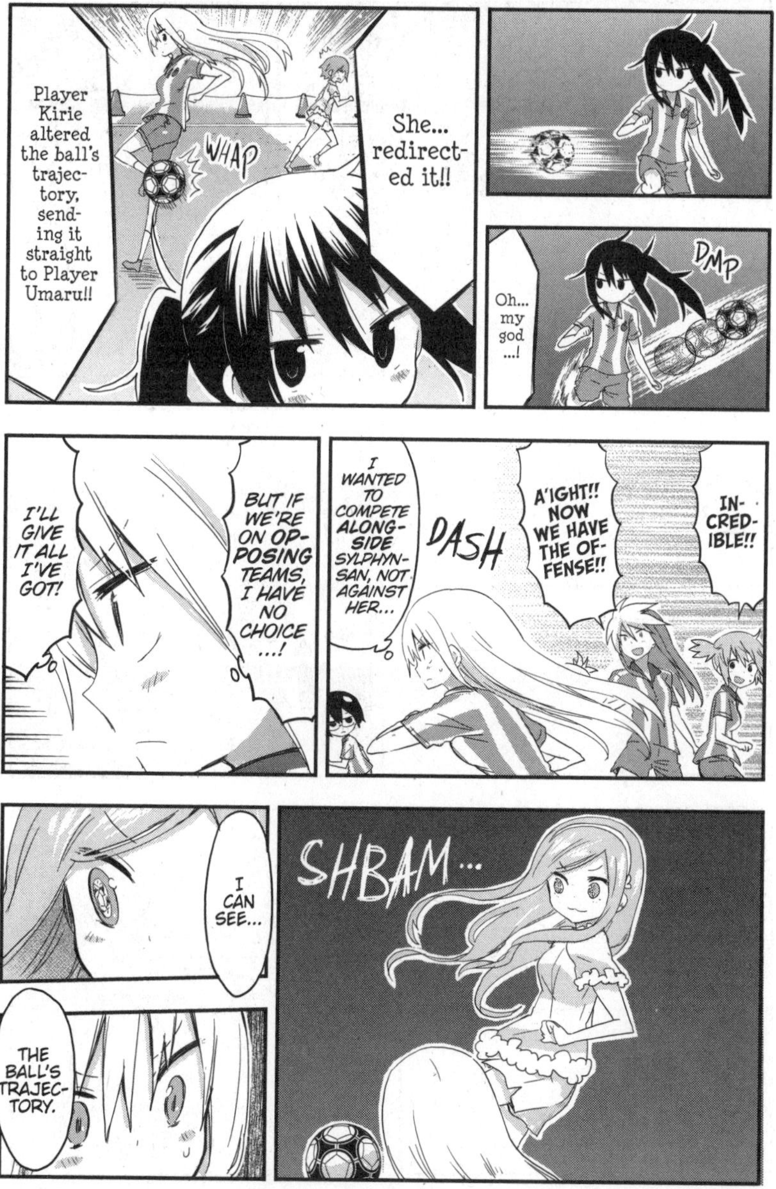
DMP
Oh... my god ...!
She... redirected it!!
Player Kirie altered the ball's trajectory, sending it straight to Player Umaru!!
WHAP
INCREDIBLE!!
A'IGHT!! NOW WE HAVE THE OFFENSE!!
DASH
I WANTED TO COMPETE ALONGSIDE SYLPHYN-SAN, NOT AGAINST HER...
BUT IF WE'RE ON OPPOSING TEAMS, I HAVE NO CHOICE ...!
I'LL GIVE IT ALL I'VE GOT!
SHBAM...
I CAN SEE...
THE BALL'S TRAJECTORY.

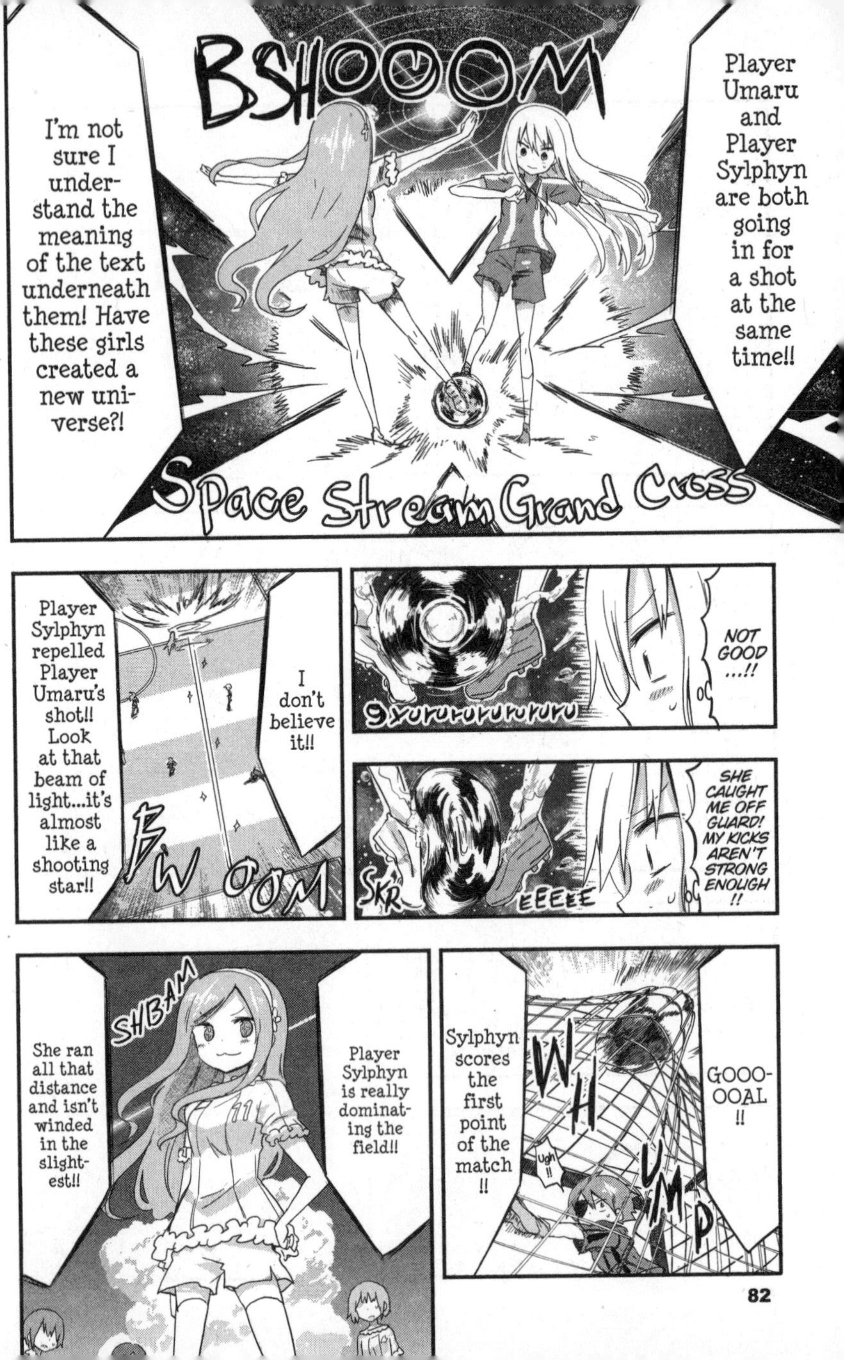

Player Umaru and Player Sylphyn are both going in for a shot at the same time!!
BSHOOOM
I'm not sure I under-stand the meaning of the text underneath them! Have these girls created a new uni-verse?!
Space Stream Grand Cross
NOT GOOD ...!!
gyururururururu
SHE CAUGHT ME OFF GUARD! MY KICKS AREN'T STRONG ENOUGH !!
SKREEEEE
Player Sylphyn repelled Player Umaru's shot!! Look at that beam of light...it's almost like a shooting star!!
I don't believe it!!
BWOOM
GOOO-OOAL !!
Sylphyn scores the first point of the match !!
WHUMP
Ugh !!
Player Sylphyn is really dominat-ing the field!!
SHBAM
She ran all that distance and isn't winded in the slight-est!!

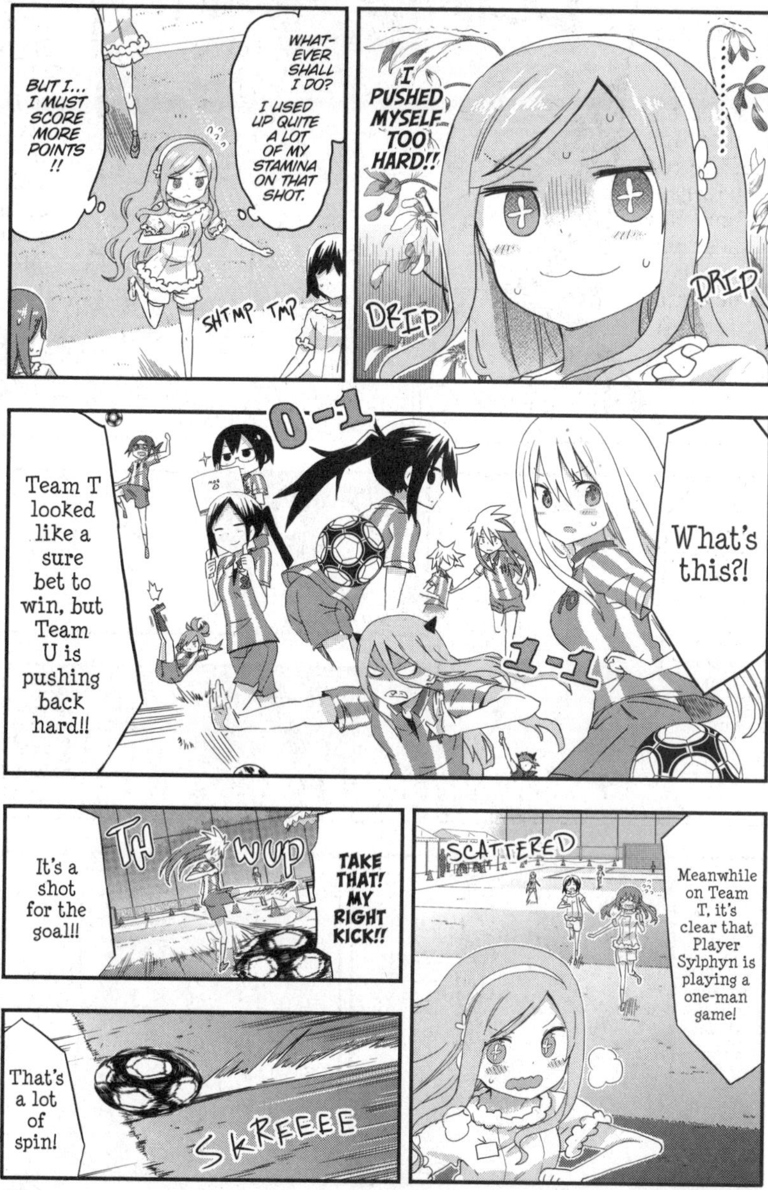
I PUSHED MYSELF TOO HARD!!
DRIP
DRIP
WHAT-EVER SHALL I DO?
I USED UP QUITE A LOT OF MY STAMINA ON THAT SHOT.
BUT I... I MUST SCORE MORE POINTS!!
SHTMP TMP
What's this?!
0-1
1-1
Team T looked like a sure bet to win, but Team U is pushing back hard!!
Meanwhile on Team T, it's clear that Player Sylphyn is playing a one-man game!
SCATTERED
TH WUP
TAKE THAT! MY RIGHT KICK!!
It's a shot for the goal!!
That's a lot of spin!
SKRFEEE

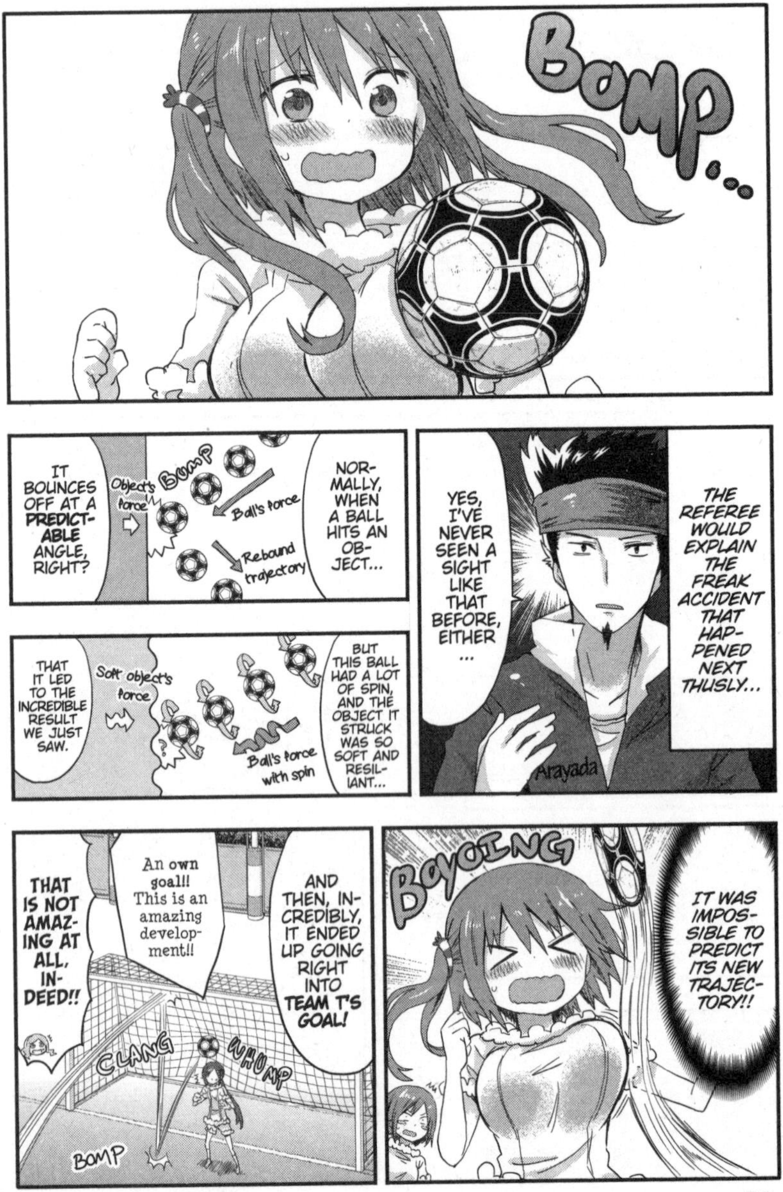
BOMP...
THE REFEREE WOULD EXPLAIN THE FREAK ACCIDENT THAT HAPPENED NEXT THUSLY...
YES, I'VE NEVER SEEN A SIGHT LIKE THAT BEFORE, EITHER...
Arayada
NORMALLY, WHEN A BALL HITS AN OBJECT...
BUMP
Object's force
Ball's force
Rebound trajectory
IT BOUNCES OFF AT A PREDICTABLE ANGLE, RIGHT?
BUT THIS BALL HAD A LOT OF SPIN, AND THE OBJECT IT STRUCK WAS SO SOFT AND RESILIANT...
Soft object's force
Ball's force with spin
THAT IT LED TO THE INCREDIBLE RESULT WE JUST SAW.
BOYOING
IT WAS IMPOSSIBLE TO PREDICT ITS NEW TRAJECTORY!!
AND THEN, INCREDIBLY, IT ENDED UP GOING RIGHT INTO TEAM T'S GOAL!
An own goal!! This is an amazing development!!
THAT IS NOT AMAZING AT ALL, INDEED!!
CLANG
WHUMP
BOMP

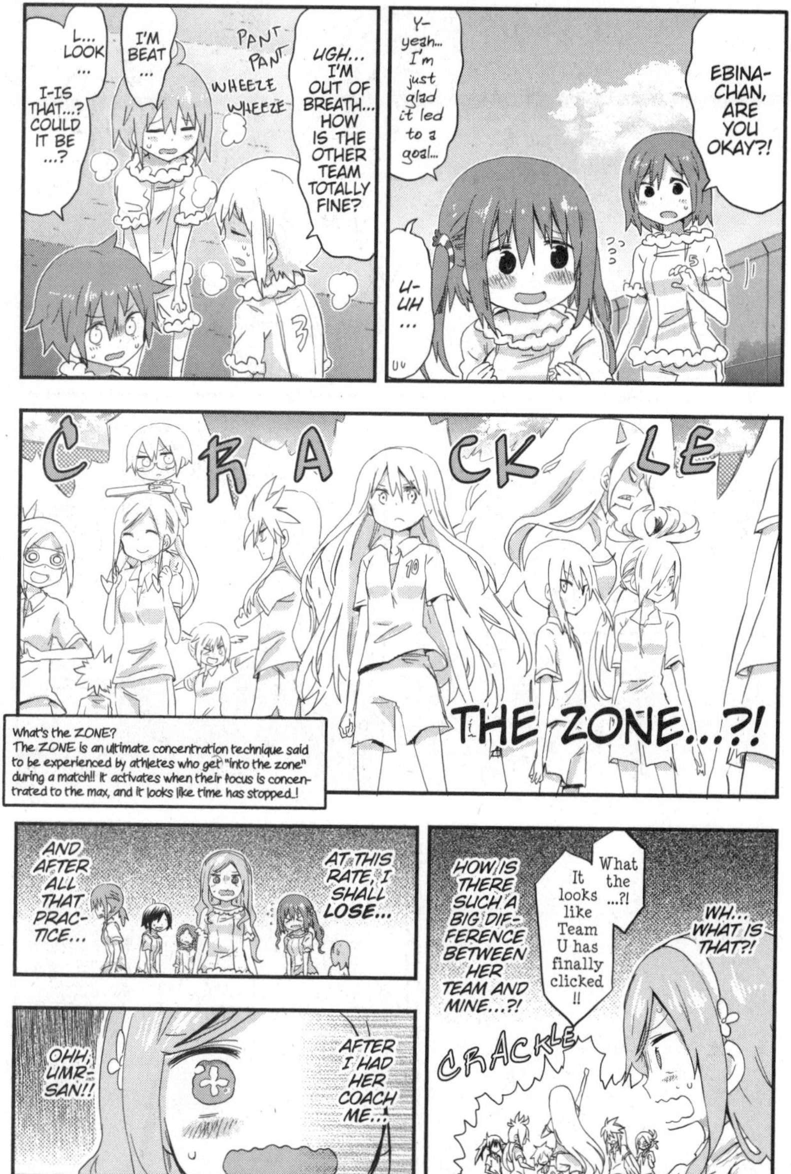
EBINA-CHAN, ARE YOU OKAY?!
Y-yeah... I'm just glad it led to a goal...
U-UH...
UGH... I'M OUT OF BREATH... HOW IS THE OTHER TEAM TOTALLY FINE?
PANT PANT
WHEEZE WHEEZE
I'M BEAT...
L... LOOK...
I-IS THAT...? COULD IT BE...?
CRACKLE
THE ZONE...?!
What's the ZONE?
The ZONE is an ultimate concentration technique said to be experienced by athletes who get "into the zone" during a match!! It activates when their focus is concentrated to the max, and it looks like time has stopped!
WH... WHAT IS THAT?!
What the ...?!
It looks like Team U has finally clicked !!
HOW IS THERE SUCH A BIG DIFFERENCE BETWEEN HER TEAM AND MINE...?!
CRACKLE
AT THIS RATE, I SHALL LOSE...
AND AFTER ALL THAT PRACTICE...
AFTER I HAD HER COACH ME...
OHH, UMR-SAN!!

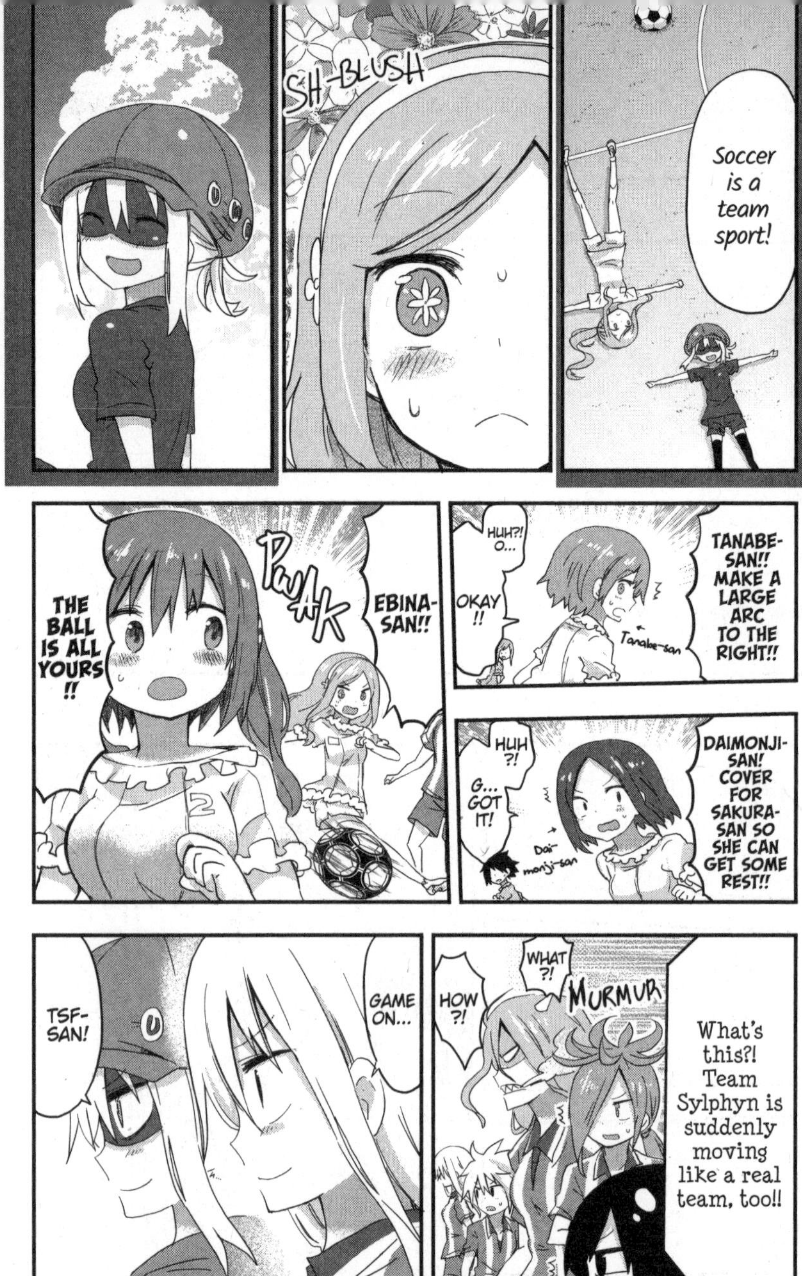

Soccer is a team sport!
SH-BLUSH
TANABE-SAN!! MAKE A LARGE ARC TO THE RIGHT!!
HUH?! O...
OKAY!!
Tanabe-san
DAIMONJI-SAN! COVER FOR SAKURA-SAN SO SHE CAN GET SOME REST!!
HUH?!
G... GOT IT!
Dai-monji-san
EBINA-SAN!!
PWAK
THE BALL IS ALL YOURS!!
What's this?! Team Sylphyn is suddenly moving like a real team, too!!
MURMUR
WHAT?!
HOW?!
GAME ON...
TSF-SAN!

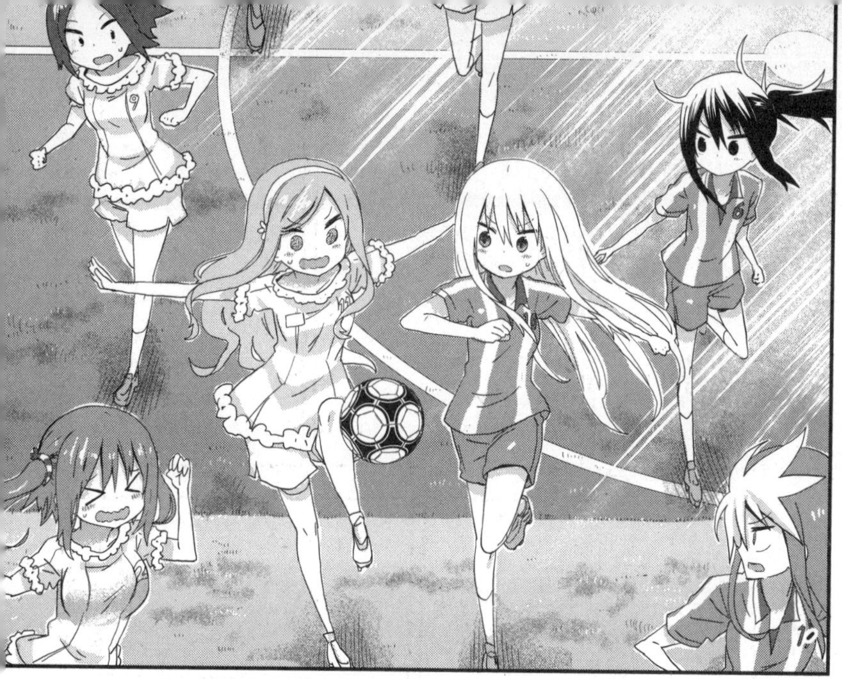

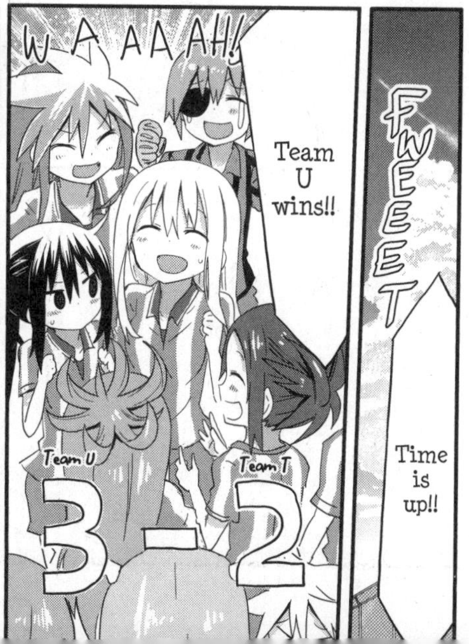
FWEEET
Time is up!!
Team U wins!!
WAAAAH!
Team U
3 - 2
Team T

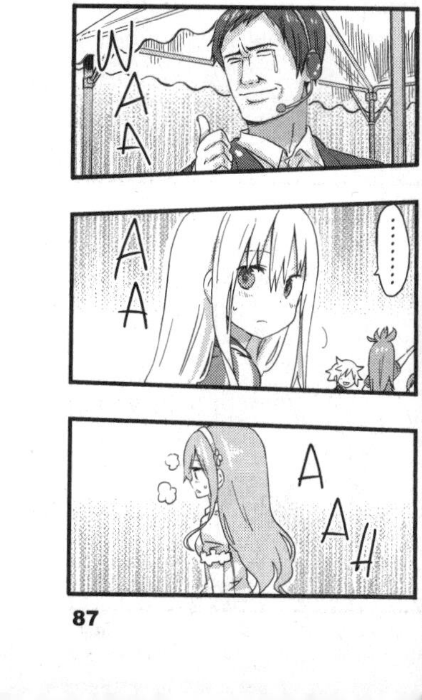
WAA
......
AA
AAH

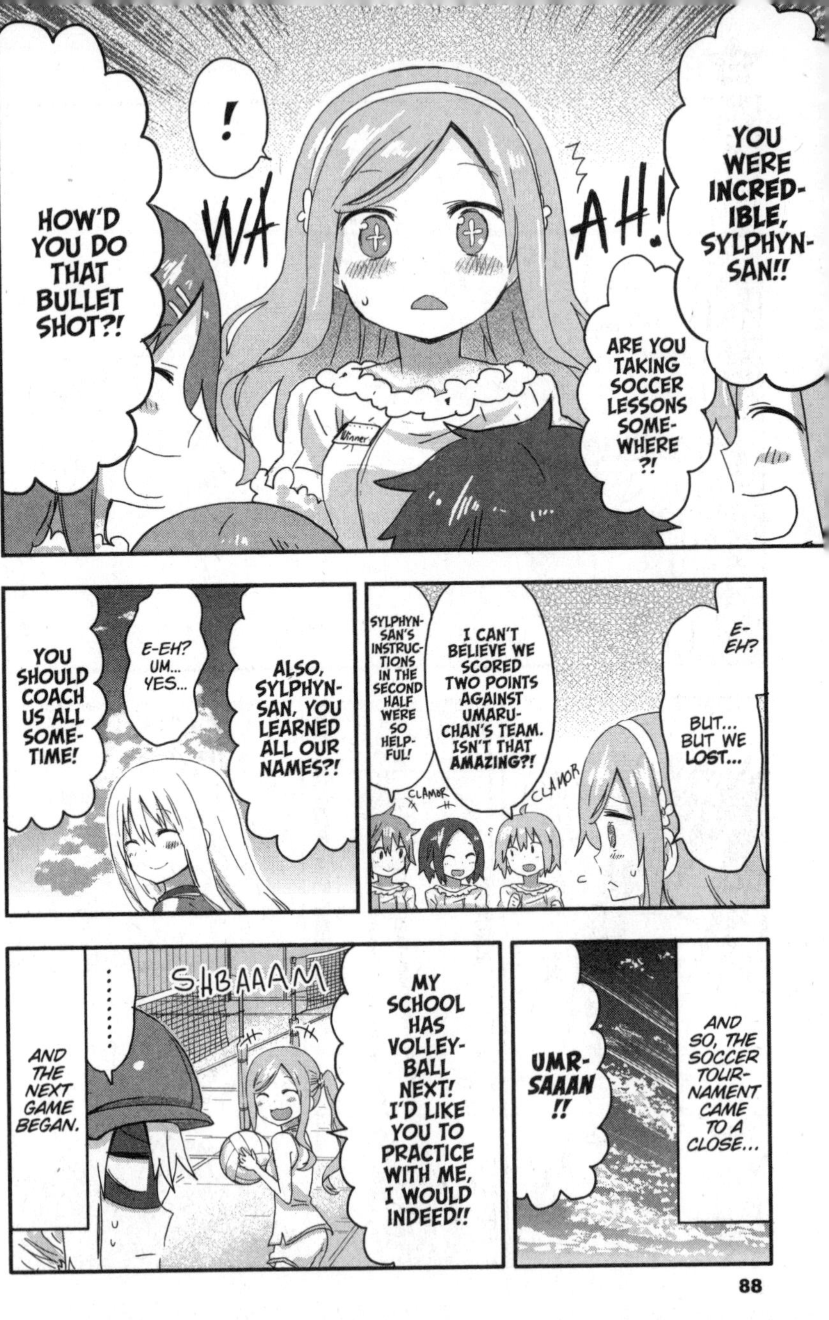
YOU WERE INCREDIBLE, SYLPHYN-SAN!!
ARE YOU TAKING SOCCER LESSONS SOMEWHERE?!
WA AH!
!
Winner
HOW'D YOU DO THAT BULLET SHOT?!
E-EH?
BUT... BUT WE LOST...
I CAN'T BELIEVE WE SCORED TWO POINTS AGAINST UMARU-CHAN'S TEAM. ISN'T THAT AMAZING?!
CLAMOR
SYLPHYN-SAN'S INSTRUCTIONS IN THE SECOND HALF WERE SO HELPFUL!
CLAMOR
ALSO, SYLPHYN-SAN, YOU LEARNED ALL OUR NAMES?!
E-EH? UM... YES...
YOU SHOULD COACH US ALL SOMETIME!
AND SO, THE SOCCER TOURNAMENT CAME TO A CLOSE...
UMR-SAAAN!!
MY SCHOOL HAS VOLLEYBALL NEXT! I'D LIKE YOU TO PRACTICE WITH ME, I WOULD INDEED!!
SHBAAAM
......
AND THE NEXT GAME BEGAN.

No. 82 Oniichan's Wrath

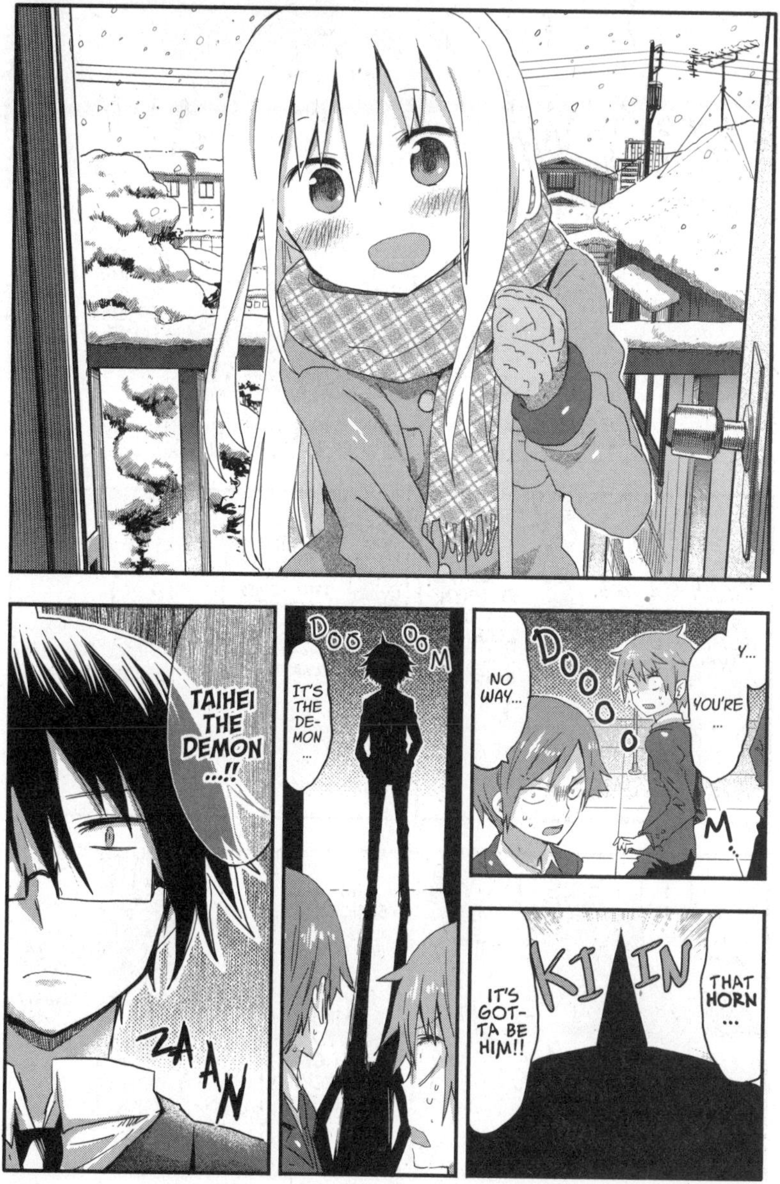
Y... YOU'RE...
NO WAY...
DOOOOOM...
THAT HORN...
IT'S GOTTA BE HIM!!
KIIIN
DOOOOM
IT'S THE DEMON...
TAIHEI THE DEMON...!!
ZAAN

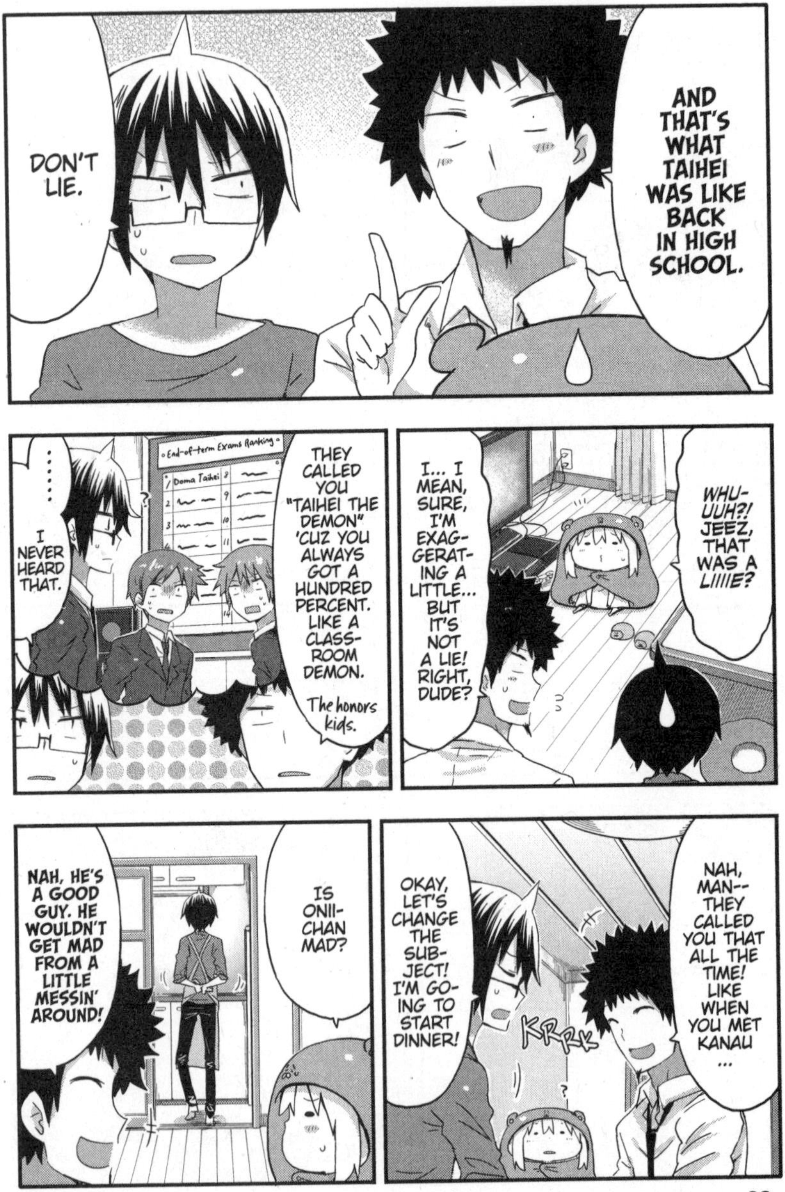
AND THAT'S WHAT TAIHEI WAS LIKE BACK IN HIGH SCHOOL.
DON'T LIE.
WHUUUH?! JEEZ, THAT WAS A LIIIIE?
I... I MEAN, SURE, I'M EXAGGERATING A LITTLE... BUT IT'S NOT A LIE! RIGHT, DUDE?
THEY CALLED YOU "TAIHEI THE DEMON" 'CUZ YOU ALWAYS GOT A HUNDRED PERCENT. LIKE A CLASSROOM DEMON.
The honors kids.
End-of-term Exams Ranking
Doma Taihei
......
I NEVER HEARD THAT.
NAH, MAN-- THEY CALLED YOU THAT ALL THE TIME! LIKE WHEN YOU MET KANAU ...
OKAY, LET'S CHANGE THE SUBJECT! I'M GOING TO START DINNER!
KRRK
IS ONII-CHAN MAD?
NAH, HE'S A GOOD GUY. HE WOULDN'T GET MAD FROM A LITTLE MESSIN' AROUND!

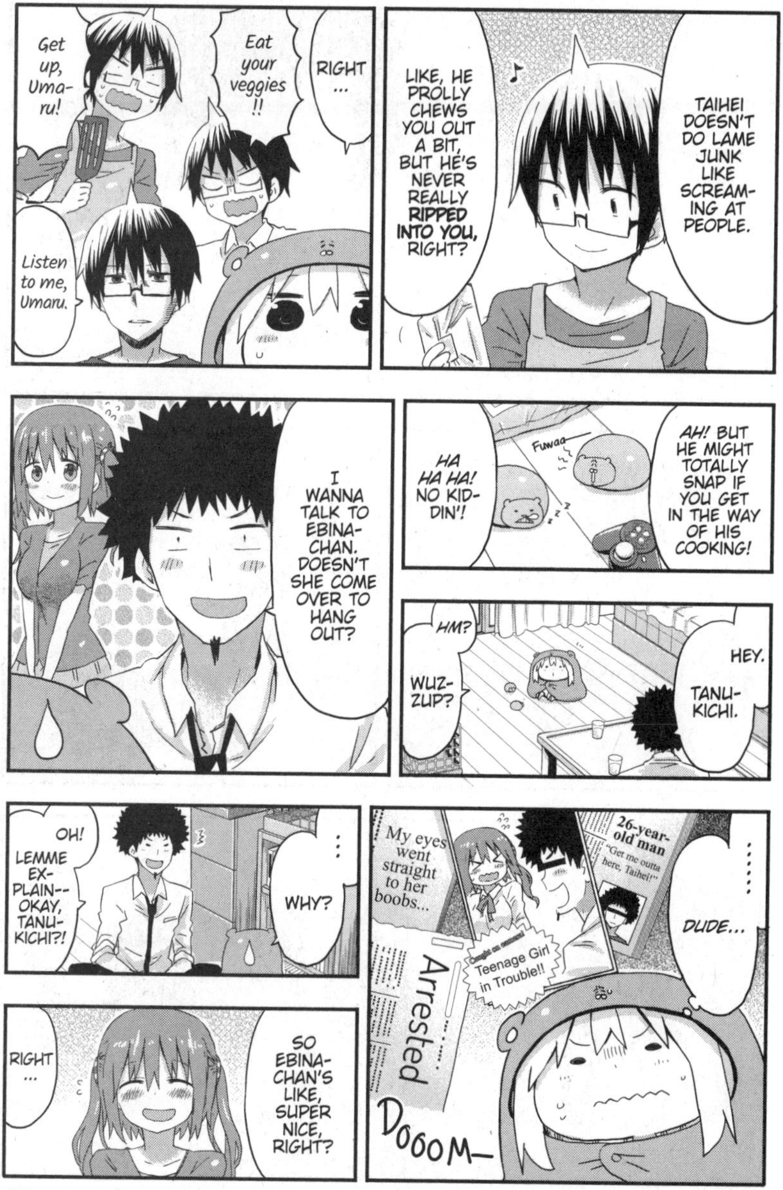
TAIHEI DOESN'T DO LAME JUNK LIKE SCREAMING AT PEOPLE.
LIKE, HE PROLLY CHEWS YOU OUT A BIT, BUT HE'S NEVER REALLY RIPPED INTO YOU, RIGHT?
RIGHT ...
Eat your veggies !!
Get up, Umaru!
Listen to me, Umaru.
AH! BUT HE MIGHT TOTALLY SNAP IF YOU GET IN THE WAY OF HIS COOKING!
Fuwaa
HA HA HA! NO KIDDIN'!
HEY.
TANUKICHI.
HM?
WUZZUP?
I WANNA TALK TO EBINA-CHAN. DOESN'T SHE COME OVER TO HANG OUT?
...
WHY?
OH! LEMME EXPLAIN--OKAY, TANUKICHI?!
SO EBINA-CHAN'S LIKE, SUPER NICE, RIGHT?
RIGHT ...
......
DUDE...
26-year-old man
"Get me outta here, Taihei!"
My eyes went straight to her boobs...
Teenage Girl in Trouble!!
Arrested
DOOOM—

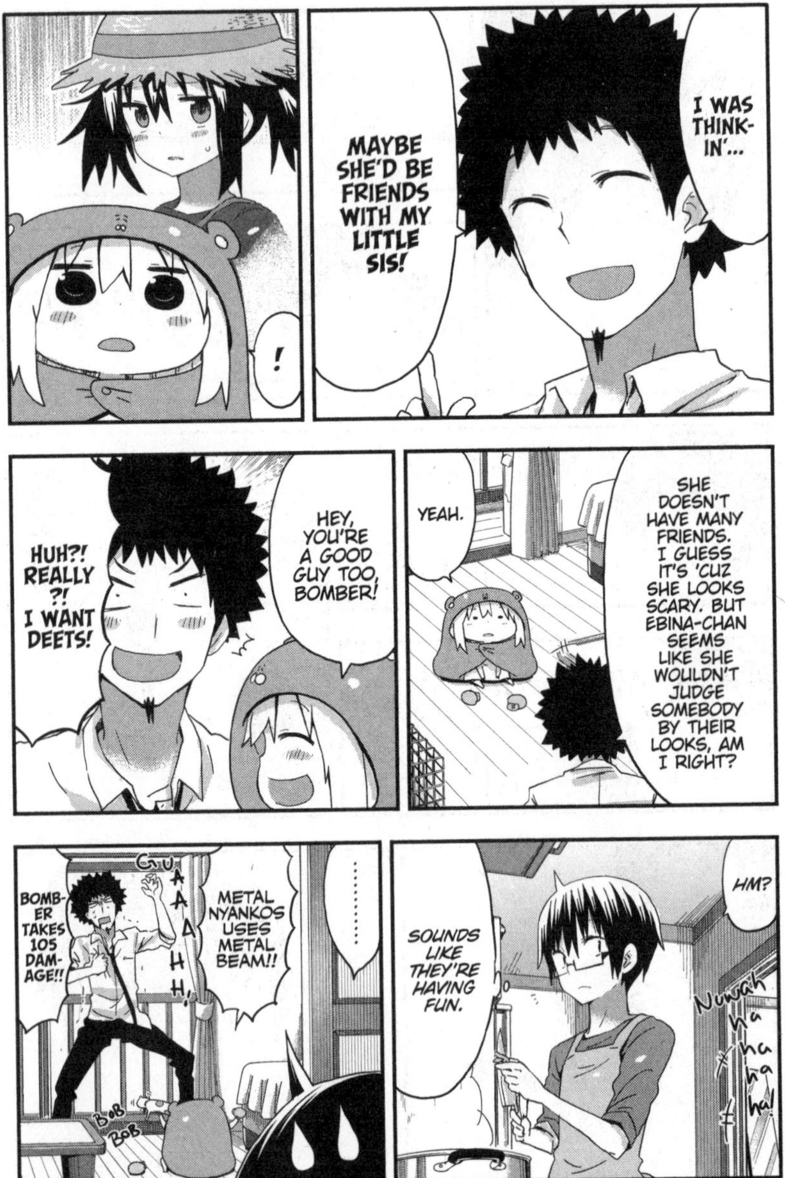
I WAS THINK-IN'...
MAYBE SHE'D BE FRIENDS WITH MY LITTLE SIS!
!
SHE DOESN'T HAVE MANY FRIENDS. I GUESS IT'S 'CUZ SHE LOOKS SCARY. BUT EBINA-CHAN SEEMS LIKE SHE WOULDN'T JUDGE SOMEBODY BY THEIR LOOKS, AM I RIGHT?
YEAH.
HEY, YOU'RE A GOOD GUY TOO, BOMBER!
HUH?! REALLY ?! I WANT DEETS!
HM?
SOUNDS LIKE THEY'RE HAVING FUN.
Nuwah ha ha ha ha!
....
METAL NYANKOS USES METAL BEAM!!
GUAAAAHH!
BOMB-ER TAKES 105 DAM-AGE!!
BOB BOB

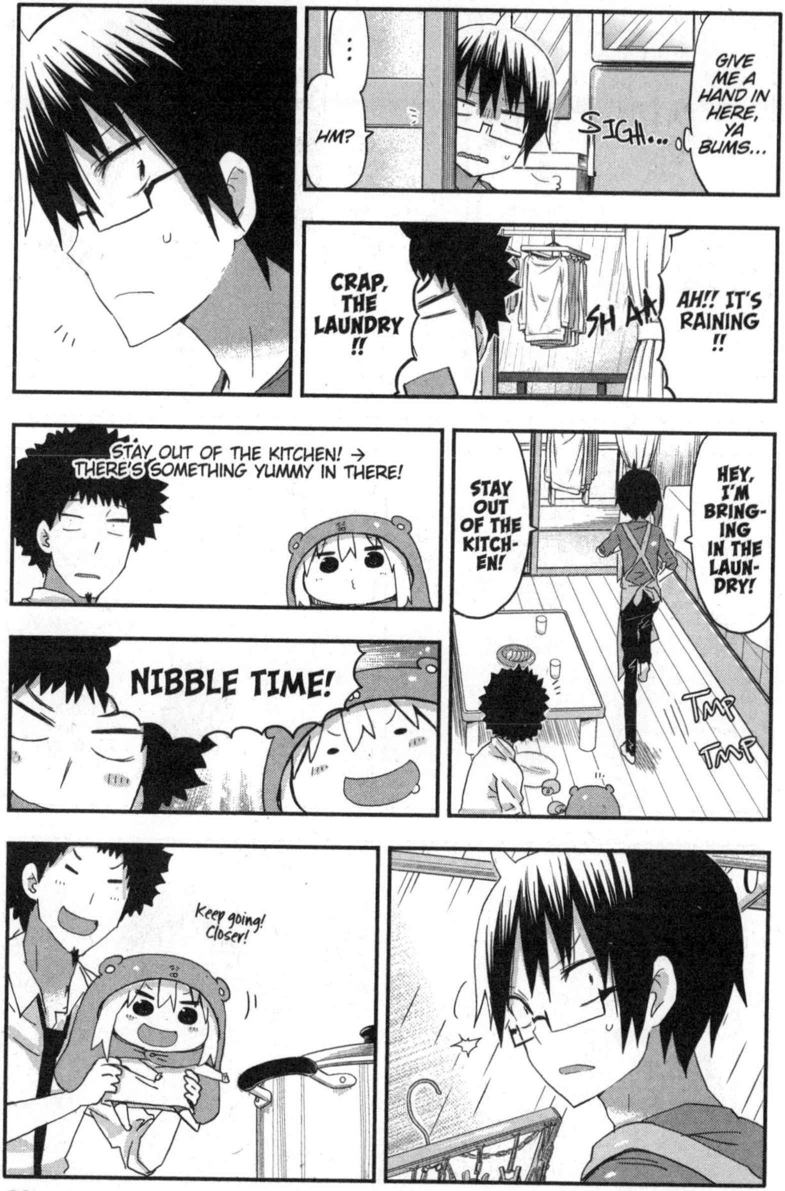
GIVE ME A HAND IN HERE, YA BUMS...
SIGH...
HM?
...
AH!! IT'S RAINING!!
SHAA
CRAP, THE LAUNDRY!!
HEY, I'M BRINGING IN THE LAUNDRY!
STAY OUT OF THE KITCHEN!
TMP
TMP
STAY OUT OF THE KITCHEN! → THERE'S SOMETHING YUMMY IN THERE!
NIBBLE TIME!
Keep going! Closer!

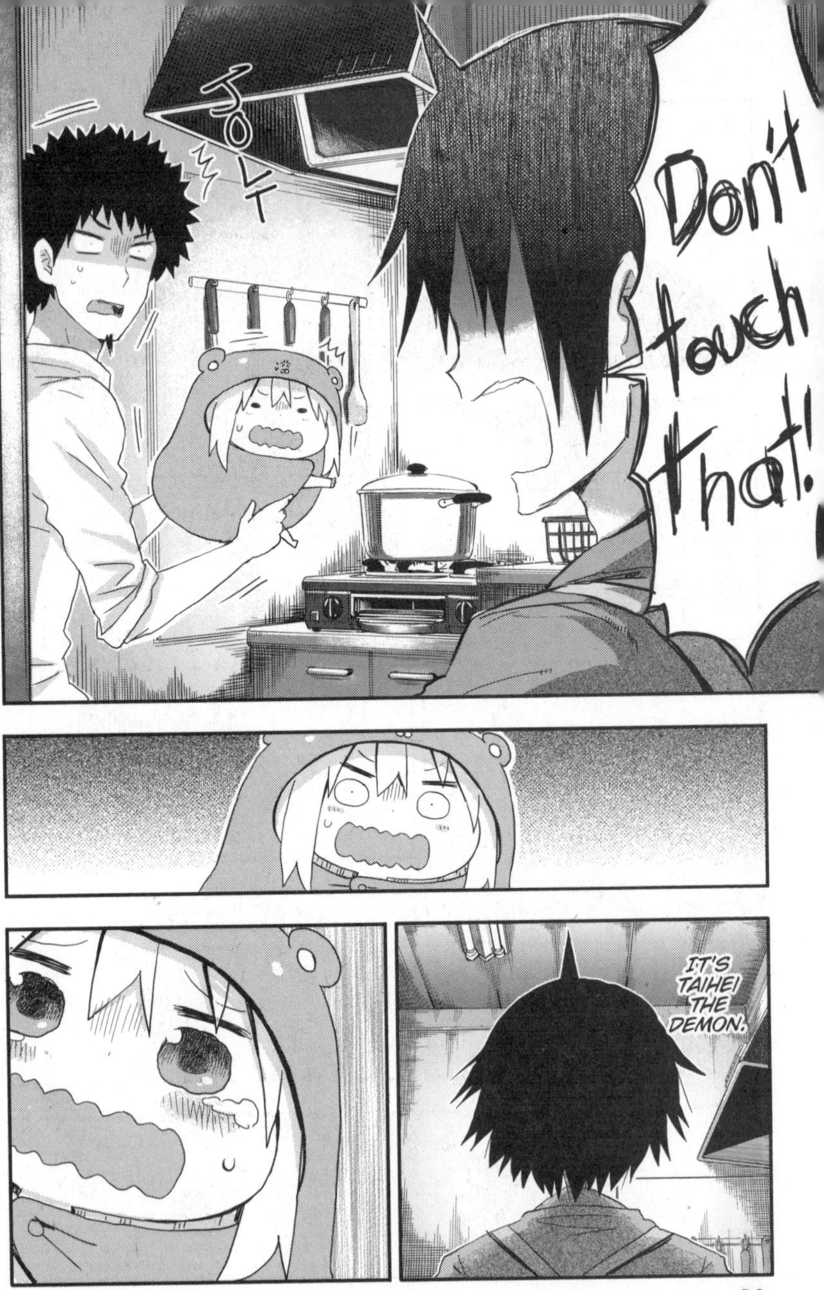
Don't touch that!
IT'S TAIHEI THE DEMON.

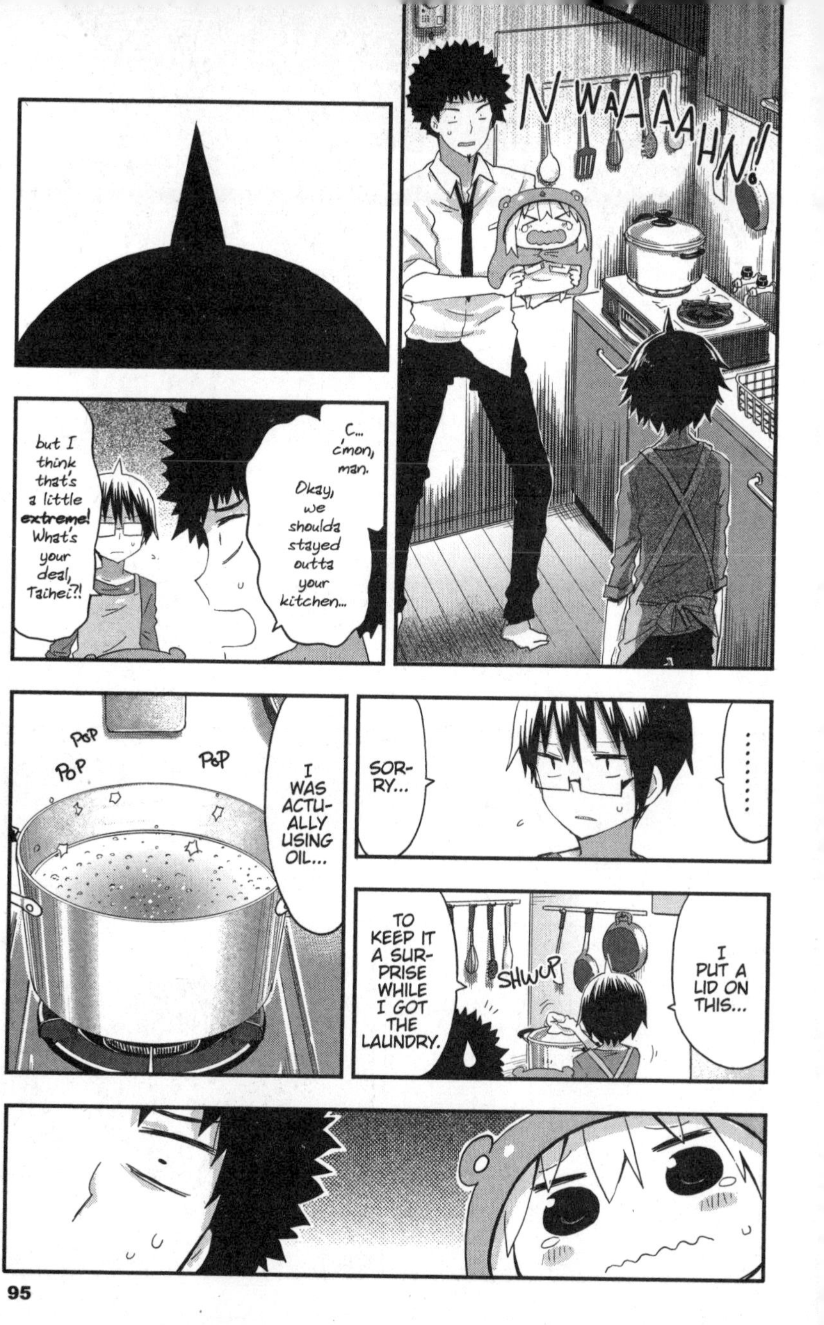
NWAAAAAHN!
C... c'mon, man.
Okay, we shoulda stayed outta your kitchen...
but I think that's a little **extreme!** What's your deal, Taihei?!
......
SORRY...
I PUT A LID ON THIS...
SHWUP
TO KEEP IT A SURPRISE WHILE I GOT THE LAUNDRY.
I WAS ACTUALLY USING OIL...
POP
POP
POP

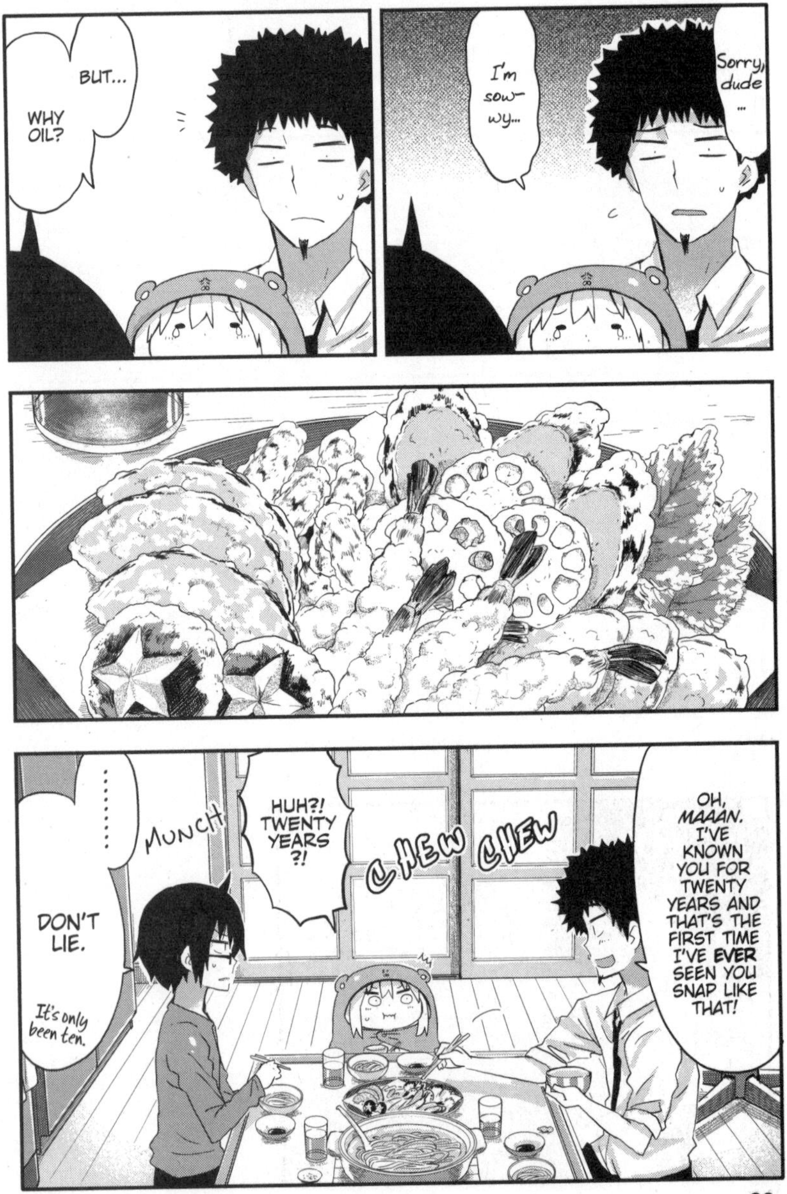

Sorry, dude ...
I'm sow-wy...
BUT...
WHY OIL?
OH, MAAAN. I'VE KNOWN YOU FOR TWENTY YEARS AND THAT'S THE FIRST TIME I'VE EVER SEEN YOU SNAP LIKE THAT!
CHEW CHEW
HUH?! TWENTY YEARS?!
MUNCH
......
DON'T LIE.
It's only been ten.

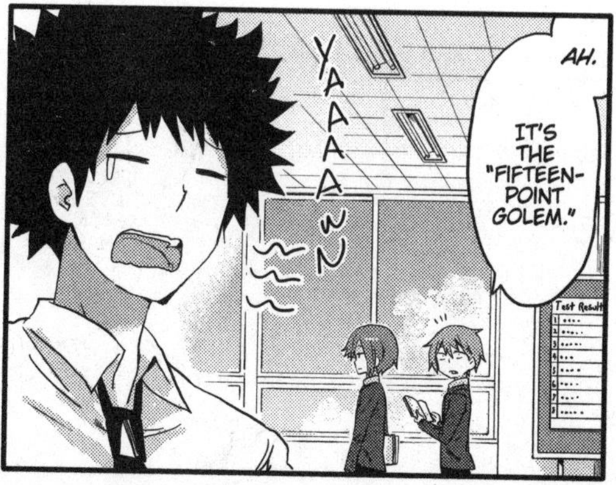
AH.
IT'S THE "FIFTEEN-POINT GOLEM."
YAAAAWN

HIMOUTO! UMARU-CHAN

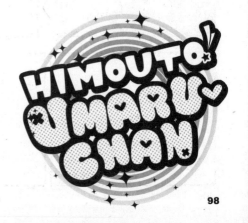

No. 83 Umaru & the Smile

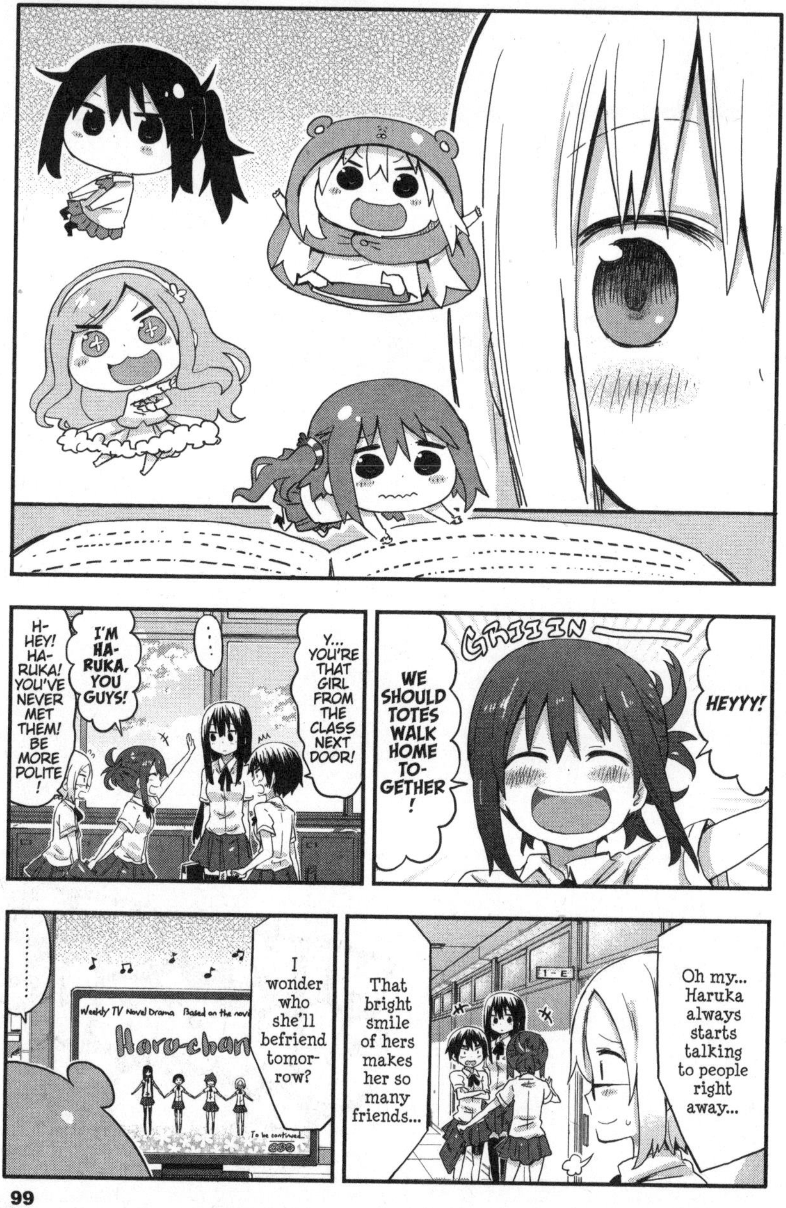

HEYYY!
GRIIIN—
WE SHOULD TOTES WALK HOME TO-GETHER!
Y... YOU'RE THAT GIRL FROM THE CLASS NEXT DOOR!
...
I'M HA-RUKA, YOU GUYS!
H-HEY! HA-RUKA! YOU'VE NEVER MET THEM! BE MORE POLITE!
Oh my... Haruka always starts talking to people right away...
1-E
That bright smile of hers makes her so many friends...
I wonder who she'll befriend tomor-row?
Weekly TV Novel Drama
Haru-chan
To be continued...
......

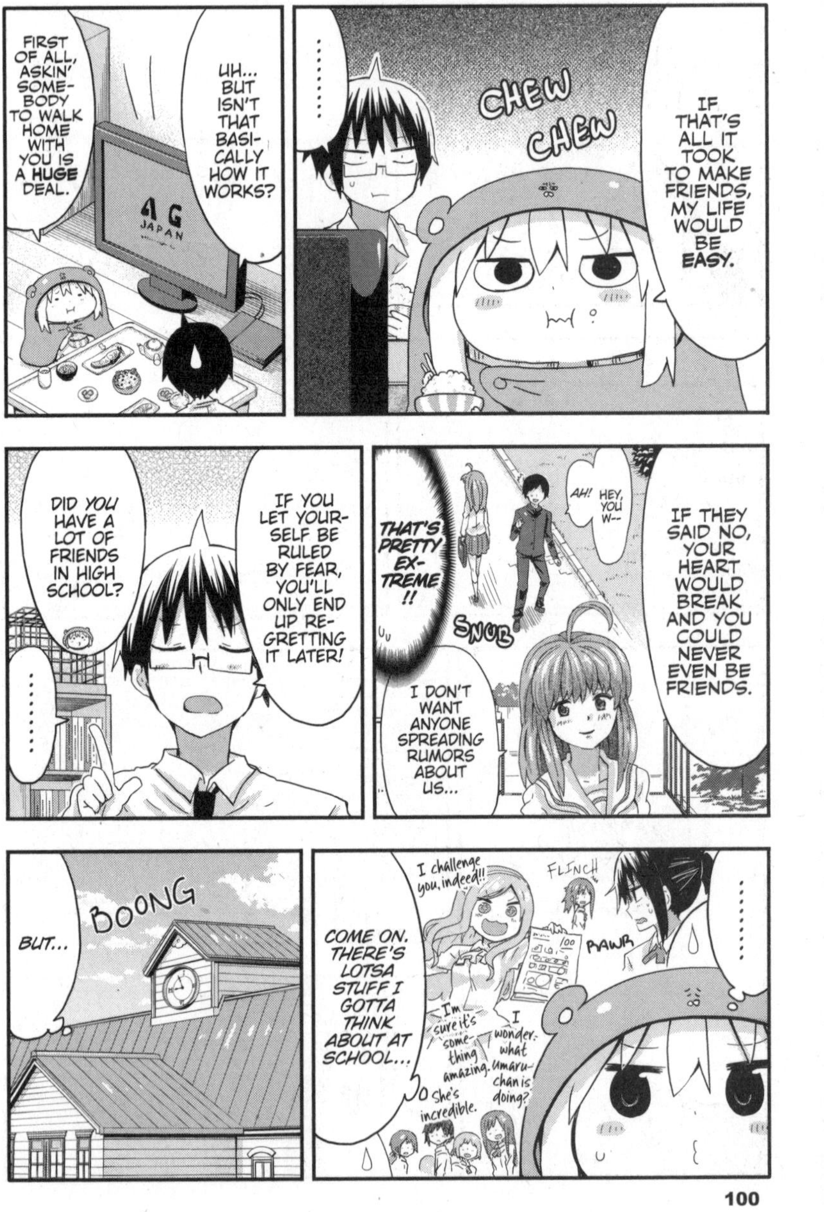
IF THAT'S ALL IT TOOK TO MAKE FRIENDS, MY LIFE WOULD BE **EASY.**
CHEW CHEW
……
UH... BUT ISN'T THAT BASICALLY HOW IT WORKS?
FIRST OF ALL, ASKIN' SOMEBODY TO WALK HOME WITH YOU IS A **HUGE** DEAL.
4G JAPAN
IF THEY SAID NO, YOUR HEART WOULD BREAK AND YOU COULD NEVER EVEN BE FRIENDS.
AH! HEY, YOU W--
THAT'S PRETTY EXTREME!!
SNUB
I DON'T WANT ANYONE SPREADING RUMORS ABOUT US...
IF YOU LET YOURSELF BE RULED BY FEAR, YOU'LL ONLY END UP REGRETTING IT LATER!
DID YOU HAVE A LOT OF FRIENDS IN HIGH SCHOOL?
……
……
FLINCH
RAWR
I challenge you, indeed!!
COME ON. THERE'S LOTSA STUFF I GOTTA THINK ABOUT AT SCHOOL...
I wonder what Umaru-chan is doing?
I'm sure it's something amazing.
She's incredible.
BOONG
BUT...

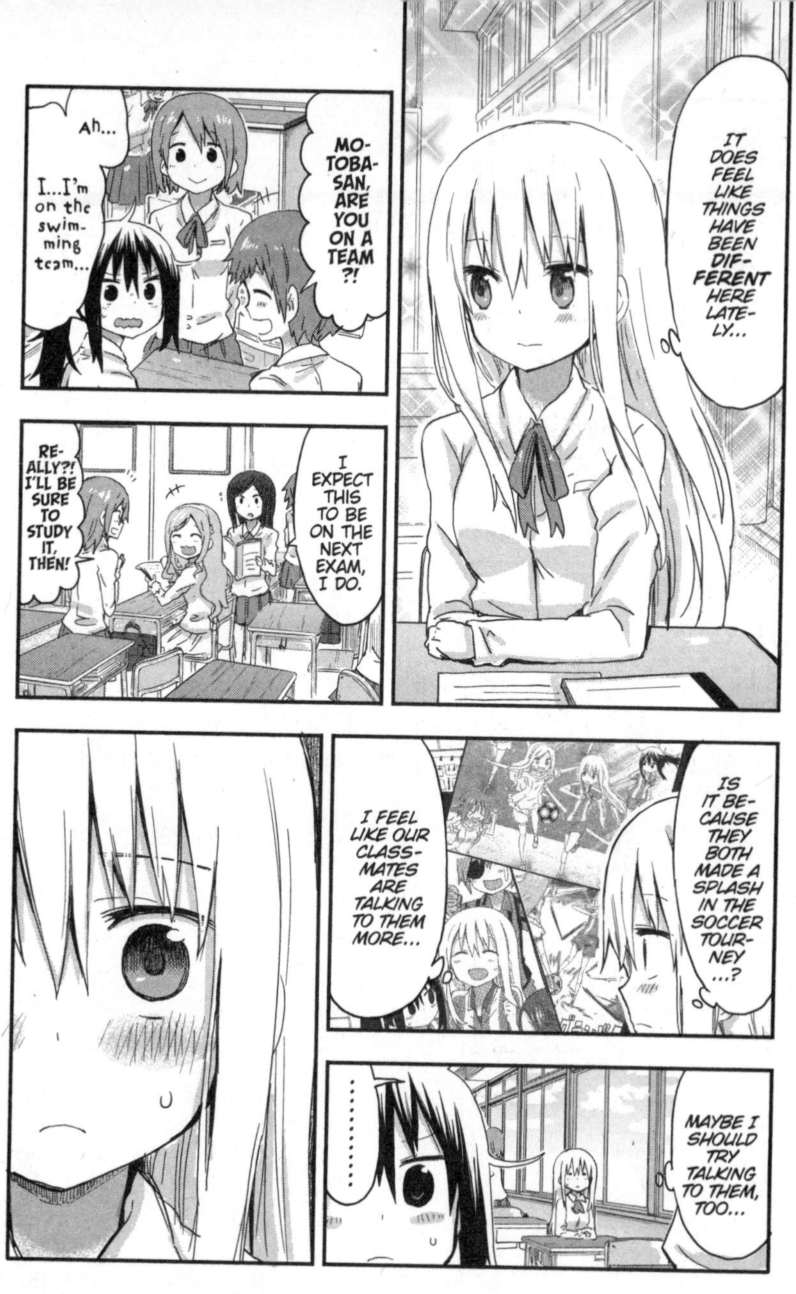
IT DOES FEEL LIKE THINGS HAVE BEEN DIFFERENT HERE LATELY...
MOTOBA-SAN, ARE YOU ON A TEAM?!
Ah...
I...I'm on the swimming team...
I EXPECT THIS TO BE ON THE NEXT EXAM, I DO.
REALLY?! I'LL BE SURE TO STUDY IT, THEN!
IS IT BECAUSE THEY BOTH MADE A SPLASH IN THE SOCCER TOURNEY...?
I FEEL LIKE OUR CLASSMATES ARE TALKING TO THEM MORE...
MAYBE I SHOULD TRY TALKING TO THEM, TOO...
......

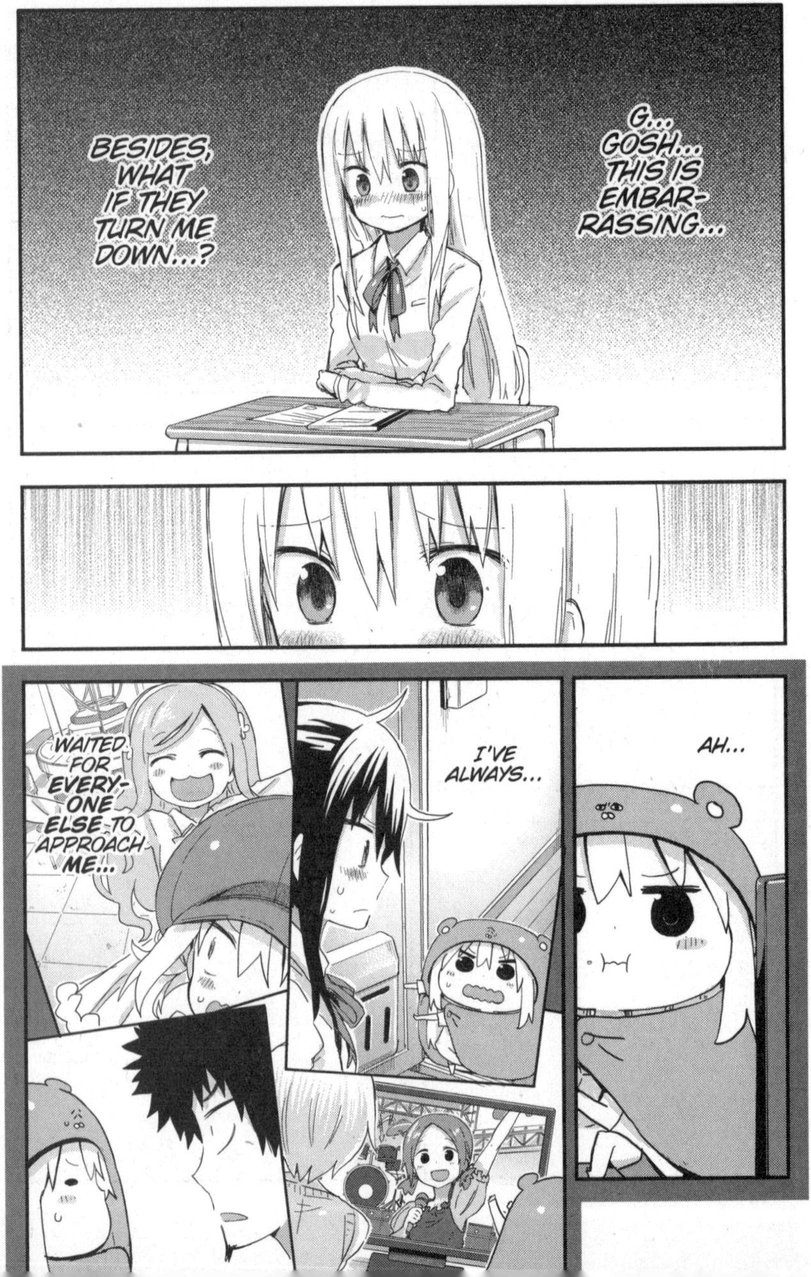
G... GOSH... THIS IS EMBARRASSING...
BESIDES, WHAT IF THEY TURN ME DOWN...?
AH...
I'VE ALWAYS...
WAITED FOR EVERYONE ELSE TO APPROACH ME...

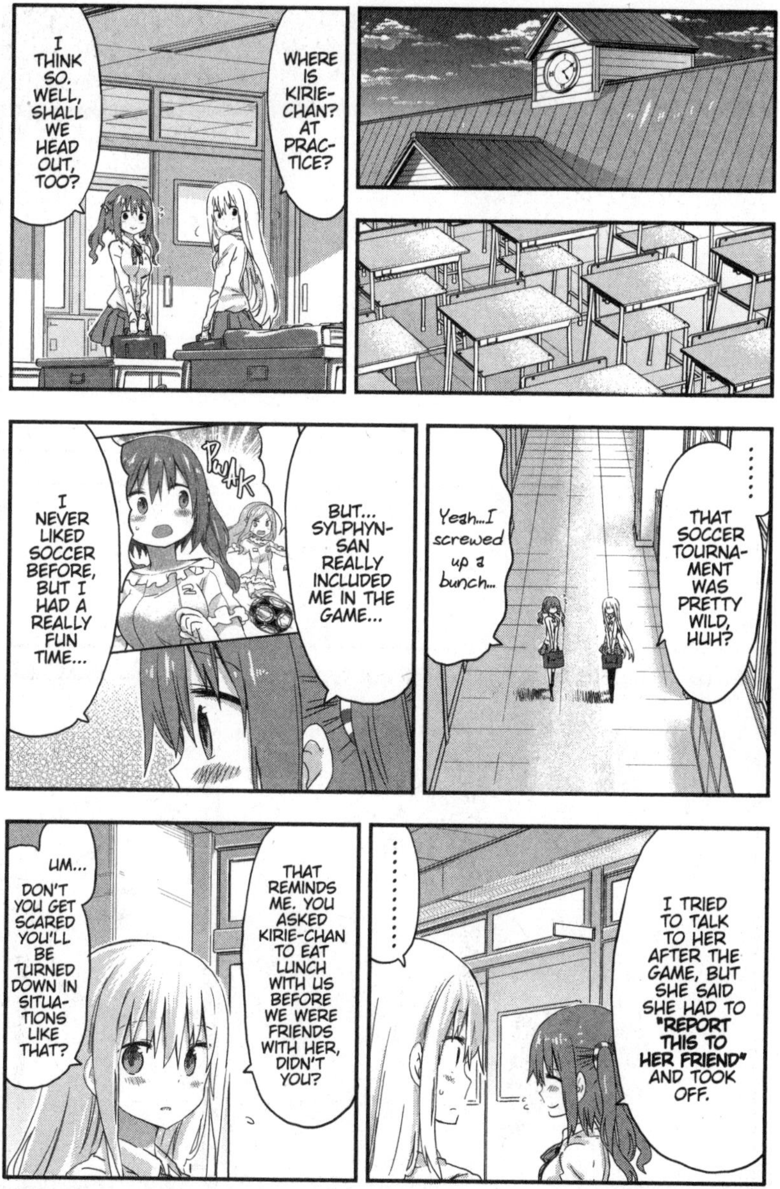
WHERE IS KIRIE-CHAN? AT PRAC-TICE?
I THINK SO. WELL, SHALL WE HEAD OUT, TOO?
......
THAT SOCCER TOURNA-MENT WAS PRETTY WILD, HUH?
Yeah...I screwed up a bunch...
BUT... SYLPHYN-SAN REALLY INCLUDED ME IN THE GAME...
PWAK
I NEVER LIKED SOCCER BEFORE, BUT I HAD A REALLY FUN TIME...
I TRIED TO TALK TO HER AFTER THE GAME, BUT SHE SAID SHE HAD TO "REPORT THIS TO HER FRIEND" AND TOOK OFF.
......
THAT REMINDS ME. YOU ASKED KIRIE-CHAN TO EAT LUNCH WITH US BEFORE WE WERE FRIENDS WITH HER, DIDN'T YOU?
UM... DON'T YOU GET SCARED YOU'LL BE TURNED DOWN IN SITUA-TIONS LIKE THAT?

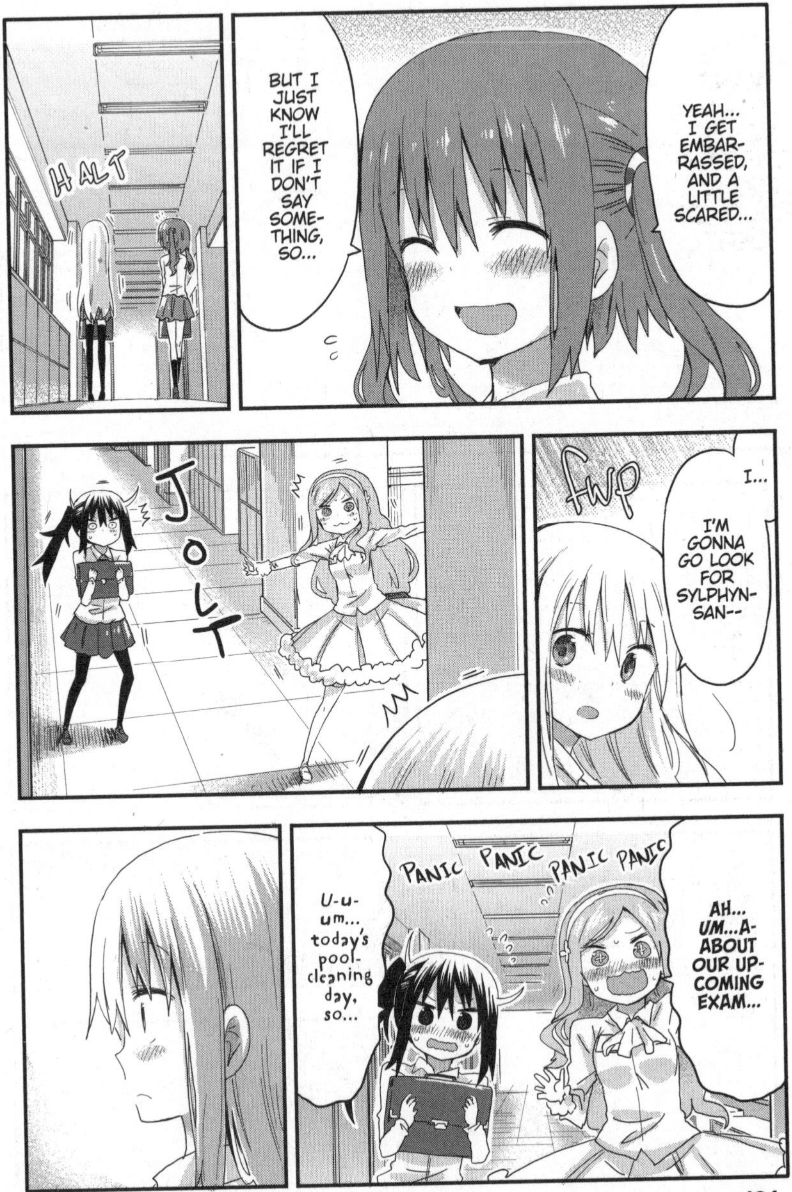
YEAH... I GET EMBAR-RASSED, AND A LITTLE SCARED...
BUT I JUST KNOW I'LL REGRET IT IF I DON'T SAY SOME-THING, SO...
HALT
FWP
I...
I'M GONNA GO LOOK FOR SYLPHYN-SAN--
JOLT
PANIC PANIC PANIC PANIC
AH... UM...A-ABOUT OUR UP-COMING EXAM...
U-u-um... today's pool-cleaning day, so...

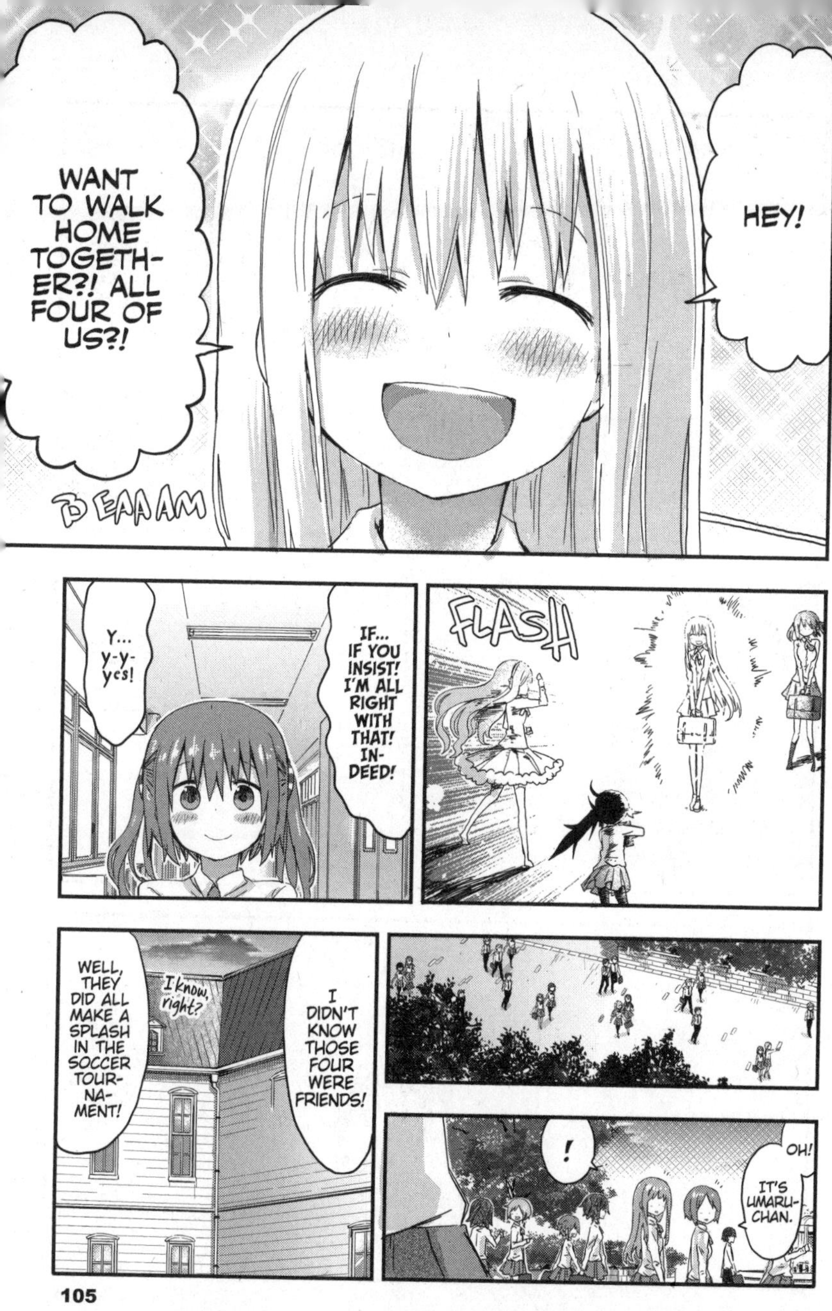
HEY!
WANT TO WALK HOME TOGETH-ER?! ALL FOUR OF US?!
BEAAAM
FLASH
IF... IF YOU INSIST! I'M ALL RIGHT WITH THAT! IN-DEED!
Y... y-y-yes!
OH!
IT'S UMARU-CHAN.
!
I DIDN'T KNOW THOSE FOUR WERE FRIENDS!
I know, right?
WELL, THEY DID ALL MAKE A SPLASH IN THE SOCCER TOUR-NA-MENT!

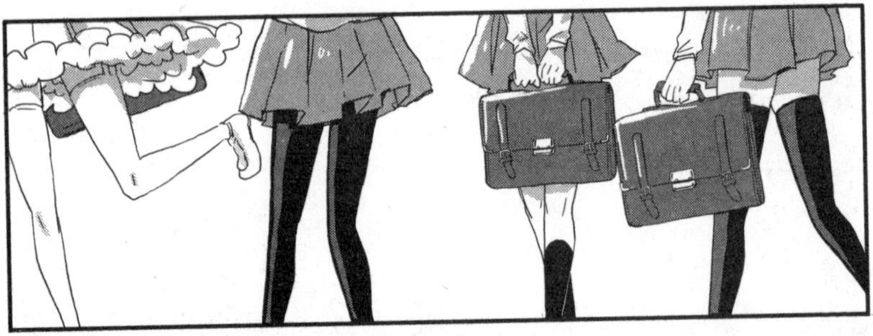
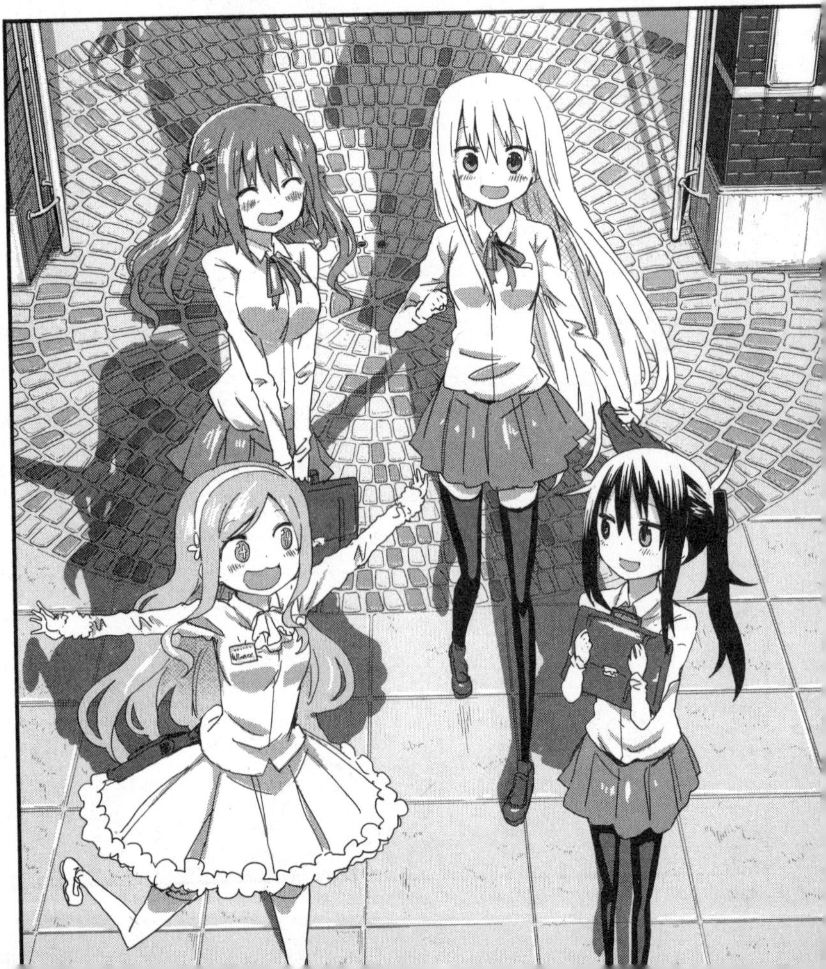

No. 84 **Umaru & the Theater**

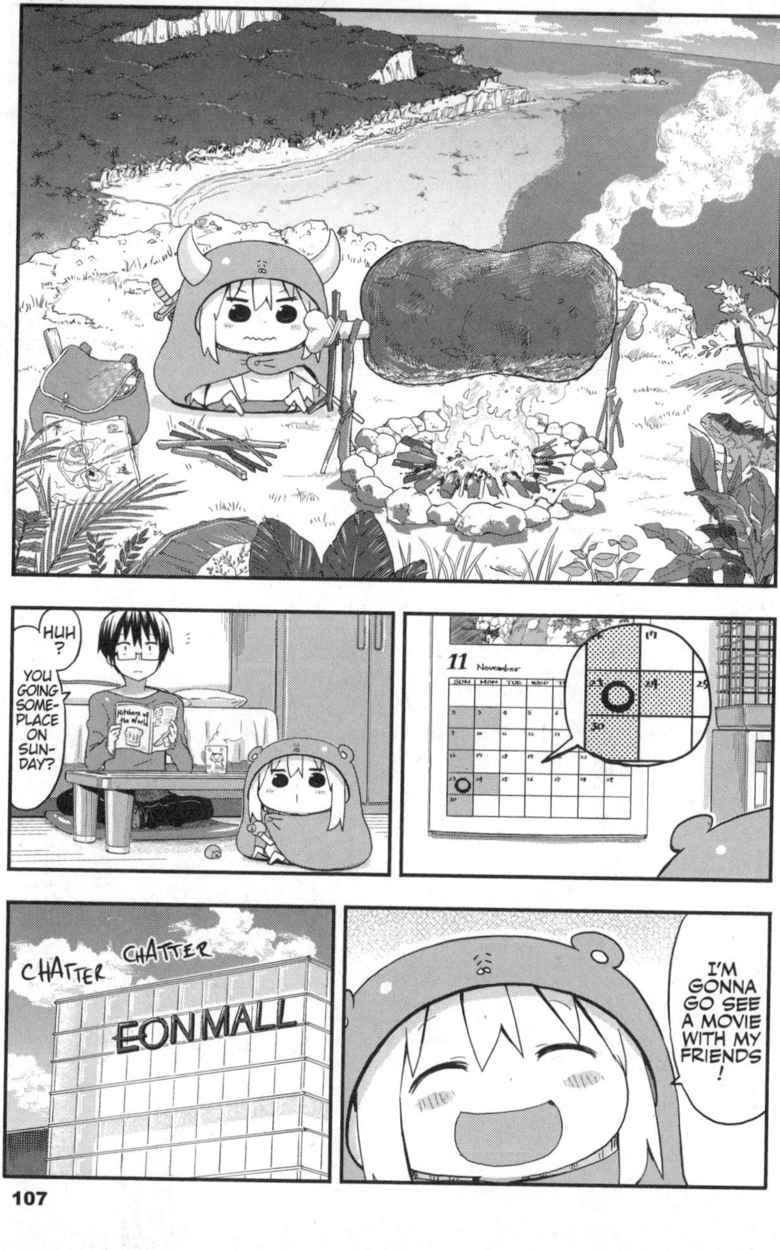
11
November
HUH?
YOU GOING SOME-PLACE ON SUN-DAY?
Kitchens of the World
I'M GONNA GO SEE A MOVIE WITH MY FRIENDS!
CHATTER
CHATTER
EON MALL

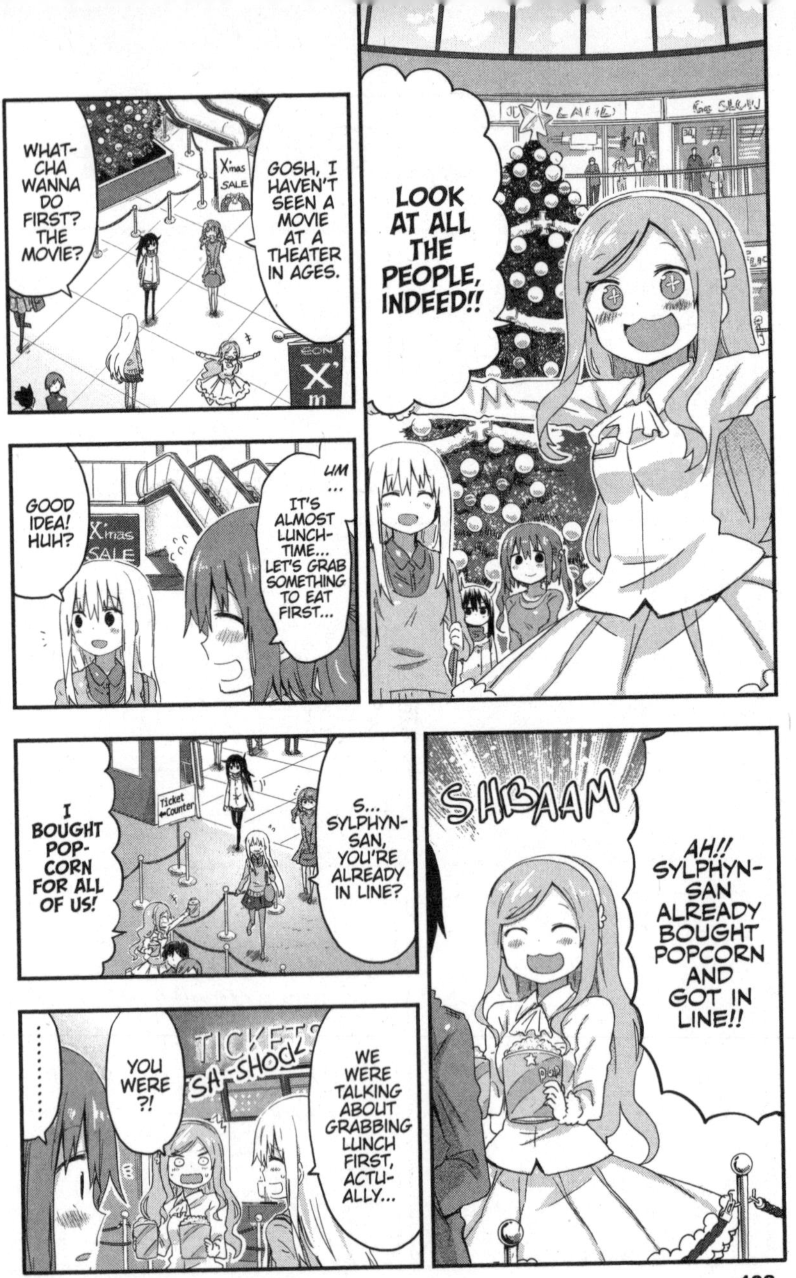
LOOK AT ALL THE PEOPLE, INDEED!!
GOSH, I HAVEN'T SEEN A MOVIE AT A THEATER IN AGES.
WHAT-CHA WANNA DO FIRST? THE MOVIE?
X'mas SALE
UM... IT'S ALMOST LUNCH-TIME... LET'S GRAB SOMETHING TO EAT FIRST...
GOOD IDEA! HUH?
Xmas SALE
SHBAAM
AH!! SYLPHYN-SAN ALREADY BOUGHT POPCORN AND GOT IN LINE!!
S... SYLPHYN-SAN, YOU'RE ALREADY IN LINE?
I BOUGHT POP-CORN FOR ALL OF US!
Ticket Counter
WE WERE TALKING ABOUT GRABBING LUNCH FIRST, ACTU-ALLY...
SA-SHOCK
YOU WERE?!
......

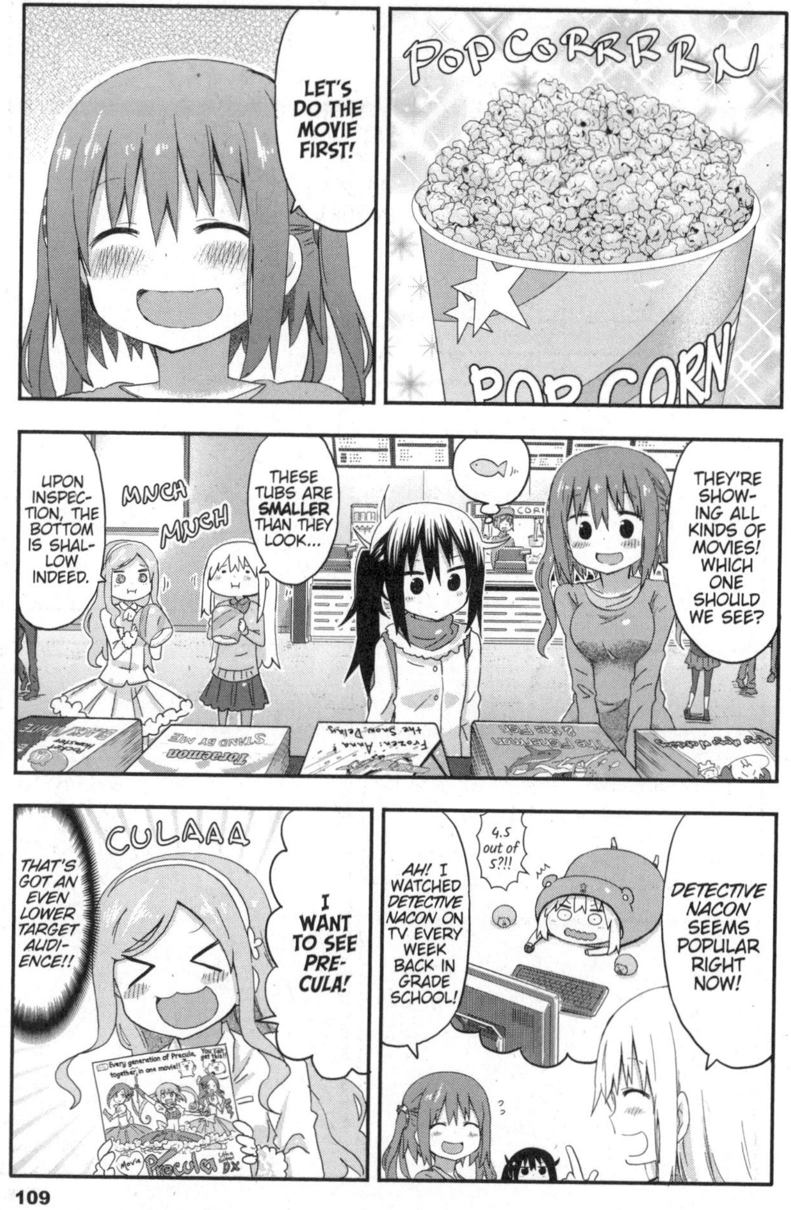
POPCORRRRN
POP CORN
LET'S DO THE MOVIE FIRST!
THEY'RE SHOWING ALL KINDS OF MOVIES! WHICH ONE SHOULD WE SEE?
THESE TUBS ARE SMALLER THAN THEY LOOK...
MNCH
MNCH
UPON INSPECTION, THE BOTTOM IS SHALLOW INDEED.
DETECTIVE NACON SEEMS POPULAR RIGHT NOW!
AH! I WATCHED DETECTIVE NACON ON TV EVERY WEEK BACK IN GRADE SCHOOL!
4.5 out of 5?!!
I WANT TO SEE PRECULA!
CULAAA
THAT'S GOT AN EVEN LOWER TARGET AUDIENCE!!
Every generation of Precula, together in one movie!!
You can get this!!
Movie Precula DX

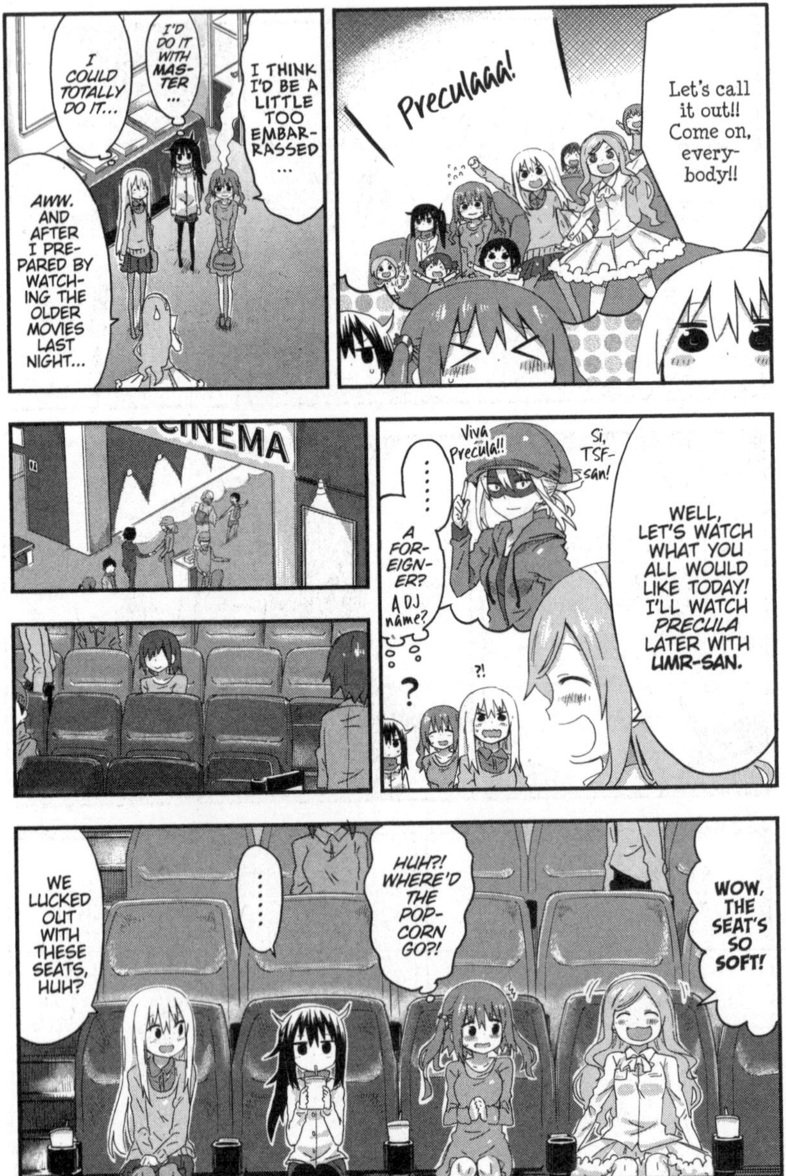
Let's call it out!! Come on, everybody!!
Preculaaa!
I THINK I'D BE A LITTLE TOO EMBARRASSED ...
I'D DO IT WITH MASTER ...
I COULD TOTALLY DO IT...
AWW. AND AFTER I PREPARED BY WATCHING THE OLDER MOVIES LAST NIGHT...
WELL, LET'S WATCH WHAT YOU ALL WOULD LIKE TODAY! I'LL WATCH *PRECULA* LATER WITH UMR-SAN.
Si, TSF-san!
Viva Precula!!
......
A FOREIGNER? A DJ name?
?!
?
CINEMA
WOW, THE SEAT'S SO SOFT!
HUH?! WHERE'D THE POPCORN GO?!
......
WE LUCKED OUT WITH THESE SEATS, HUH?

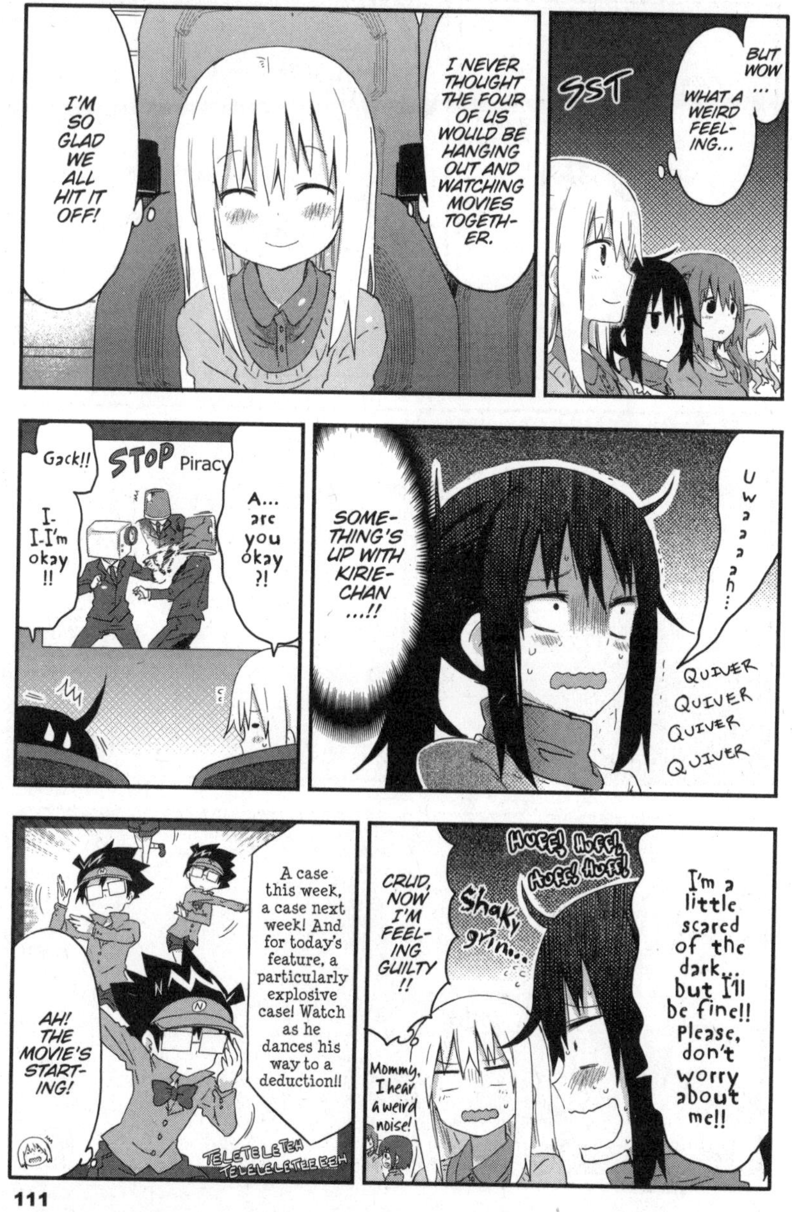
BUT WOW... WHAT A WEIRD FEELING...
SST
I NEVER THOUGHT THE FOUR OF US WOULD BE HANGING OUT AND WATCHING MOVIES TOGETHER.
I'M SO GLAD WE ALL HIT IT OFF!
Uwaaaah...
QUIVER QUIVER QUIVER QUIVER
SOMETHING'S UP WITH KIRIE-CHAN...!!
A... are you okay?!
STOP Piracy
Gack!!
I- I-I'm okay!!
I'm a little scared of the dark... but I'll be fine!! Please, don't worry about me!!
HUFF! HUFF! HUFF! HUFF!
CRUD, NOW I'M FEELING GUILTY!!
Shaky grin...
Mommy, I hear a weird noise!
A case this week, a case next week! And for today's feature, a particularly explosive case! Watch as he dances his way to a deduction!!
AH! THE MOVIE'S STARTING!
TELETELETEH TELELELETEEEEH

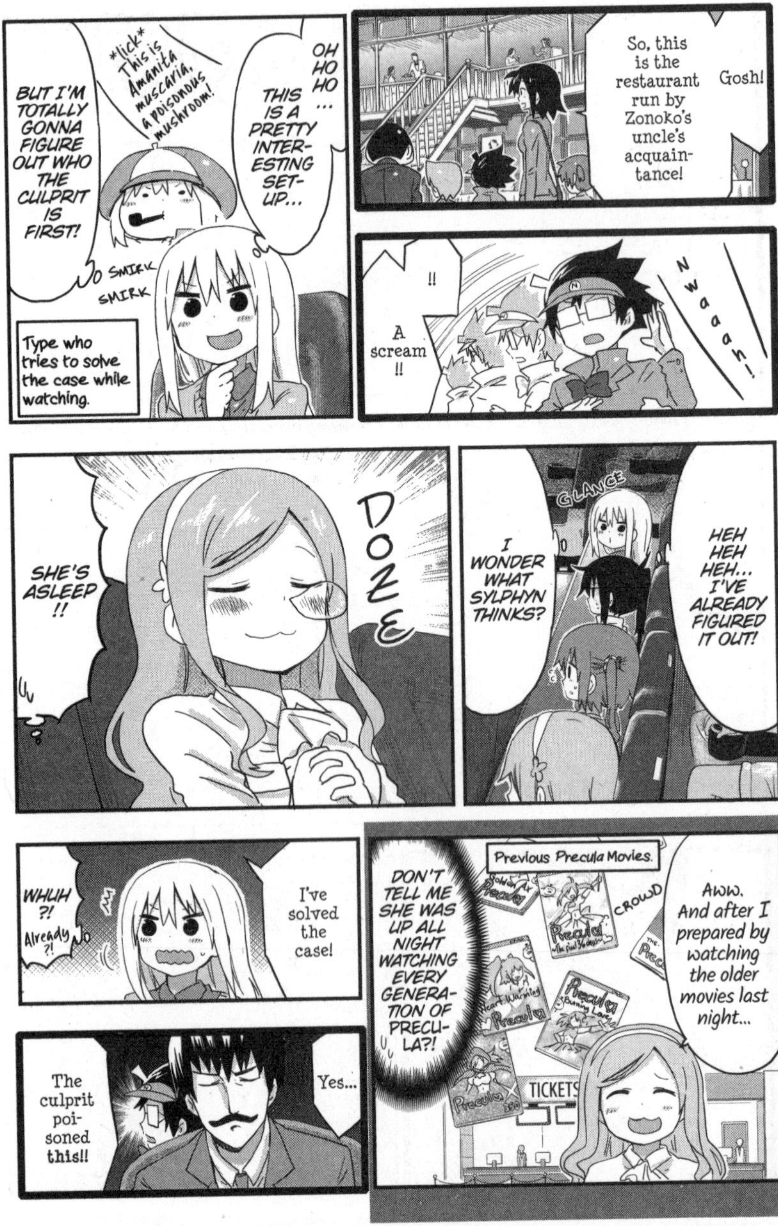
Gosh!
So, this is the restaurant run by Zonoko's uncle's acquaintance!
Nwaaah!
!!
A scream !!
OH HO HO ... THIS IS A PRETTY INTERESTING SET-UP...
lick This is Amanita muscaria, a poisonous mushroom!
BUT I'M TOTALLY GONNA FIGURE OUT WHO THE CULPRIT IS FIRST!
SMIRK SMIRK
Type who tries to solve the case while watching.
GLANCE
HEH HEH HEH... I'VE ALREADY FIGURED IT OUT!
I WONDER WHAT SYLPHYN THINKS?
DOZE
SHE'S ASLEEP !!
Previous Precula Movies.
Aww. And after I prepared by watching the older movies last night...
CROWD
DON'T TELL ME SHE WAS UP ALL NIGHT WATCHING EVERY GENERATION OF PRECULA?!
Heart Warning Precula
Precula ~Burning Love~
TICKETS
I've solved the case!
WHUH ?!
Already ?!
Yes...
The culprit poisoned this!!

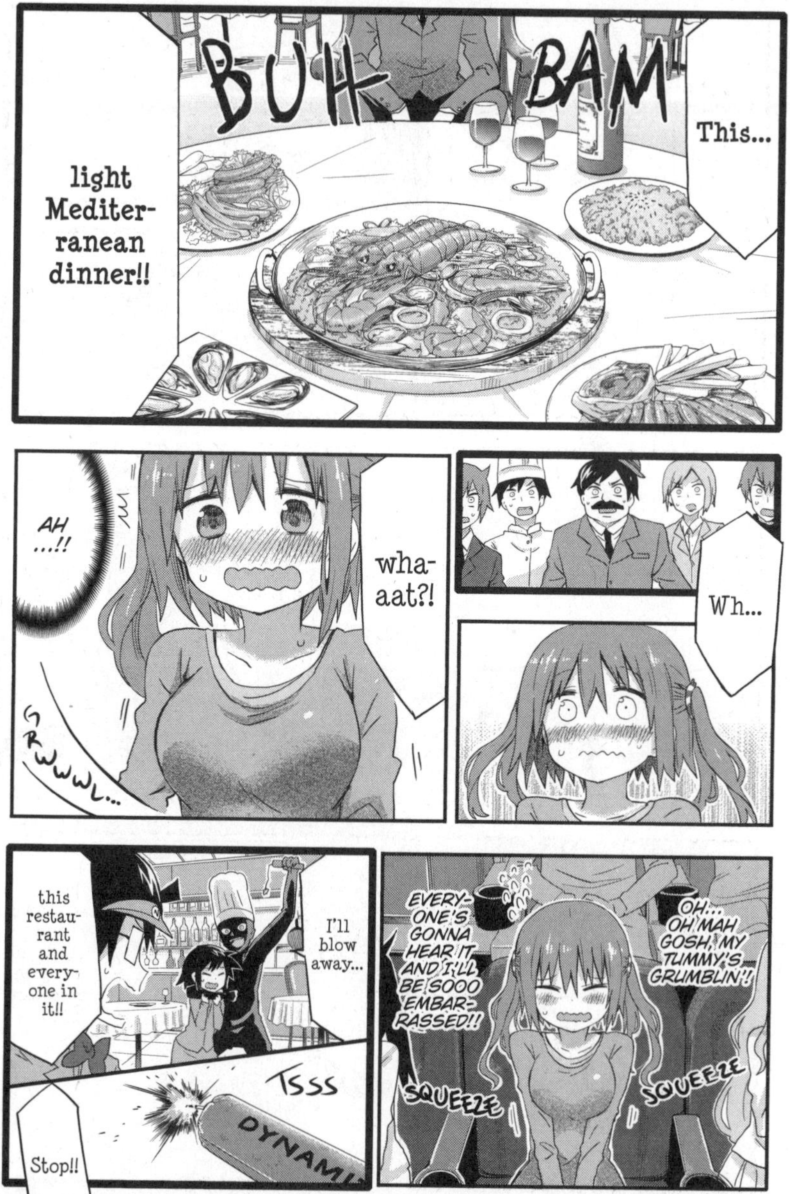
BUH BAM
This...
light Mediter-ranean dinner!!
Wh...
wha-aat?!
AH ...!!
GRWWWL...
OH... OH MAH GOSH, MY TUMMY'S GRUMBLIN'!
EVERY-ONE'S GONNA HEAR IT AND I'LL BE SOOO EMBAR-RASSED!!
SQUEEZE
SQUEEZE
I'll blow away...
this restau-rant and every-one in it!!
TSSS
DYNAMI
Stop!!

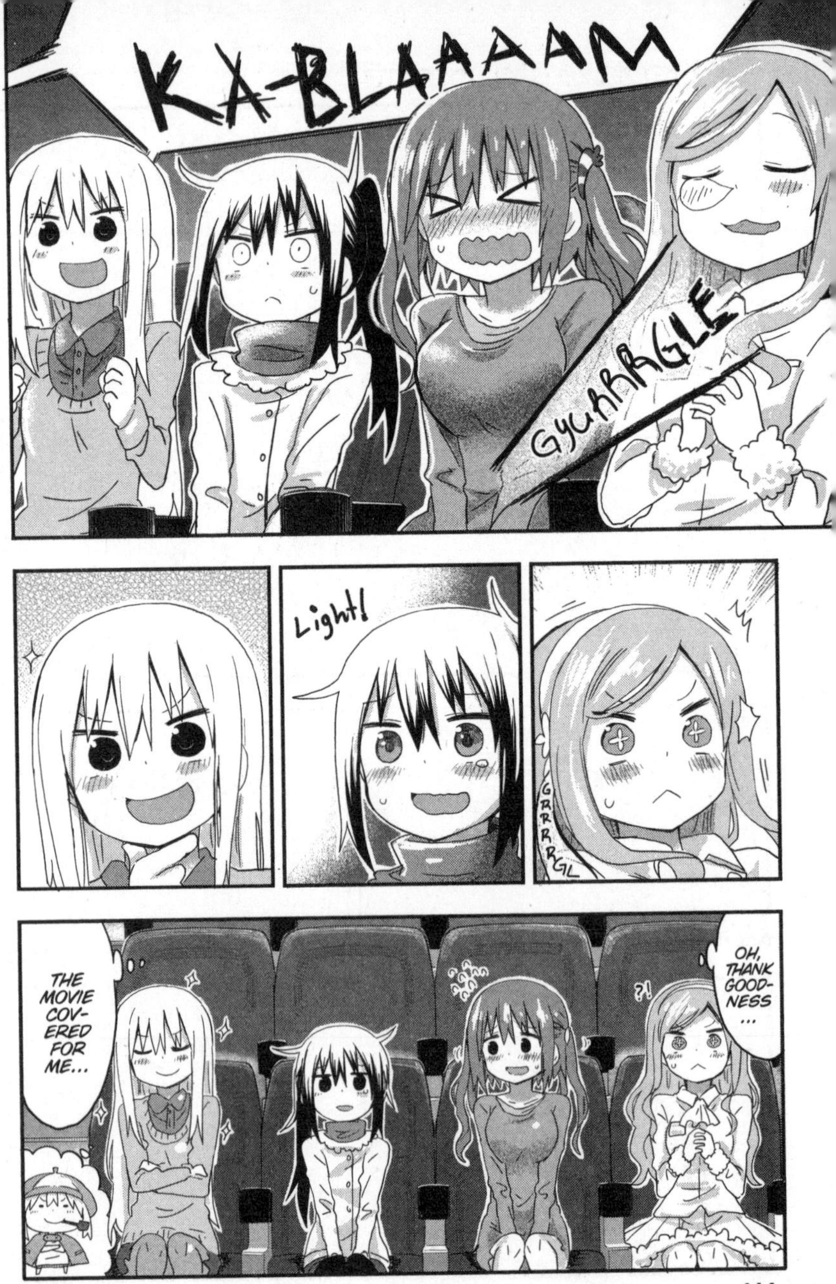
KA-BLAAAAM
GYURRGLE
GRRRRRGL
Light!
OH, THANK GOODNESS...
THE MOVIE COVERED FOR ME...

No. 85 **Umaru & the Present**

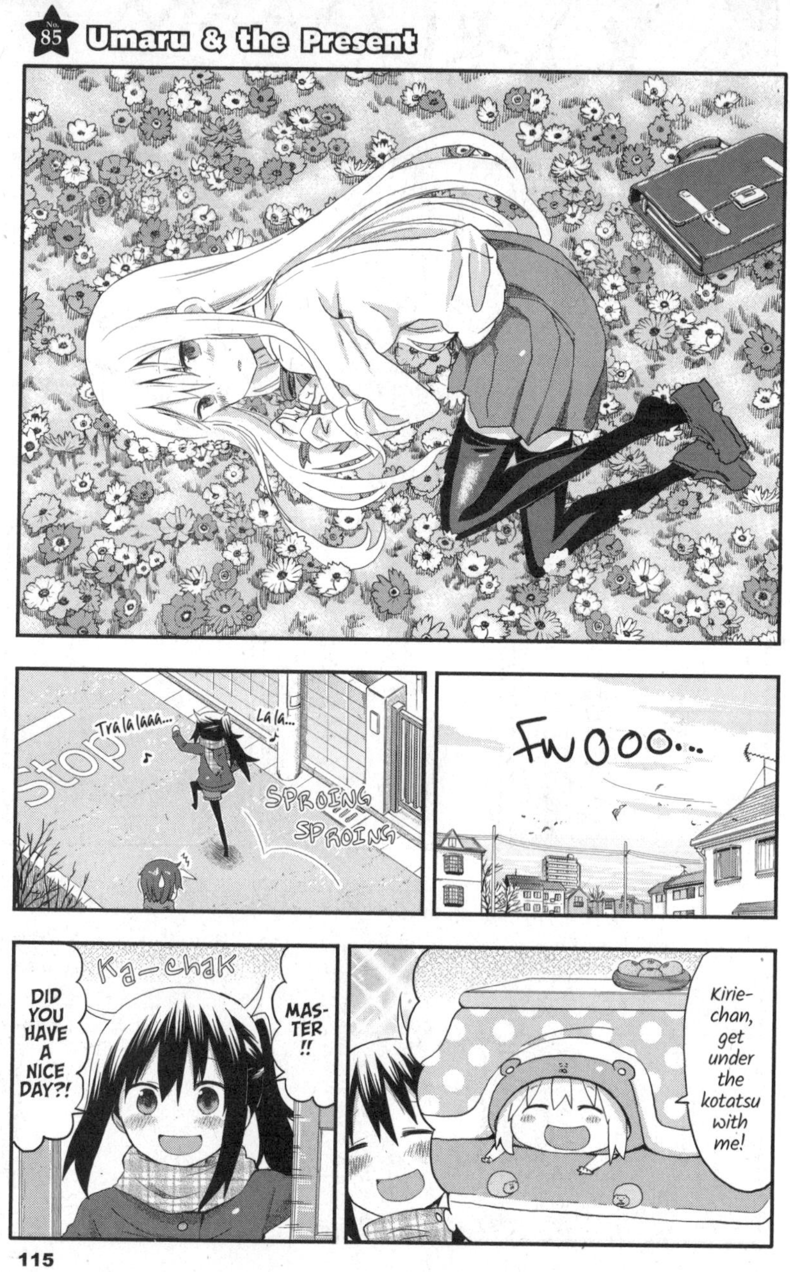

Fwooo...
La la...
Tralalaaa...
Stop
SPROING SPROING
Kirie-chan, get under the kotatsu with me!
Ka-chak
MAS-TER!!
DID YOU HAVE A NICE DAY?!

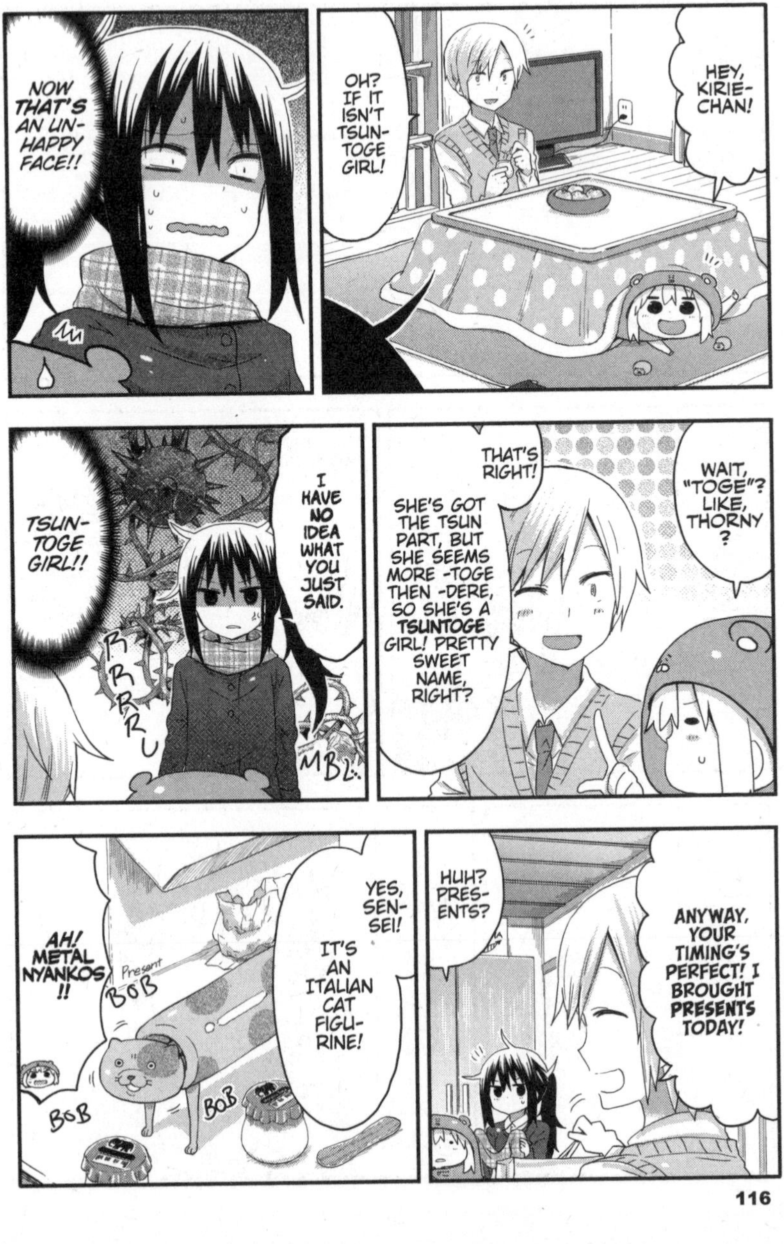
HEY, KIRIE-CHAN!
OH? IF IT ISN'T TSUN-TOGE GIRL!
NOW THAT'S AN UN-HAPPY FACE!!
WAIT, "TOGE"? LIKE, THORNY?
THAT'S RIGHT!
SHE'S GOT THE TSUN PART, BUT SHE SEEMS MORE -TOGE THEN -DERE, SO SHE'S A **TSUNTOGE** GIRL! PRETTY SWEET NAME, RIGHT?
I HAVE **NO** IDEA WHAT YOU JUST SAID.
TSUN-TOGE GIRL!!
ANYWAY, YOUR TIMING'S PERFECT! I BROUGHT **PRESENTS** TODAY!
HUH? PRES-ENTS?
YES, SEN-SEI!
IT'S AN ITALIAN CAT FIGU-RINE!
AH! METAL NYANKOS!!
Present
BOB

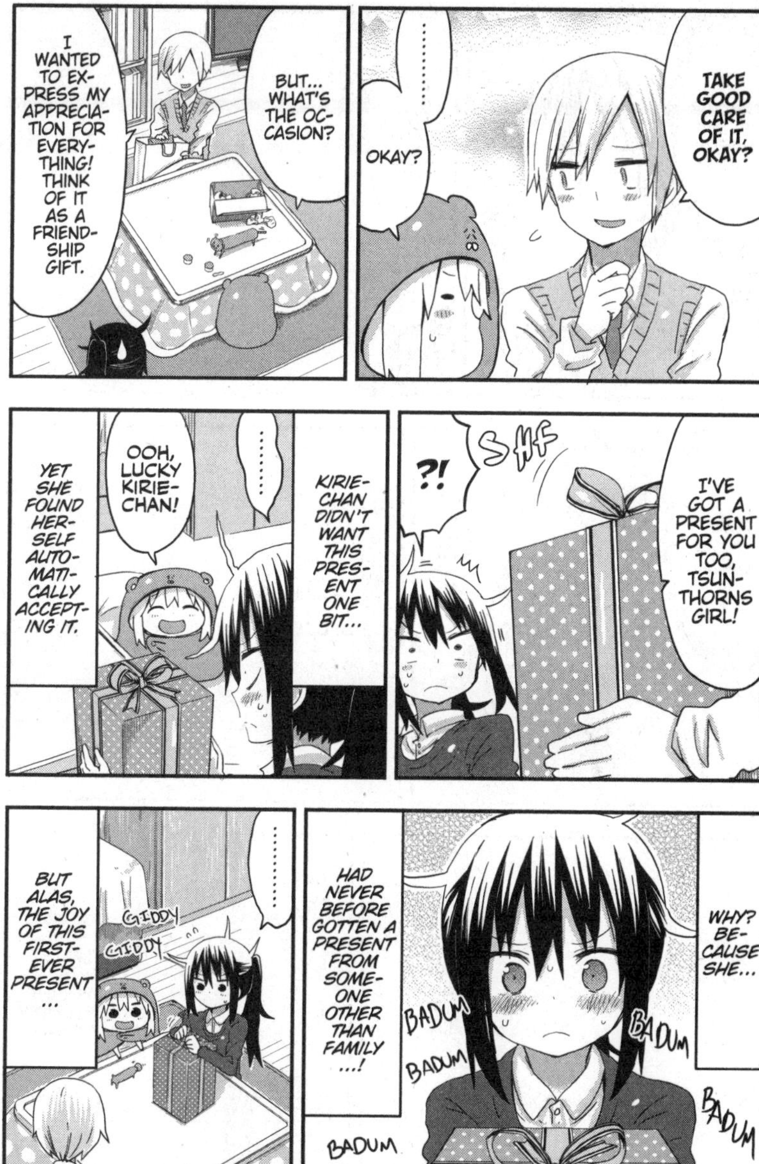

TAKE GOOD CARE OF IT, OKAY?
......
OKAY?
BUT... WHAT'S THE OCCASION?
I WANTED TO EXPRESS MY APPRECIATION FOR EVERYTHING! THINK OF IT AS A FRIENDSHIP GIFT.
I'VE GOT A PRESENT FOR YOU TOO, TSUN-THORNS GIRL!
SHF
?!
KIRIE-CHAN DIDN'T WANT THIS PRESENT ONE BIT...
......
OOH, LUCKY KIRIE-CHAN!
YET SHE FOUND HERSELF AUTOMATICALLY ACCEPTING IT.
WHY? BECAUSE SHE...
HAD NEVER BEFORE GOTTEN A PRESENT FROM SOMEONE OTHER THAN FAMILY...!
BADUM
BADUM
BADUM
BADUM
BADUM
......
GIDDY
GIDDY
BUT ALAS, THE JOY OF THIS FIRST-EVER PRESENT...

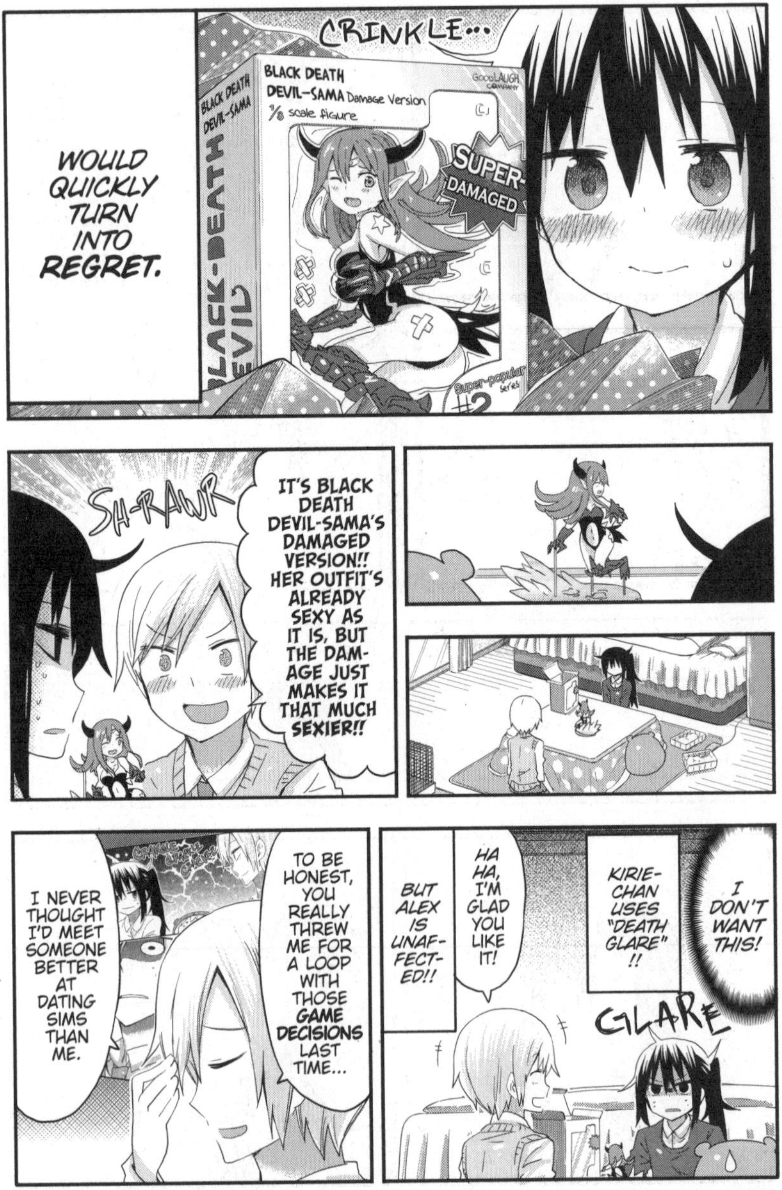
CRINKLE...
GOOD LAUGH COMPANY
BLACK DEATH DEVIL-SAMA Damage Version
1/8 scale figure
SUPER-DAMAGED
Super-popular series
#2
BLACK DEATH DEVIL-SAMA
BLACK-DEATH DEVIL
WOULD QUICKLY TURN INTO REGRET.
SH-RAWR
IT'S BLACK DEATH DEVIL-SAMA'S DAMAGED VERSION!! HER OUTFIT'S ALREADY SEXY AS IT IS, BUT THE DAMAGE JUST MAKES IT THAT MUCH SEXIER!!
I DON'T WANT THIS!
KIRIE-CHAN USES "DEATH GLARE" !!
HA HA, I'M GLAD YOU LIKE IT!
BUT ALEX IS UNAFFECTED!!
GLARE
TO BE HONEST, YOU REALLY THREW ME FOR A LOOP WITH THOSE GAME DECISIONS LAST TIME...
I NEVER THOUGHT I'D MEET SOMEONE BETTER AT DATING SIMS THAN ME.

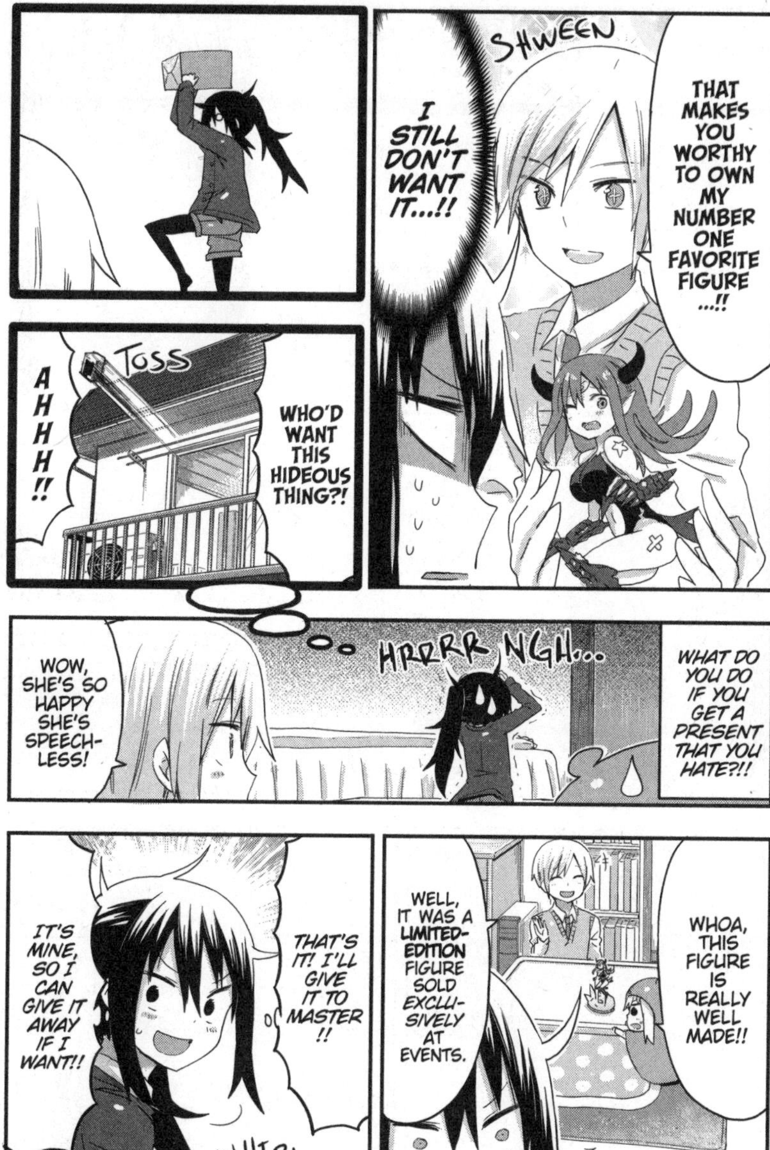
SHWEEN
THAT MAKES YOU WORTHY TO OWN MY NUMBER ONE FAVORITE FIGURE ...!!
I STILL DON'T WANT IT...!!
WHO'D WANT THIS HIDEOUS THING?!
TOSS
AHHHH!!
WHAT DO YOU DO IF YOU GET A PRESENT THAT YOU HATE?!!
HRRRR NGH...
WOW, SHE'S SO HAPPY SHE'S SPEECHLESS!
WHOA, THIS FIGURE IS REALLY WELL MADE!!
WELL, IT WAS A LIMITED-EDITION FIGURE SOLD EXCLUSIVELY AT EVENTS.
THAT'S IT! I'LL GIVE IT TO MASTER!!
IT'S MINE, SO I CAN GIVE IT AWAY IF I WANT!!
WHIRL

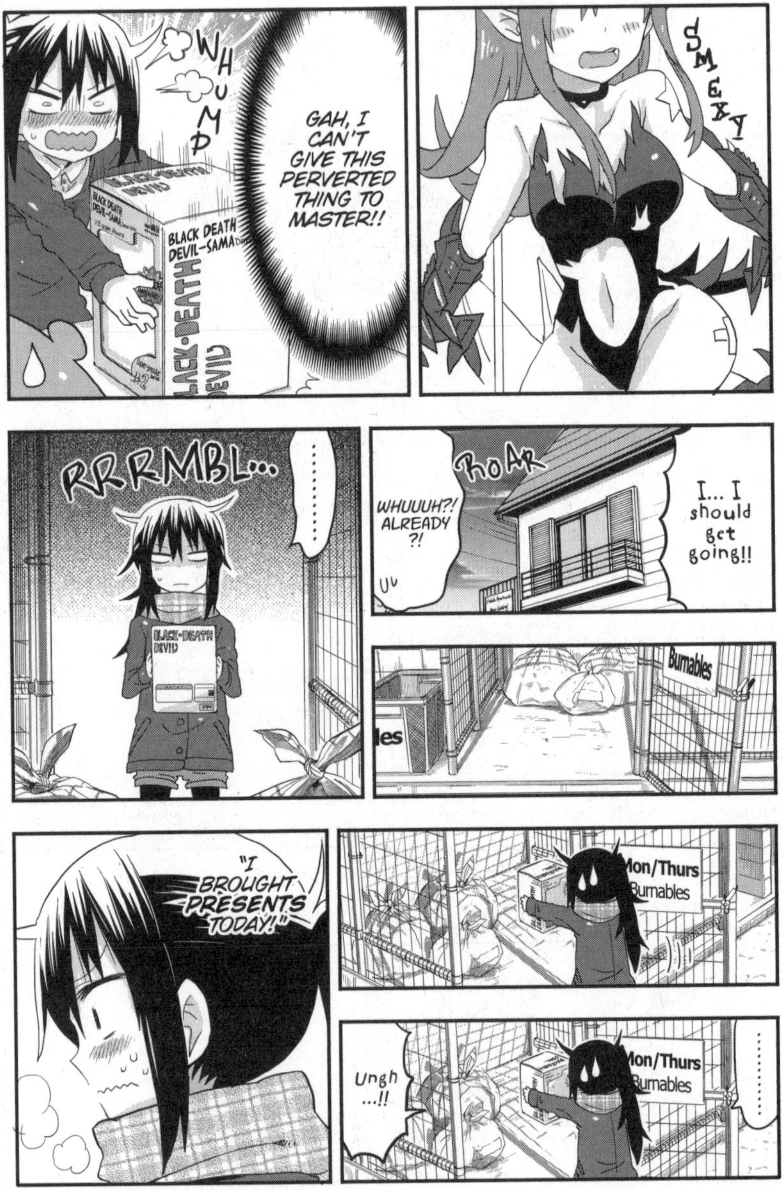
SMEXY
WHUMP
GAH, I CAN'T GIVE THIS PERVERTED THING TO MASTER!!
BLACK DEATH DEVIL-SAMA
BLACK-DEATH DEVIL
ROAR
WHUUUH?! ALREADY ?!
I... I should get going!!
Burnables
RRRMBL...
......
Mon/Thurs Burnables
Mon/Thurs Burnables
Ungh ...!!
......
"I BROUGHT PRESENTS TODAY!"

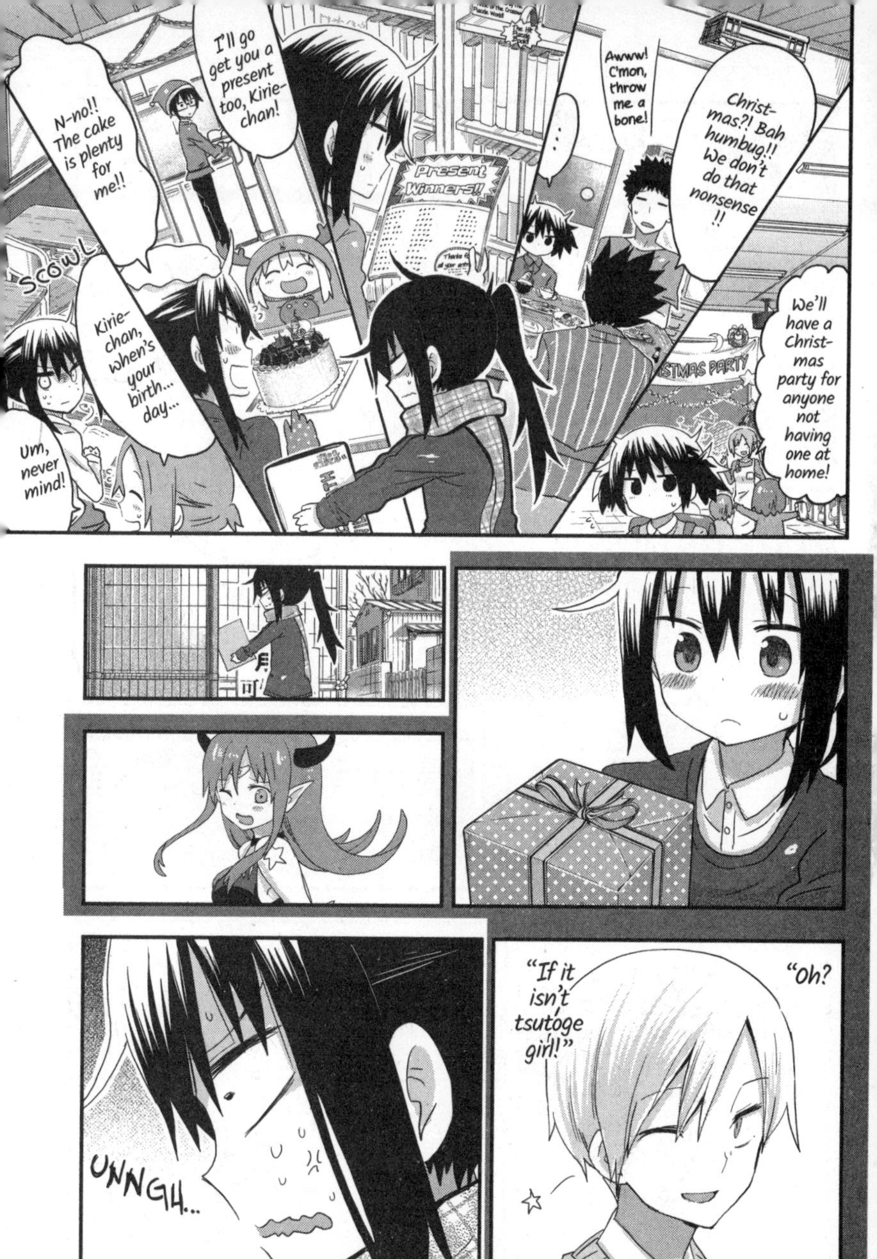
Christmas?! Bah humbug!! We don't do that nonsense!!
Awww! C'mon, throw me a bone!
...
We'll have a Christmas party for anyone not having one at home!
CHRISTMAS PARTY
Present Winners!!
I'll go get you a present too, Kirie-chan!
N-no!! The cake is plenty for me!!
SCOWL
Kirie-chan, when's your birth... day...
Um, never mind!
"Oh?
"If it isn't tsutoge girl!"
UNNGH...

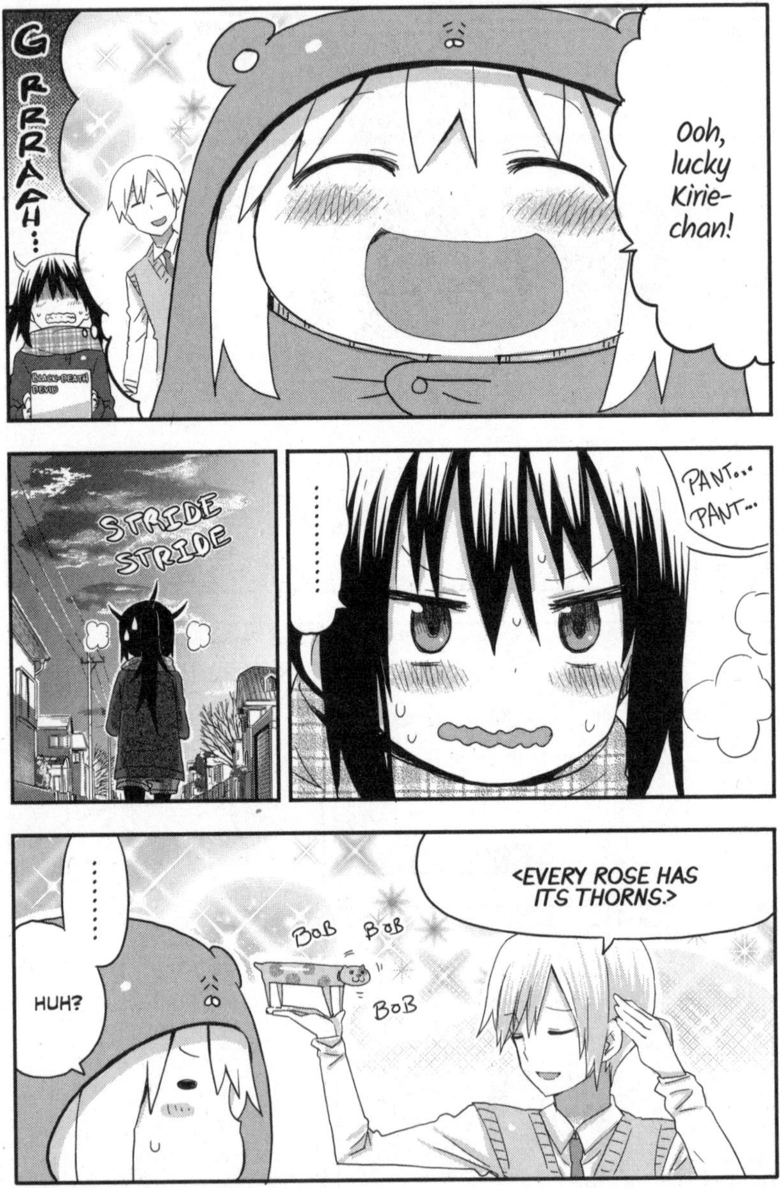
Ooh, lucky Kirie-chan!
GRRRAGH...
BLACK-DEATH DEVIL
PANT... PANT...
......
STRIDE STRIDE
<EVERY ROSE HAS ITS THORNS.>
BOB BOB
BOB
......
HUH?

No. 86 **Umaru & Yakiniku**

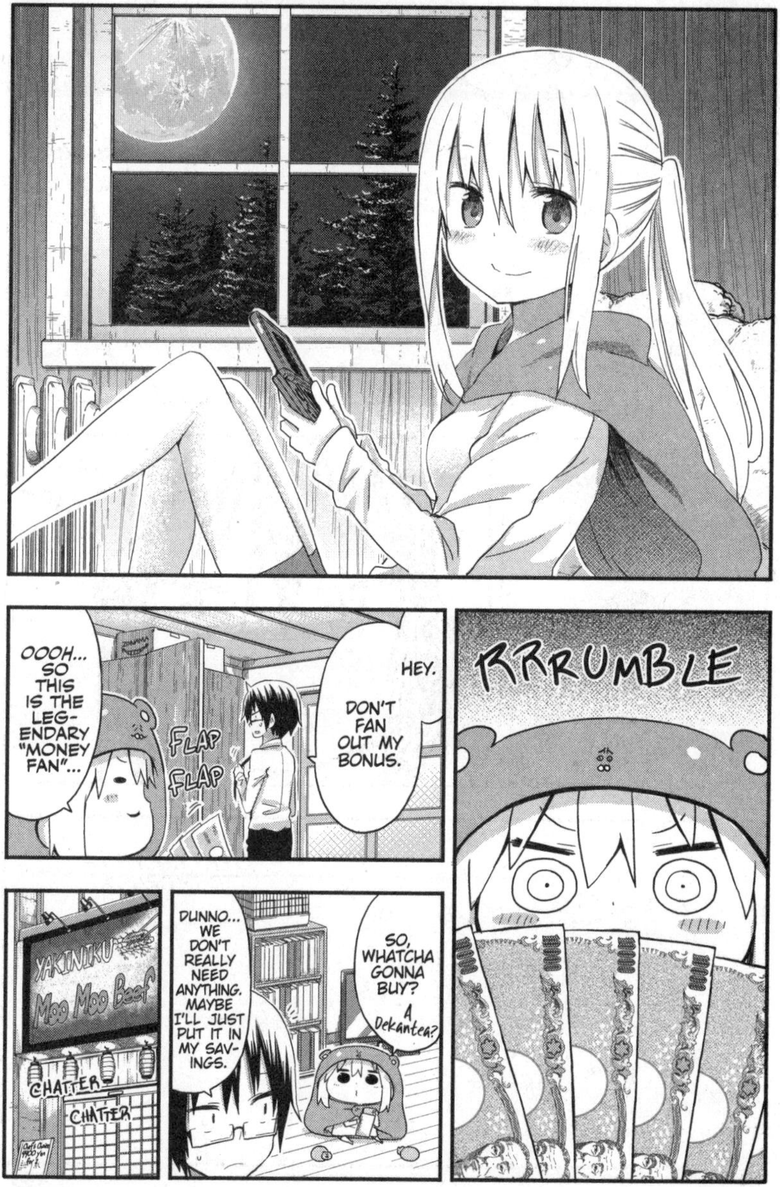
RRRUMBLE
HEY.
DON'T FAN OUT MY BONUS.
OOOH... SO THIS IS THE LEGENDARY "MONEY FAN"...
FLAP FLAP
SO, WHATCHA GONNA BUY?
A Dekantea?
DUNNO... WE DON'T REALLY NEED ANYTHING. MAYBE I'LL JUST PUT IT IN MY SAVINGS.
YAKINIKU
Moo Moo Beef
CHATTER
CHATTER

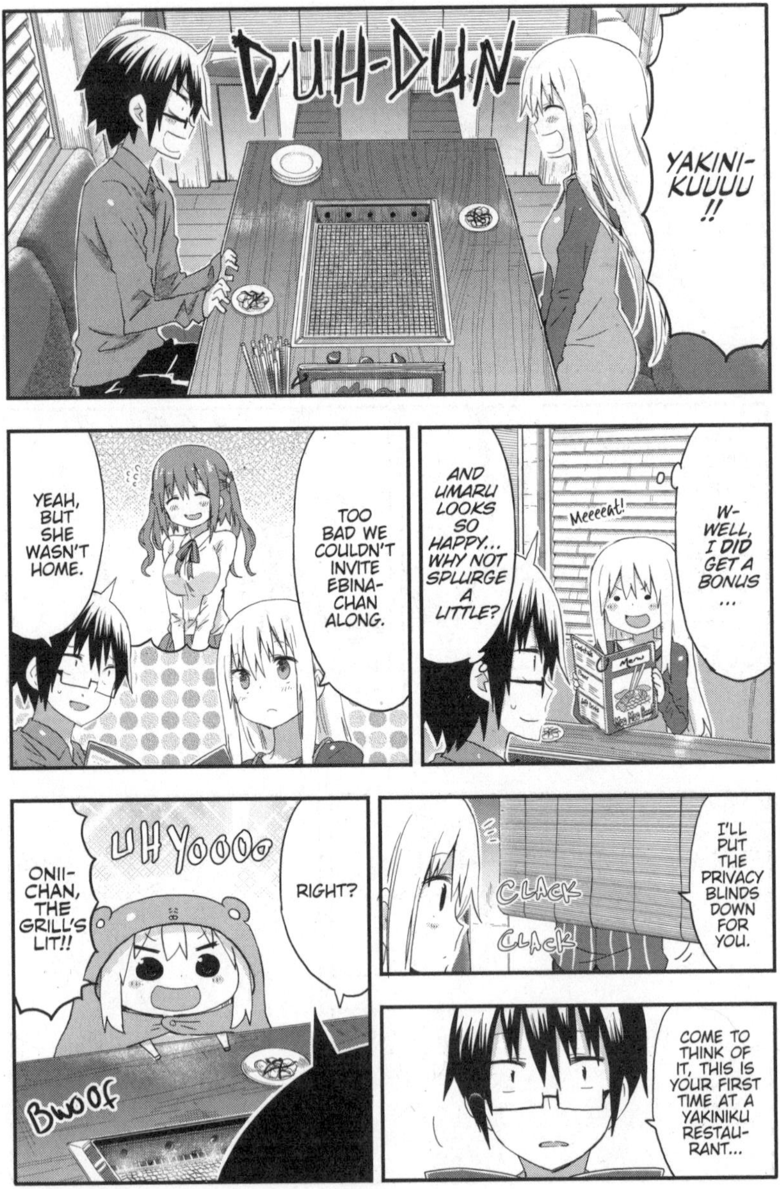
DUH-DUN
YAKINI-KUUUU!!
W-WELL, I DID GET A BONUS...
Meeeeat!
AND UMARU LOOKS SO HAPPY... WHY NOT SPLURGE A LITTLE?
TOO BAD WE COULDN'T INVITE EBINA-CHAN ALONG.
YEAH, BUT SHE WASN'T HOME.
I'LL PUT THE PRIVACY BLINDS DOWN FOR YOU.
CLACK
CLACK
COME TO THINK OF IT, THIS IS YOUR FIRST TIME AT A YAKINIKU RESTAURANT...
RIGHT?
UHYOOO
ONII-CHAN, THE GRILL'S LIT!!
Bwoof

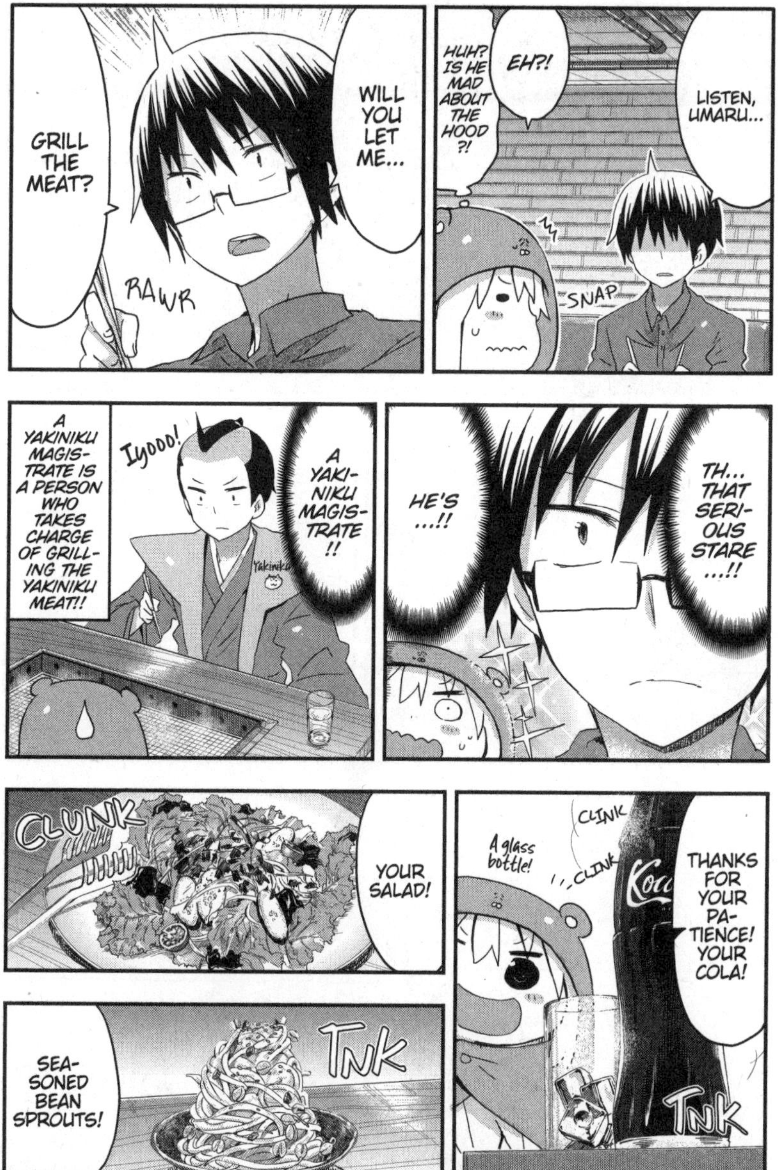
LISTEN, UMARU...
EH?!
HUH? IS HE MAD ABOUT THE HOOD ?!
SNAP
WILL YOU LET ME...
GRILL THE MEAT?
RAWR
TH... THAT SERIOUS STARE ...!!
HE'S ...!!
A YAKINIKU MAGISTRATE !!
Iyooo!
A YAKINIKU MAGISTRATE IS A PERSON WHO TAKES CHARGE OF GRILLING THE YAKINIKU MEAT!!
Yakiniku
THANKS FOR YOUR PATIENCE! YOUR COLA!
CLINK
A glass bottle!
CLINK
TNK
YOUR SALAD!
CLUNK
SEASONED BEAN SPROUTS!
TNK

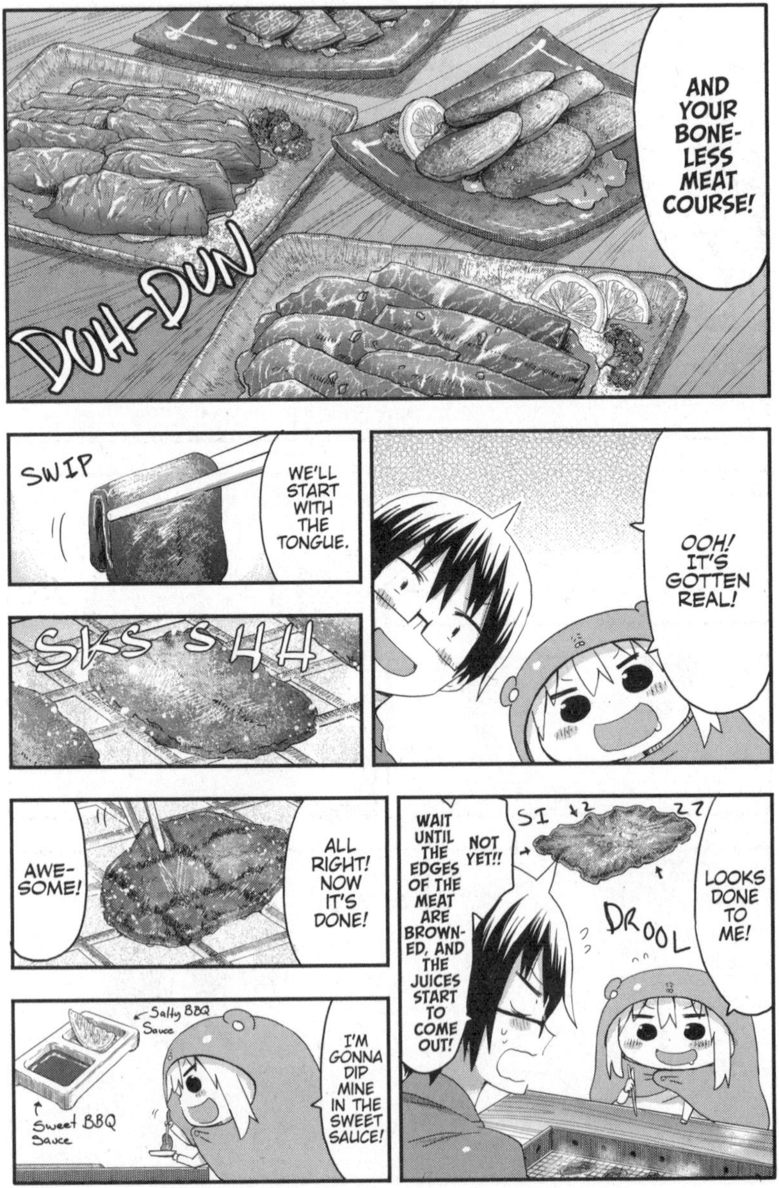
AND YOUR BONE-LESS MEAT COURSE!
DUH-DUN
OOH! IT'S GOTTEN REAL!
SWIP
WE'LL START WITH THE TONGUE.
SKS SHH
LOOKS DONE TO ME!
SI
Z
ZZ
DROOL
NOT YET!!
WAIT UNTIL THE EDGES OF THE MEAT ARE BROWNED, AND THE JUICES START TO COME OUT!
ALL RIGHT! NOW IT'S DONE!
AWE-SOME!
I'M GONNA DIP MINE IN THE SWEET SAUCE!
Salty BBQ Sauce
Sweet BBQ Sauce

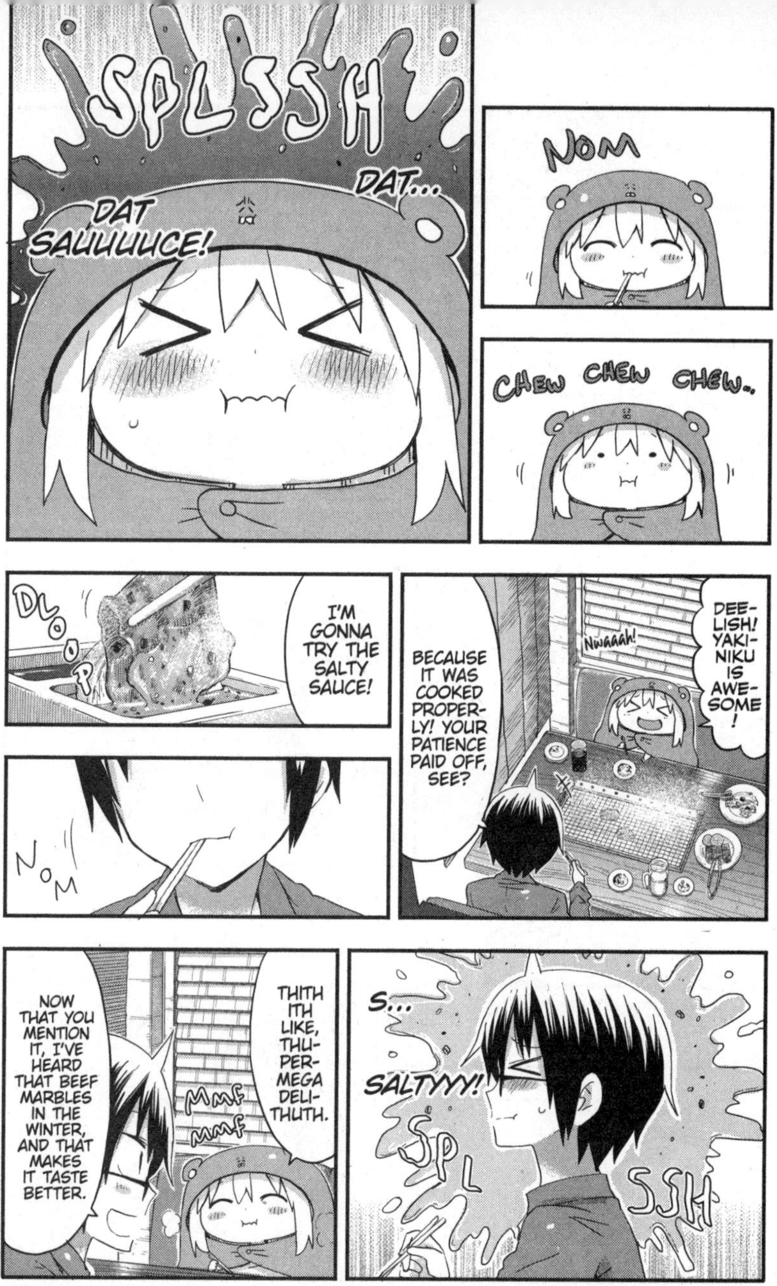
NOM
CHEW CHEW CHEW..
SPLSSH
DAT...
DAT SAUUUUUCE!
Nwaaah!
DEE-LISH! YAKI-NIKU IS AWE-SOME!
BECAUSE IT WAS COOKED PROPER-LY! YOUR PATIENCE PAID OFF, SEE?
I'M GONNA TRY THE SALTY SAUCE!
DLOOP
NOM
S...
SALTYYY!
SPLSSH
THITH ITH LIKE, THUPER-MEGA DELI-THUTH.
Mmf mmf
NOW THAT YOU MENTION IT, I'VE HEARD THAT BEEF MARBLES IN THE WINTER, AND THAT MAKES IT TASTE BETTER.

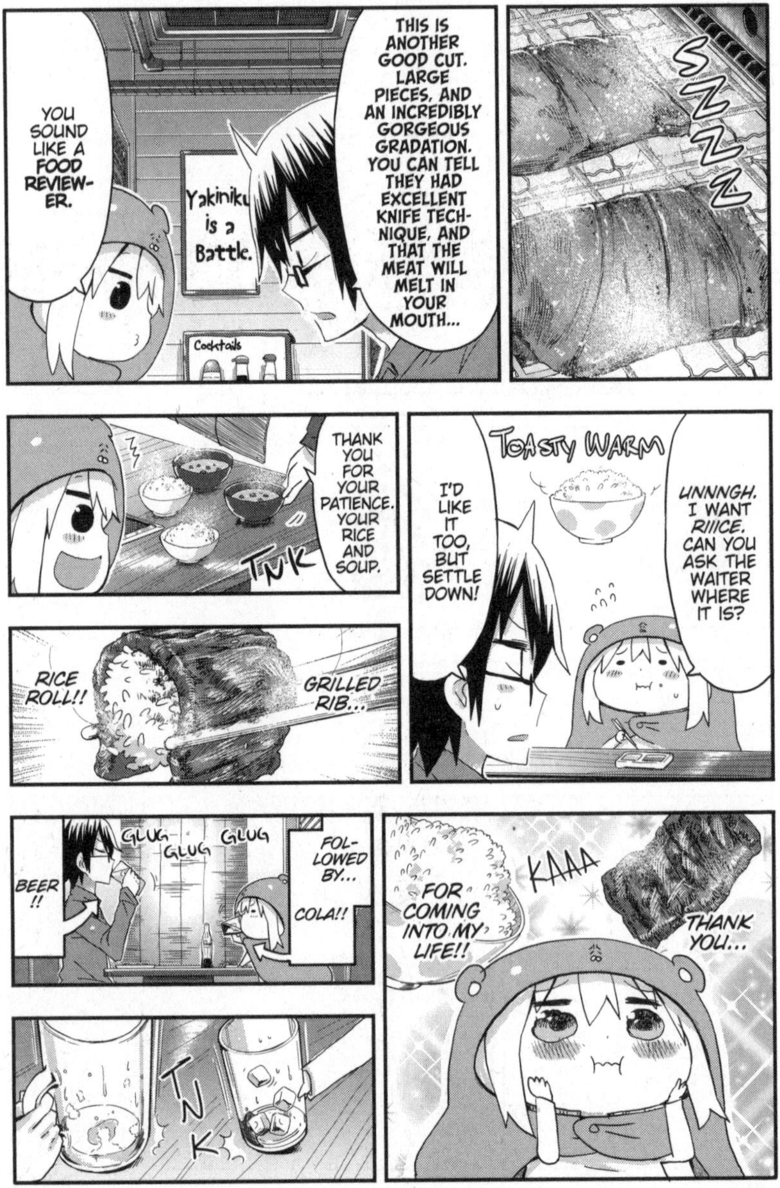
SZZZZ
THIS IS ANOTHER GOOD CUT. LARGE PIECES, AND AN INCREDIBLY GORGEOUS GRADATION. YOU CAN TELL THEY HAD EXCELLENT KNIFE TECH-NIQUE, AND THAT THE MEAT WILL MELT IN YOUR MOUTH...
Yakiniku is a Battle.
Cocktails
YOU SOUND LIKE A FOOD REVIEWER-ER.
TOASTY WARM
UNNNGH. I WANT RIIICE. CAN YOU ASK THE WAITER WHERE IT IS?
I'D LIKE IT TOO, BUT SETTLE DOWN!
THANK YOU FOR YOUR PATIENCE. YOUR RICE AND SOUP.
TNK
GRILLED RIB...
RICE ROLL!!
KAAA
THANK YOU...
FOR COMING INTO MY LIFE!!
GLUG GLUG GLUG
BEER!!
FOL-LOWED BY...
COLA!!
TNK

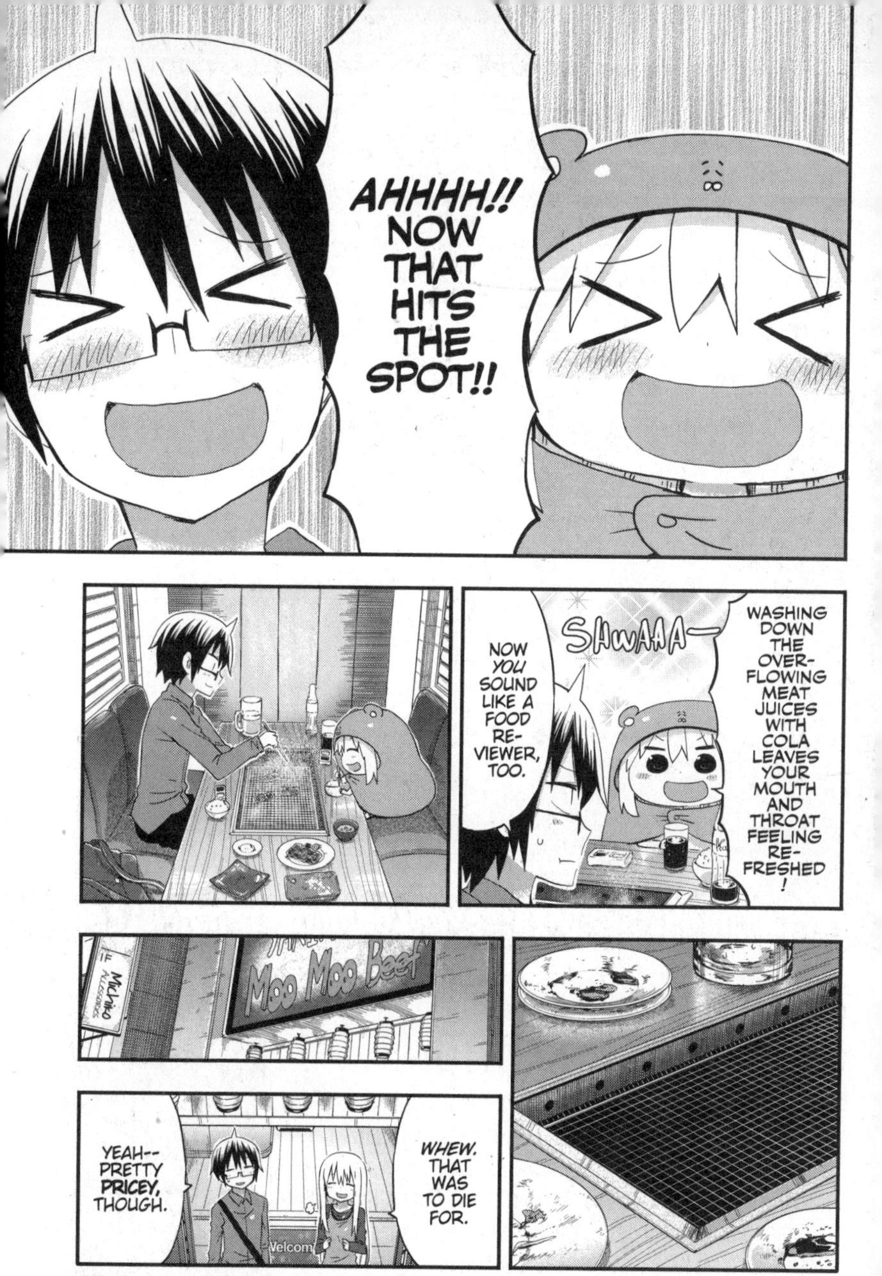
AHHHH!! NOW THAT HITS THE SPOT!!
WASHING DOWN THE OVER-FLOWING MEAT JUICES WITH COLA LEAVES YOUR MOUTH AND THROAT FEELING RE-FRESHED!
SHWAAA–
NOW YOU SOUND LIKE A FOOD RE-VIEWER, TOO.
Moo Moo Beef
1F Michiko Accessories
WHEW. THAT WAS TO DIE FOR.
YEAH-- PRETTY PRICEY, THOUGH.

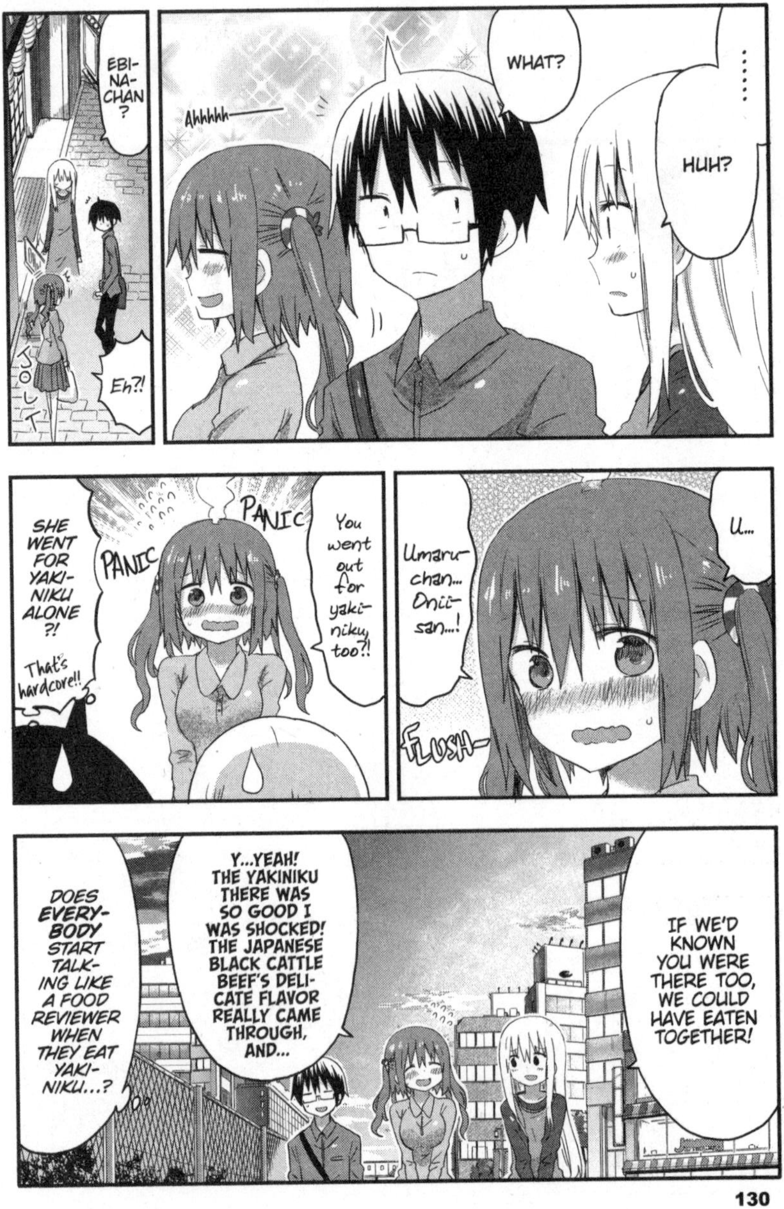
……
HUH?
WHAT?
Ahhhhh——
EBI-NA-CHAN?
JOLT
Eh?!
U...
Umaru-chan... Onii-san...!
FLUSH-
You went out for yaki-niku, too?!
PANIC
PANIC
SHE WENT FOR YAKI-NIKU ALONE?!
That's hardcore!!
IF WE'D KNOWN YOU WERE THERE TOO, WE COULD HAVE EATEN TOGETHER!
Y...YEAH! THE YAKINIKU THERE WAS SO GOOD I WAS SHOCKED! THE JAPANESE BLACK CATTLE BEEF'S DELICATE FLAVOR REALLY CAME THROUGH, AND...
DOES EVERYBODY START TALKING LIKE A FOOD REVIEWER WHEN THEY EAT YAKINIKU...?

No. 87 Umaru & the Anime Shop

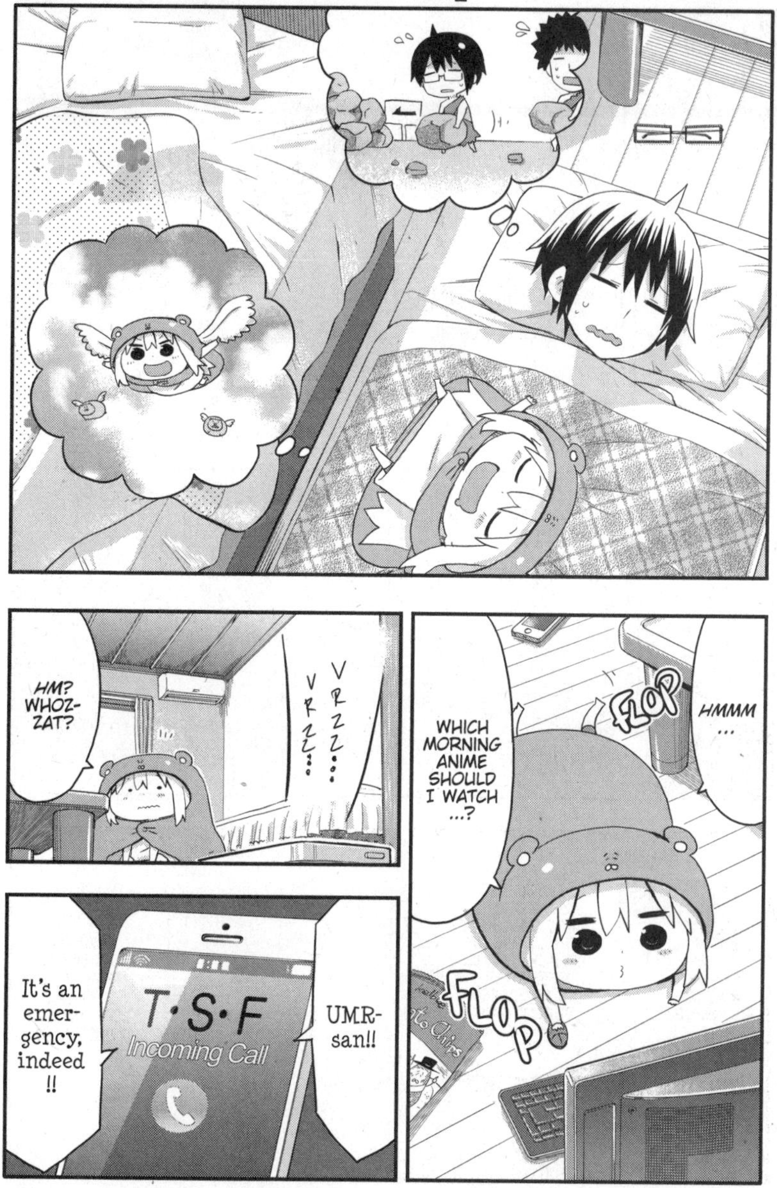
HMMM ...
FLOP
WHICH MORNING ANIME SHOULD I WATCH ...?
FLOP
VRZZ...
VRZZ...
HM? WHOZZAT?
UMR-san!!
T·S·F
Incoming Call
It's an emergency, indeed!!

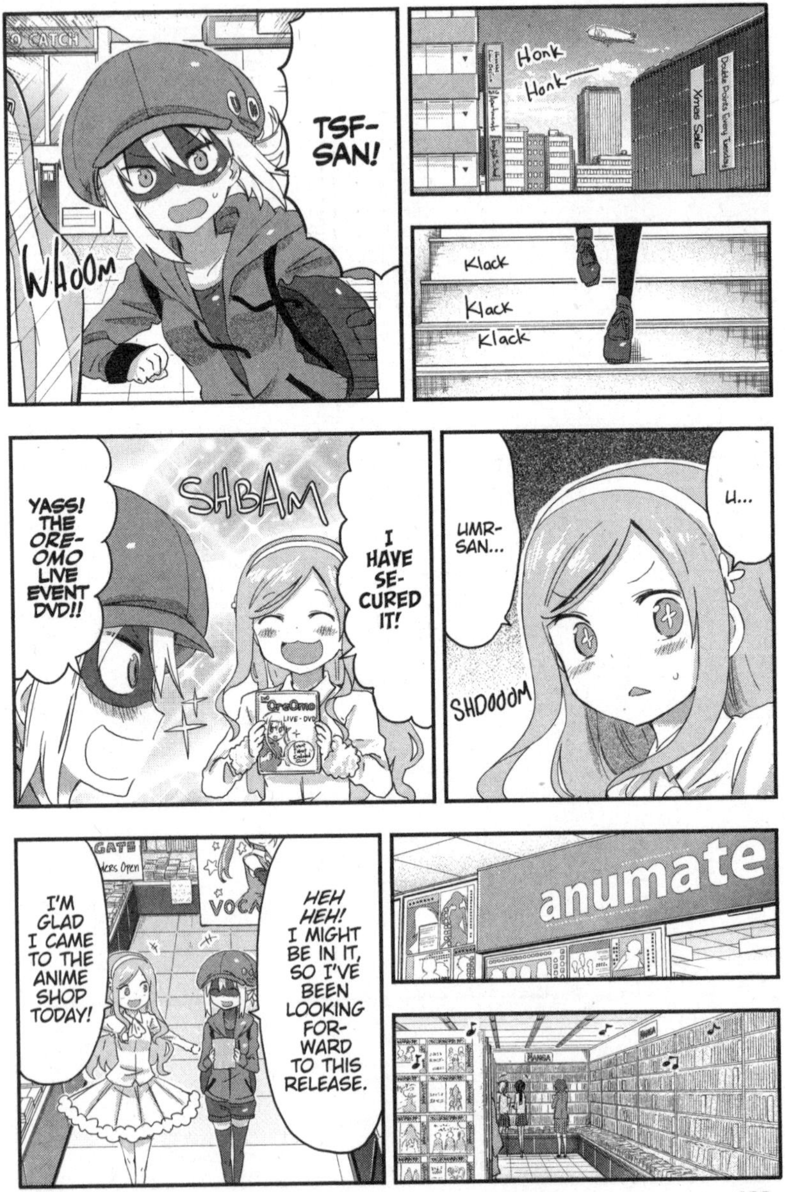
Honk
Honk
Double Points Every Tuesday
Xmas Sale
Klack
Klack
Klack
TSF-SAN!
WHOOM
U...
UMR-SAN...
SHDOOOM
SHBAM
I HAVE SE-CURED IT!
YASS! THE ORE-OMO LIVE EVENT DVD!!
OreOmo
LIVE-DVD
anumate
HEH HEH! I MIGHT BE IN IT, SO I'VE BEEN LOOKING FOR-WARD TO THIS RELEASE.
I'M GLAD I CAME TO THE ANIME SHOP TODAY!

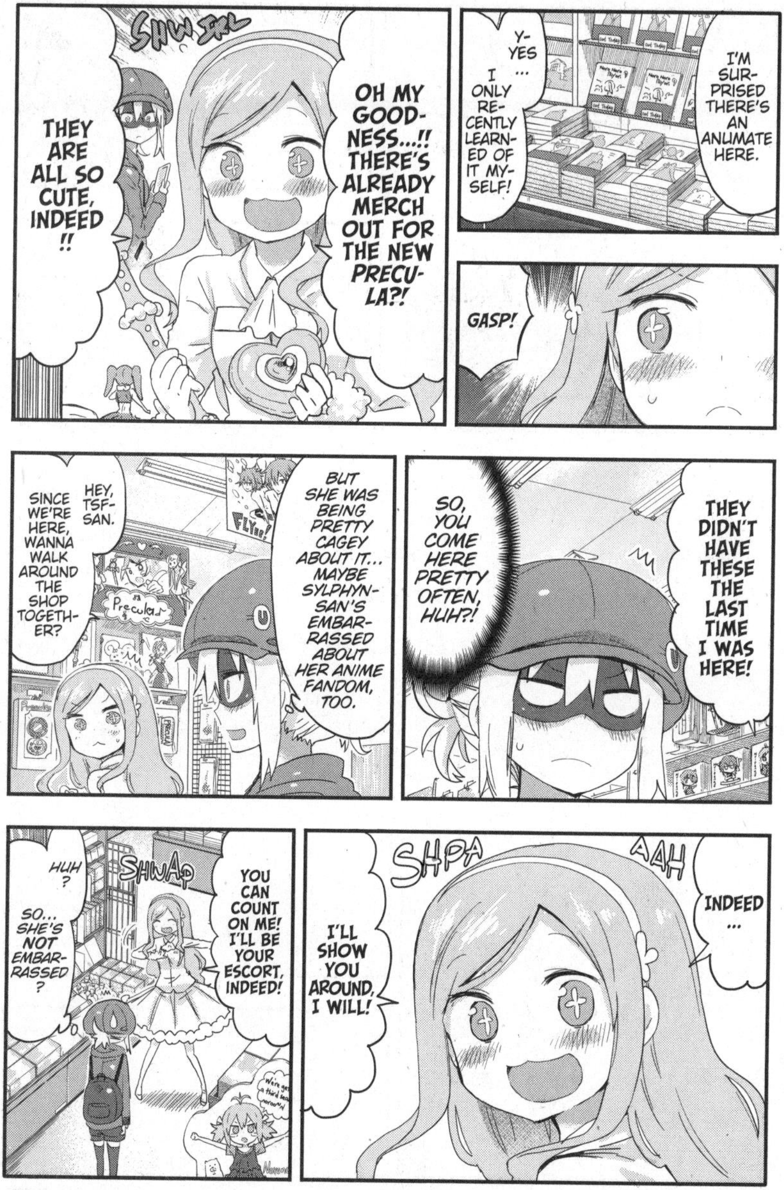
I'M SURPRISED THERE'S AN ANUMATE HERE.
Y-YES... I ONLY RECENTLY LEARNED OF IT MYSELF!
GASP!
SHWIRL
OH MY GOODNESS...!! THERE'S ALREADY MERCH OUT FOR THE NEW PRECULA?!
THEY ARE ALL SO CUTE, INDEED!!
THEY DIDN'T HAVE THESE THE LAST TIME I WAS HERE!
SO, YOU COME HERE PRETTY OFTEN, HUH?!
BUT SHE WAS BEING PRETTY CAGEY ABOUT IT... MAYBE SYLPHYN-SAN'S EMBARRASSED ABOUT HER ANIME FANDOM, TOO.
HEY, TSF-SAN.
SINCE WE'RE HERE, WANNA WALK AROUND THE SHOP TOGETHER?
SHPA AAH
INDEED...
I'LL SHOW YOU AROUND, I WILL!
SHWAP
YOU CAN COUNT ON ME! I'LL BE YOUR ESCORT, INDEED!
HUH?
SO... SHE'S NOT EMBARRASSED?

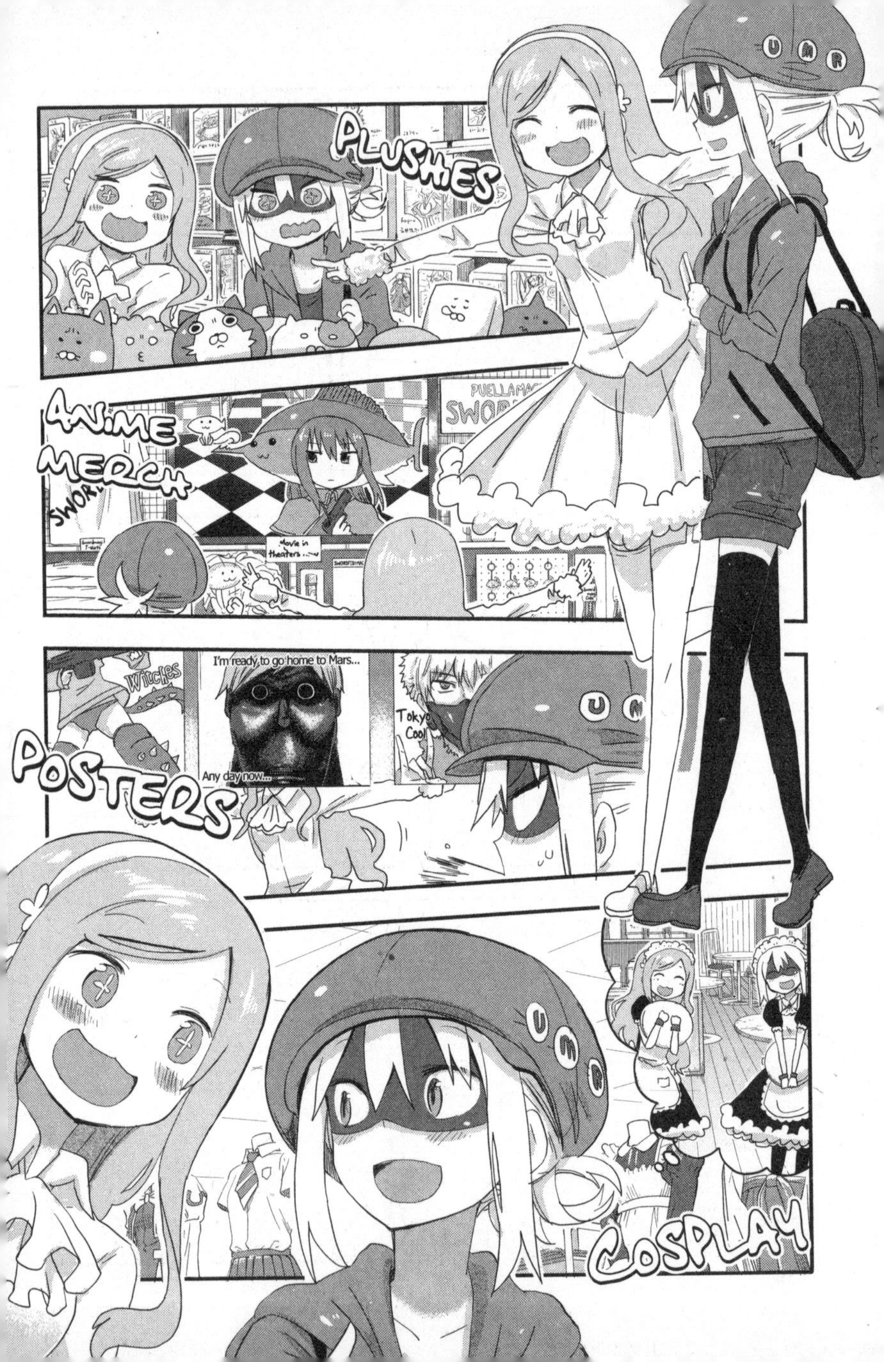

PLUSHES
ANIME MERCH
Movie in theaters...
Tokyo Cool
I'm ready to go home to Mars...
Any day now...
Witches
POSTERS
COSPLAY

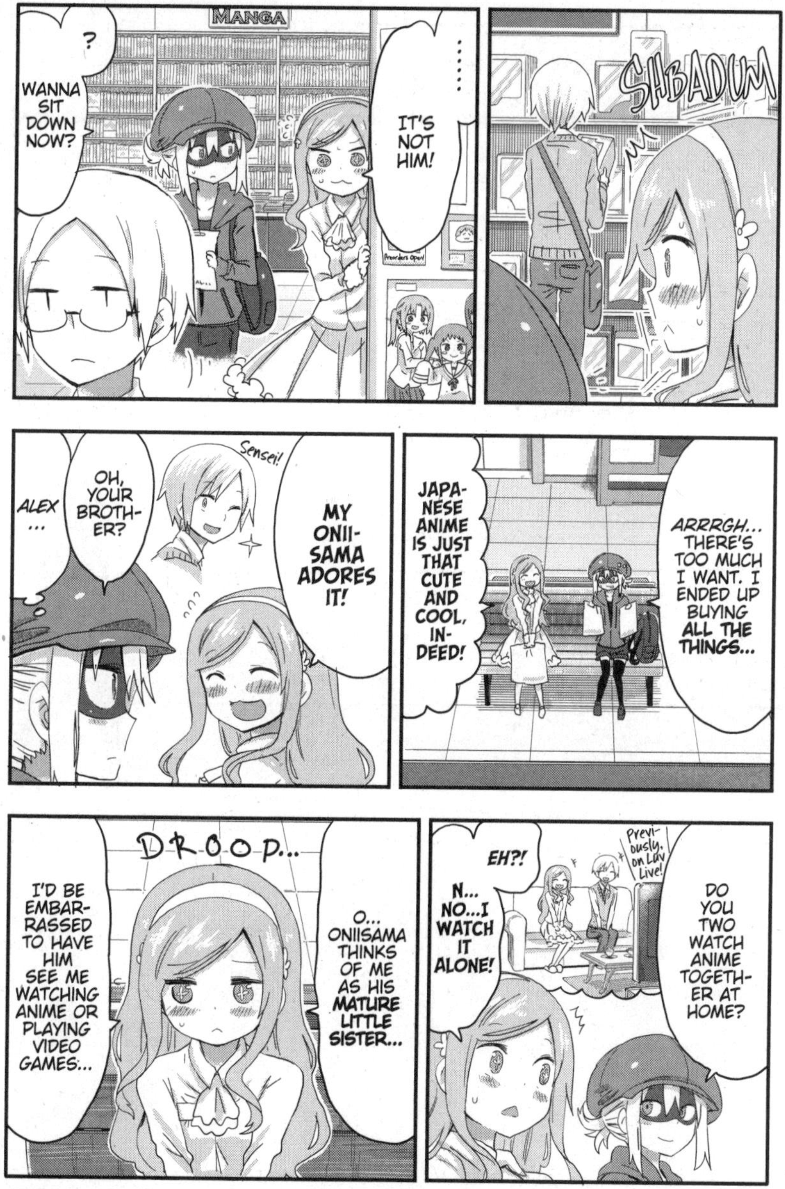
SHBADUM
MANGA
......
IT'S NOT HIM!
?
WANNA SIT DOWN NOW?
Preorders Open!
ARRRGH... THERE'S TOO MUCH I WANT. I ENDED UP BUYING ALL THE THINGS...
JAPANESE ANIME IS JUST THAT CUTE AND COOL, INDEED!
MY ONIISAMA ADORES IT!
Sensei!
OH, YOUR BROTHER?
ALEX ...
DO YOU TWO WATCH ANIME TOGETHER AT HOME?
Previously, on Lov Live!
EH?!
N... NO...I WATCH IT ALONE!
O... ONIISAMA THINKS OF ME AS HIS MATURE LITTLE SISTER...
DROOP...
I'D BE EMBARRASSED TO HAVE HIM SEE ME WATCHING ANIME OR PLAYING VIDEO GAMES...

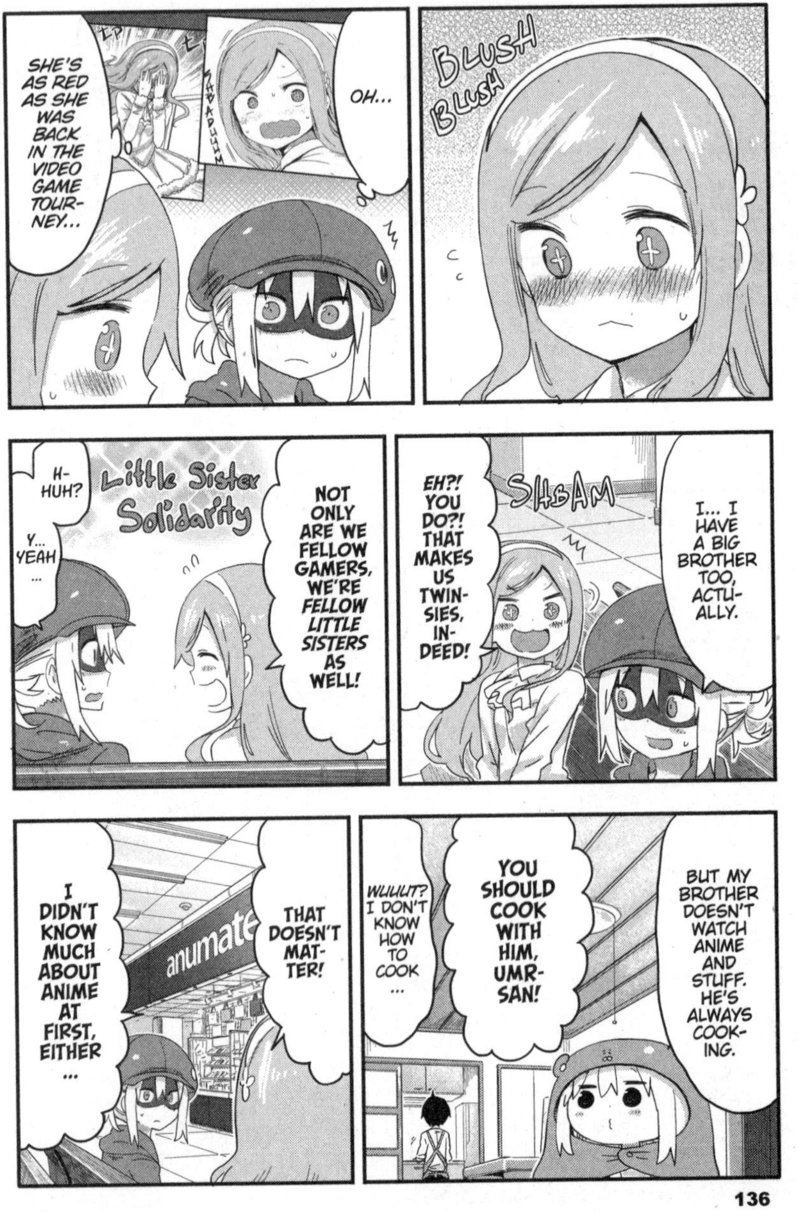
BLUSH BLUSH
OH...
SHE'S AS RED AS SHE WAS BACK IN THE VIDEO GAME TOURNEY...
I... I HAVE A BIG BROTHER TOO, ACTUALLY.
SHBAM
EH?! YOU DO?! THAT MAKES US TWINSIES, INDEED!
NOT ONLY ARE WE FELLOW GAMERS, WE'RE FELLOW LITTLE SISTERS AS WELL!
Little Sister Solidarity
H-HUH?
Y... YEAH ...
BUT MY BROTHER DOESN'T WATCH ANIME AND STUFF. HE'S ALWAYS COOKING.
YOU SHOULD COOK WITH HIM, UMR-SAN!
WUUUT? I DON'T KNOW HOW TO COOK ...
THAT DOESN'T MATTER!
anumate
I DIDN'T KNOW MUCH ABOUT ANIME AT FIRST, EITHER ...

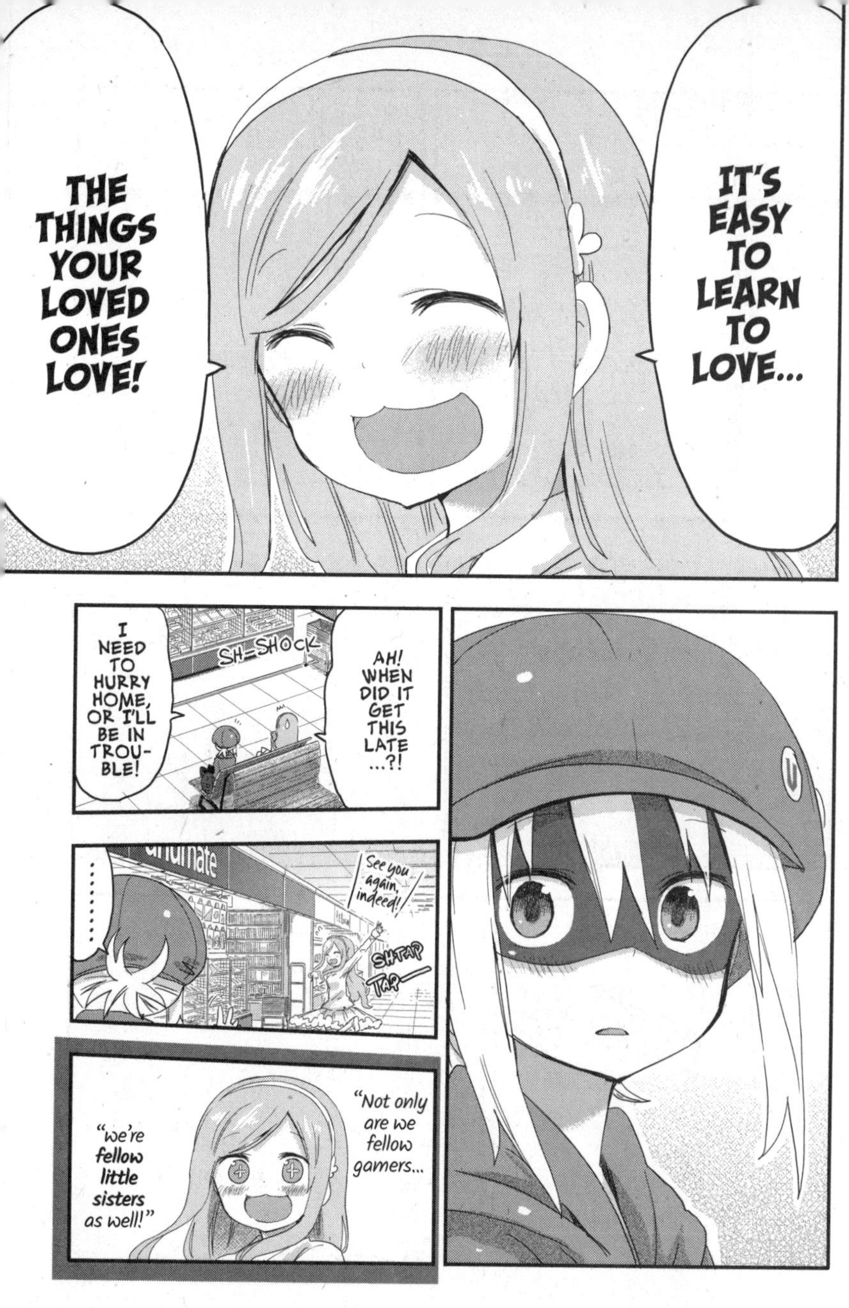
IT'S EASY TO LEARN TO LOVE...
THE THINGS YOUR LOVED ONES LOVE!
AH! WHEN DID IT GET THIS LATE ...?!
SH-SHOCK
I NEED TO HURRY HOME, OR I'LL BE IN TROU-BLE!
See you again, indeed!
SHTAP
TAP—
......
"Not only are we fellow gamers...
"we're fellow little sisters as well!"

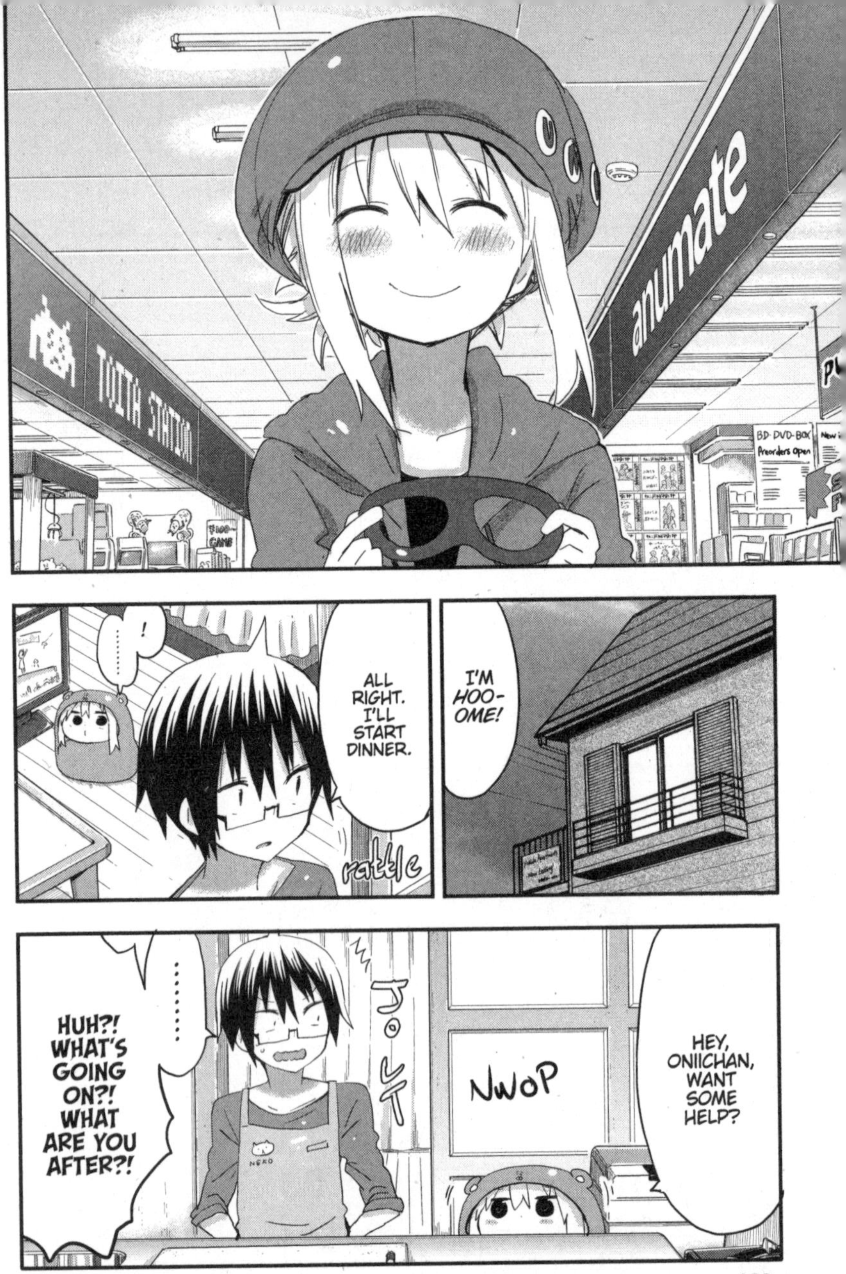
anumate
TOOTH STATION
BD·DVD·BOX
Preorders Open
I'M HOO-OME!
......!
ALL RIGHT. I'LL START DINNER.
rattle
HEY, ONIICHAN, WANT SOME HELP?
NWOP
....
HUH?! WHAT'S GOING ON?! WHAT ARE YOU AFTER?!
NEKO

The OreOmo Live DVD

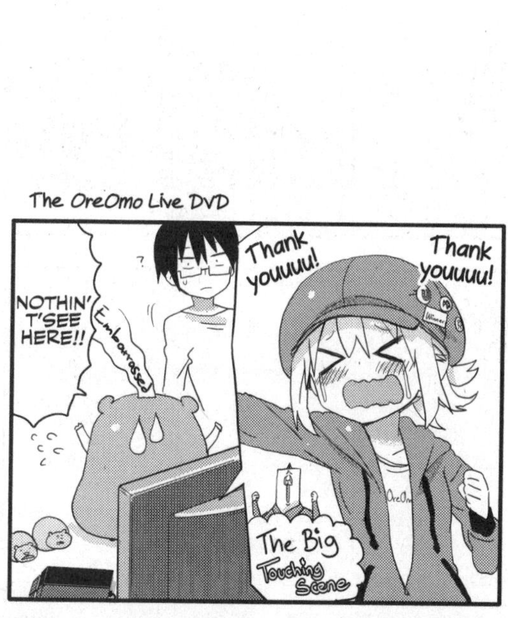
Thank youuuu!
Thank youuuu!
NOTHIN' T'SEE HERE!!
Embarrassed
OreOmo
The Big Touching Scene

Himouto! Umaru-chan

※This popularity poll ran in *Weekly Young Jump* 2014 No. 40.

Best Sibling Pair

+Selection General Election ♪

Tachibana Alex

Tachibana Sylphynford

Ebina Nana

Section Chief Kanau

2nd	Ebina X Taihei	123 votes
3rd	Outside Umaru X Taihei	97 votes
4th	Inside Umaru X Outside Umaru	81 votes
5th	Outside Umaru X Ebina	80 votes
6th	Inside Umaru X Kirie	34 votes
7th	UMR X Sylphyn	33 votes
8th	Inside Umaru X Ebina	33 votes
9th	Inside Umaru X Nekolumbus	31 votes
10th	Outside Umaru X Sylphyn	20 votes

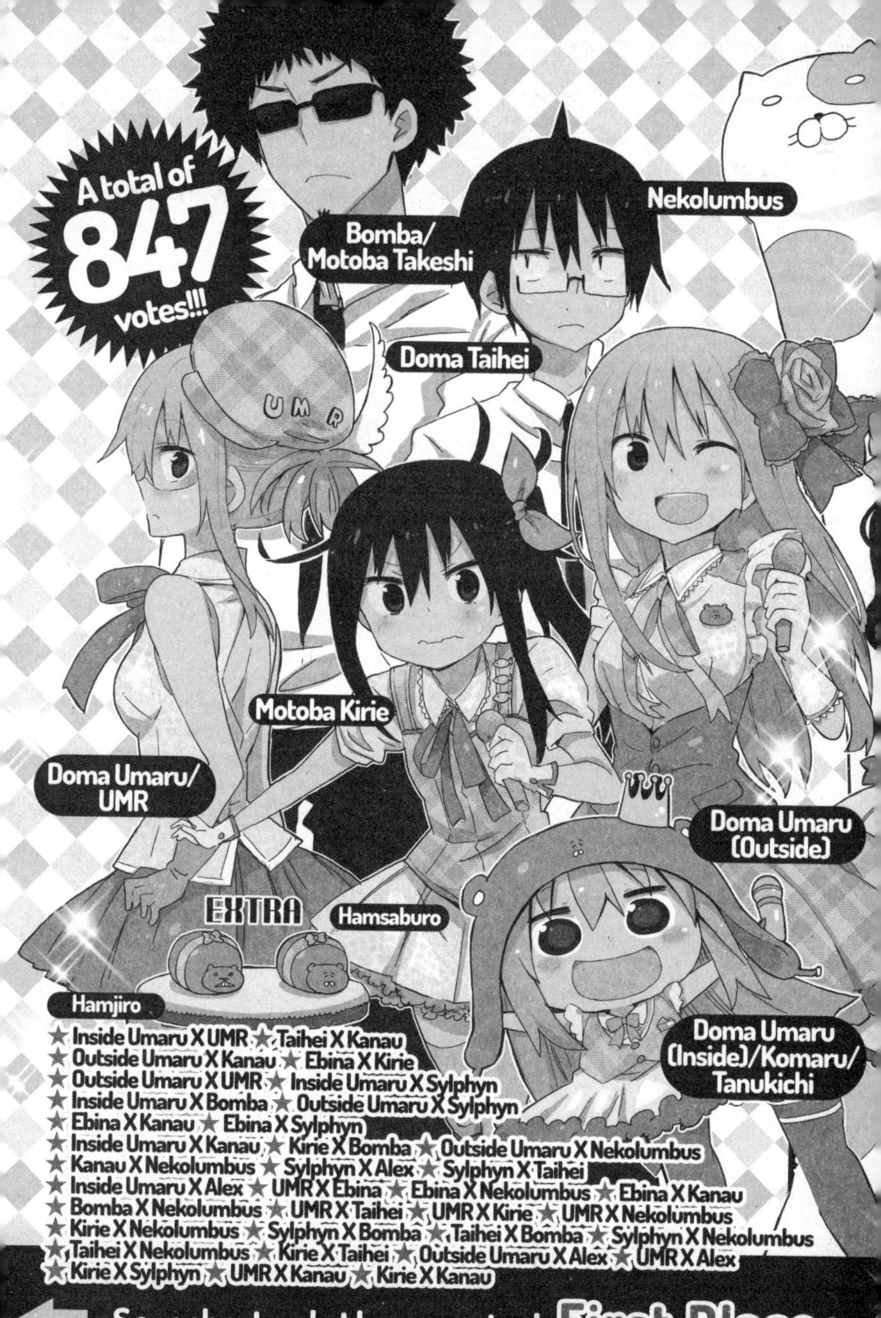
A total of 847 votes!!!
Nekolumbus
Bomba/ Motoba Takeshi
Doma Taihei
U M R
Motoba Kirie
Doma Umaru/ UMR
Doma Umaru (Outside)
EXTRA
Hamsaburo
Hamjiro
Doma Umaru (Inside)/Komaru/ Tanukichi
★ Inside Umaru X UMR ★ Taihei X Kanau
★ Outside Umaru X Kanau ★ Ebina X Kirie
★ Outside Umaru X UMR ★ Inside Umaru X Sylphyn
★ Inside Umaru X Bomba ★ Outside Umaru X Sylphyn
★ Ebina X Kanau ★ Ebina X Sylphyn
★ Inside Umaru X Kanau ★ Kirie X Bomba ★ Outside Umaru X Nekolumbus
★ Kanau X Nekolumbus ★ Sylphyn X Alex ★ Sylphyn X Taihei
★ Inside Umaru X Alex ★ UMR X Ebina ★ Ebina X Nekolumbus ★ Ebina X Kanau
★ Bomba X Nekolumbus ★ UMR X Taihei ★ UMR X Kirie ★ UMR X Nekolumbus
★ Kirie X Nekolumbus ★ Sylphyn X Bomba ★ Taihei X Bomba ★ Sylphyn X Nekolumbus
★ Taihei X Nekolumbus ★ Kirie X Taihei ★ Outside Umaru X Alex ★ UMR X Alex
★ Kirie X Sylphyn ★ UMR X Kanau ★ Kirie X Kanau

So, who took the coveted **First Place**?

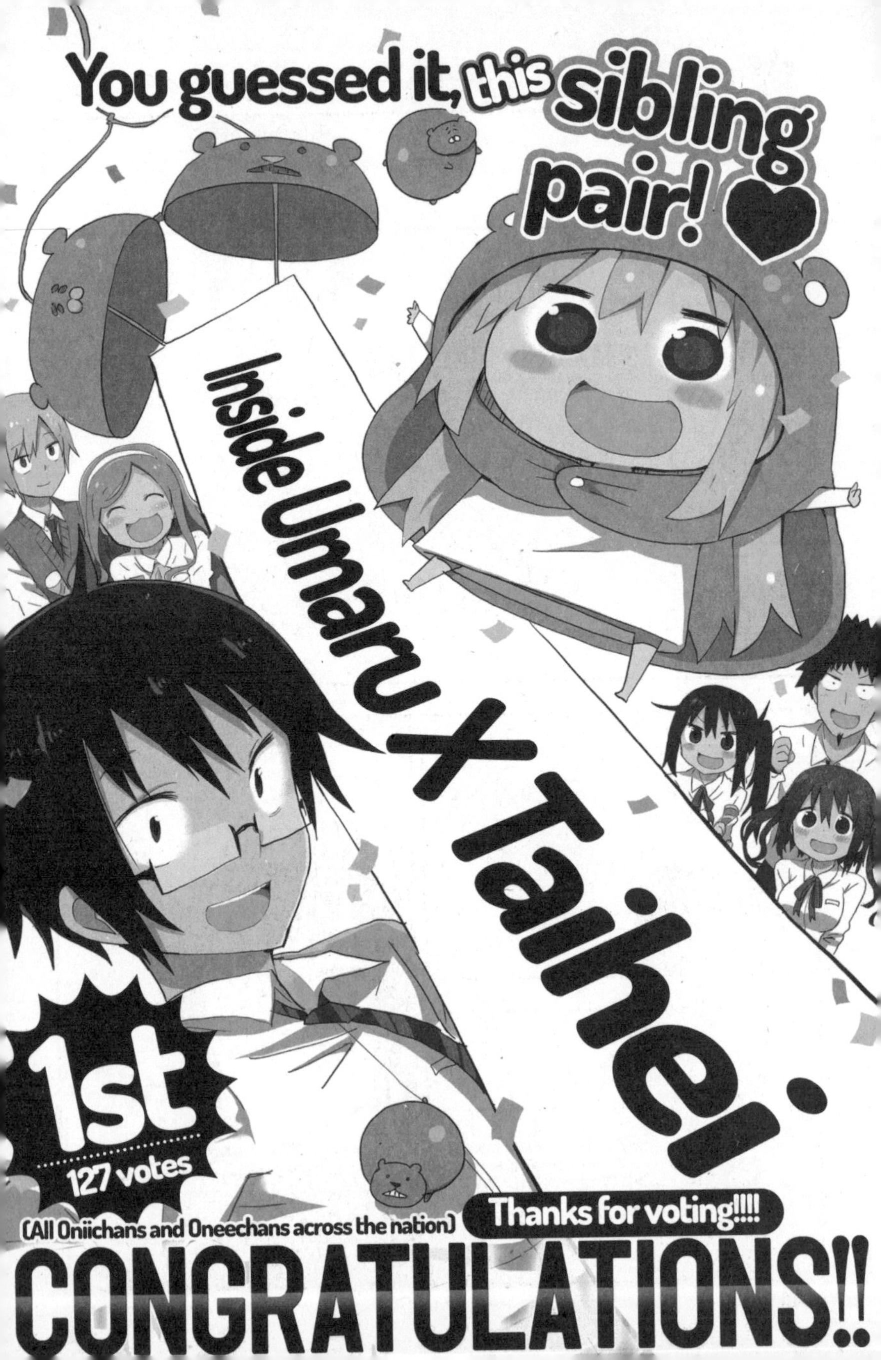
You guessed it, this sibling pair! ♥
Inside Umaru x Taihei!
1st
127 votes
(All Oniichans and Oneechans across the nation)
Thanks for voting!!!!
CONGRATULATIONS!!

No. 88 Umaru & the Christmas Party: Part 1

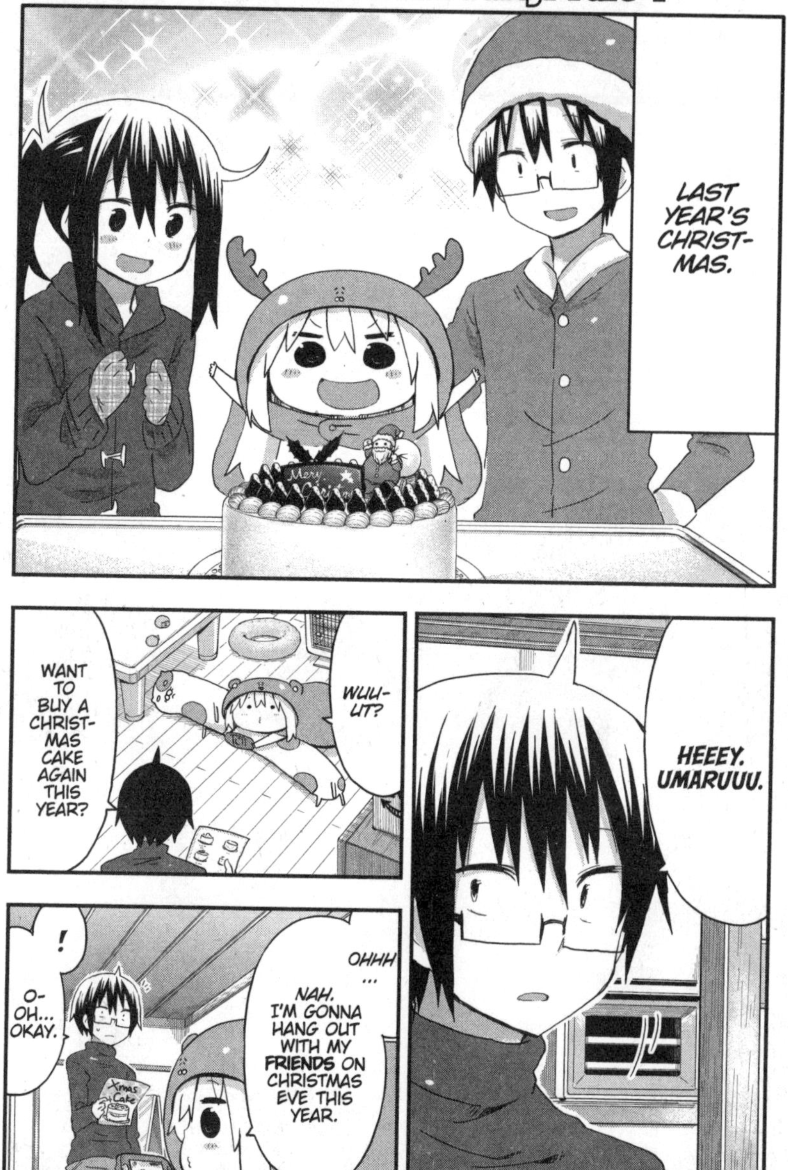
LAST YEAR'S CHRIST-MAS.
Merry Christmas
HEEEY. UMARUUU.
WUU-UT?
WANT TO BUY A CHRIST-MAS CAKE AGAIN THIS YEAR?
OHHH ...
NAH. I'M GONNA HANG OUT WITH MY **FRIENDS** ON CHRISTMAS EVE THIS YEAR.
!
O-OH... OKAY.
Xmas Cake

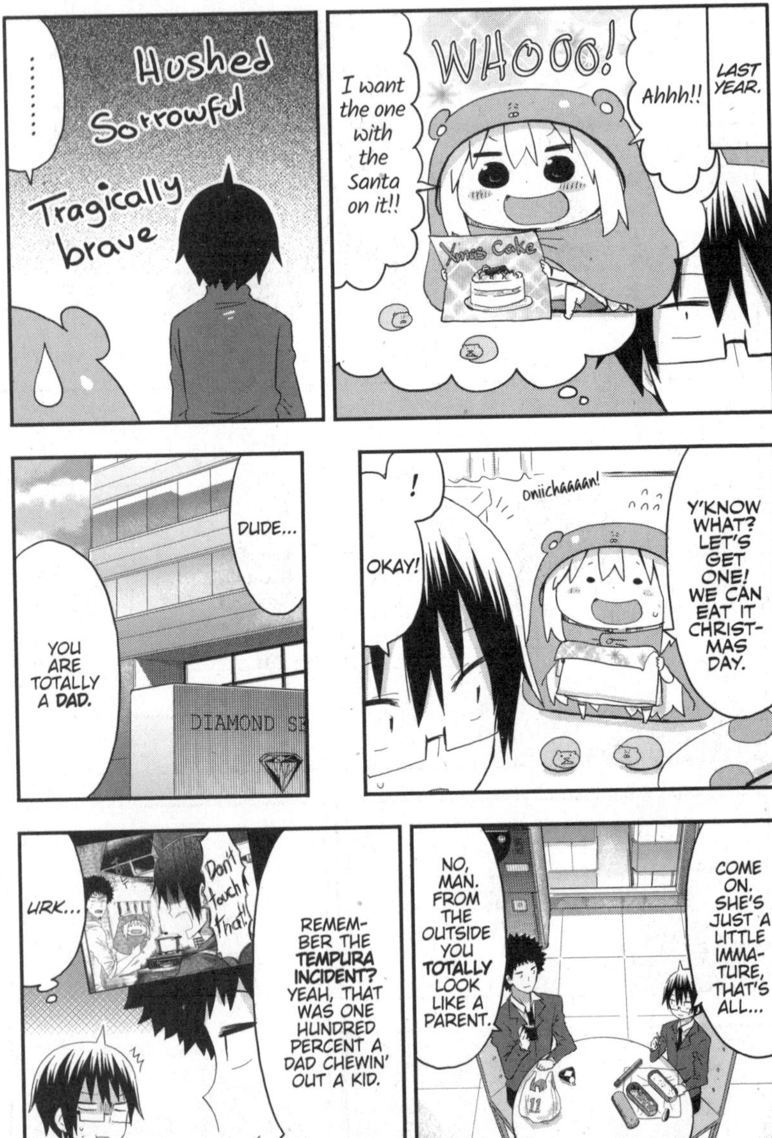
LAST YEAR.
Ahhh!!
WHOOO!
I want the one with the Santa on it!!
Xmas Cake
......
Hushed
Sorrowful
Tragically brave
Y'KNOW WHAT? LET'S GET ONE! WE CAN EAT IT CHRISTMAS DAY.
Oniichaaaaan!
!
OKAY!
DUDE...
YOU ARE TOTALLY A DAD.
DIAMOND S
COME ON. SHE'S JUST A LITTLE IMMATURE, THAT'S ALL...
NO, MAN. FROM THE OUTSIDE YOU TOTALLY LOOK LIKE A PARENT.
REMEMBER THE TEMPURA INCIDENT? YEAH, THAT WAS ONE HUNDRED PERCENT A DAD CHEWIN' OUT A KID.
Don't touch that!!
URK...

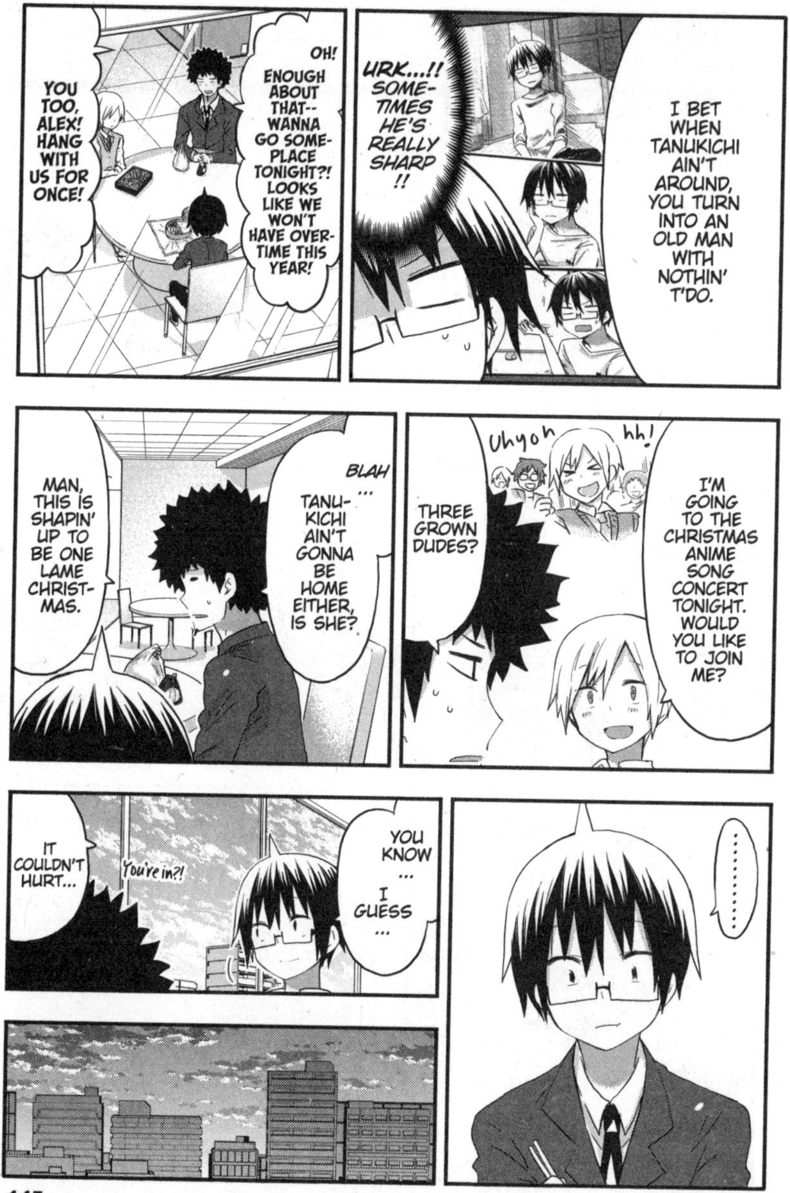
I BET WHEN TANUKICHI AIN'T AROUND, YOU TURN INTO AN OLD MAN WITH NOTHIN' T'DO.
URK...!! SOMETIMES HE'S REALLY SHARP!!
OH! ENOUGH ABOUT THAT--WANNA GO SOMEPLACE TONIGHT?! LOOKS LIKE WE WON'T HAVE OVERTIME THIS YEAR!
YOU TOO, ALEX! HANG WITH US FOR ONCE!
I'M GOING TO THE CHRISTMAS ANIME SONG CONCERT TONIGHT. WOULD YOU LIKE TO JOIN ME?
Uhyohhh!
THREE GROWN DUDES?
BLAH...
TANUKICHI AIN'T GONNA BE HOME EITHER, IS SHE?
MAN, THIS IS SHAPIN' UP TO BE ONE LAME CHRISTMAS.
....
YOU KNOW... I GUESS...
You're in?!
IT COULDN'T HURT...

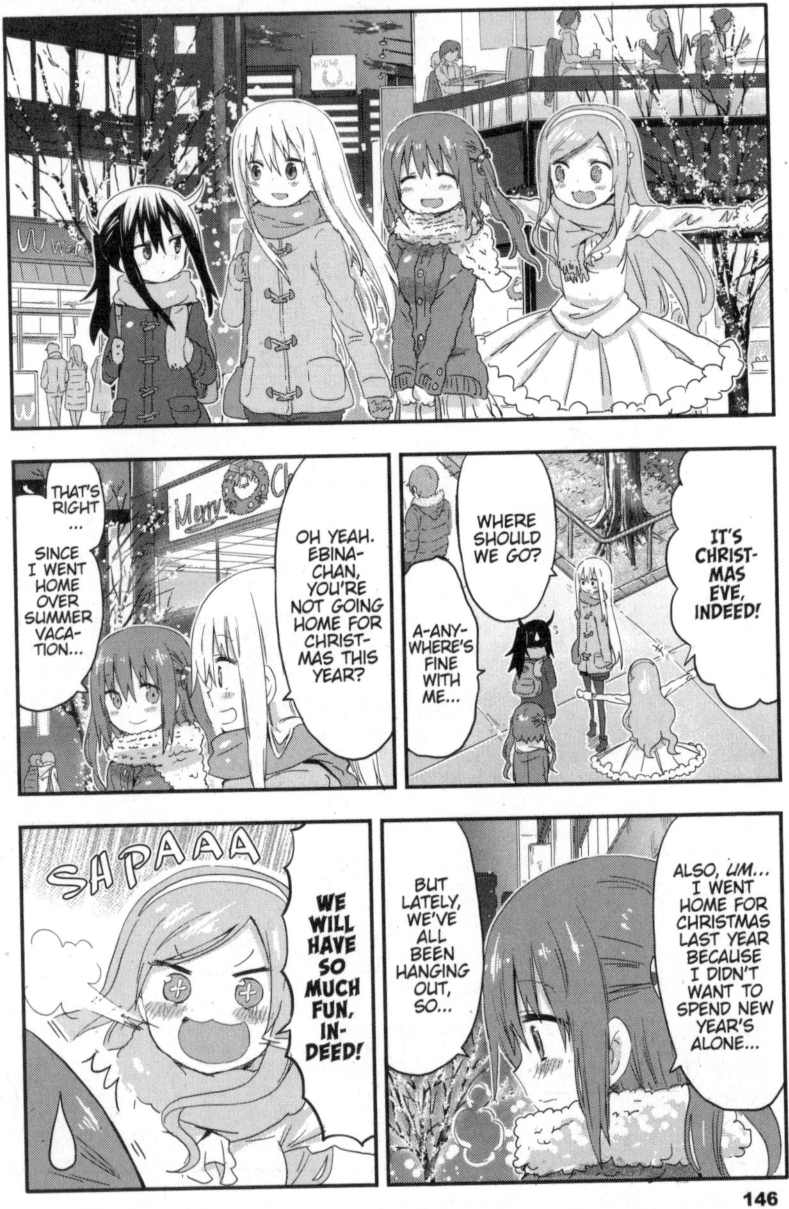
IT'S CHRISTMAS EVE, INDEED!
WHERE SHOULD WE GO?
A-ANYWHERE'S FINE WITH ME...
OH YEAH. EBINA-CHAN, YOU'RE NOT GOING HOME FOR CHRISTMAS THIS YEAR?
THAT'S RIGHT...
SINCE I WENT HOME OVER SUMMER VACATION...
ALSO, UM... I WENT HOME FOR CHRISTMAS LAST YEAR BECAUSE I DIDN'T WANT TO SPEND NEW YEAR'S ALONE...
BUT LATELY, WE'VE ALL BEEN HANGING OUT, SO...
SHPAAAA
WE WILL HAVE SO MUCH FUN, INDEED!

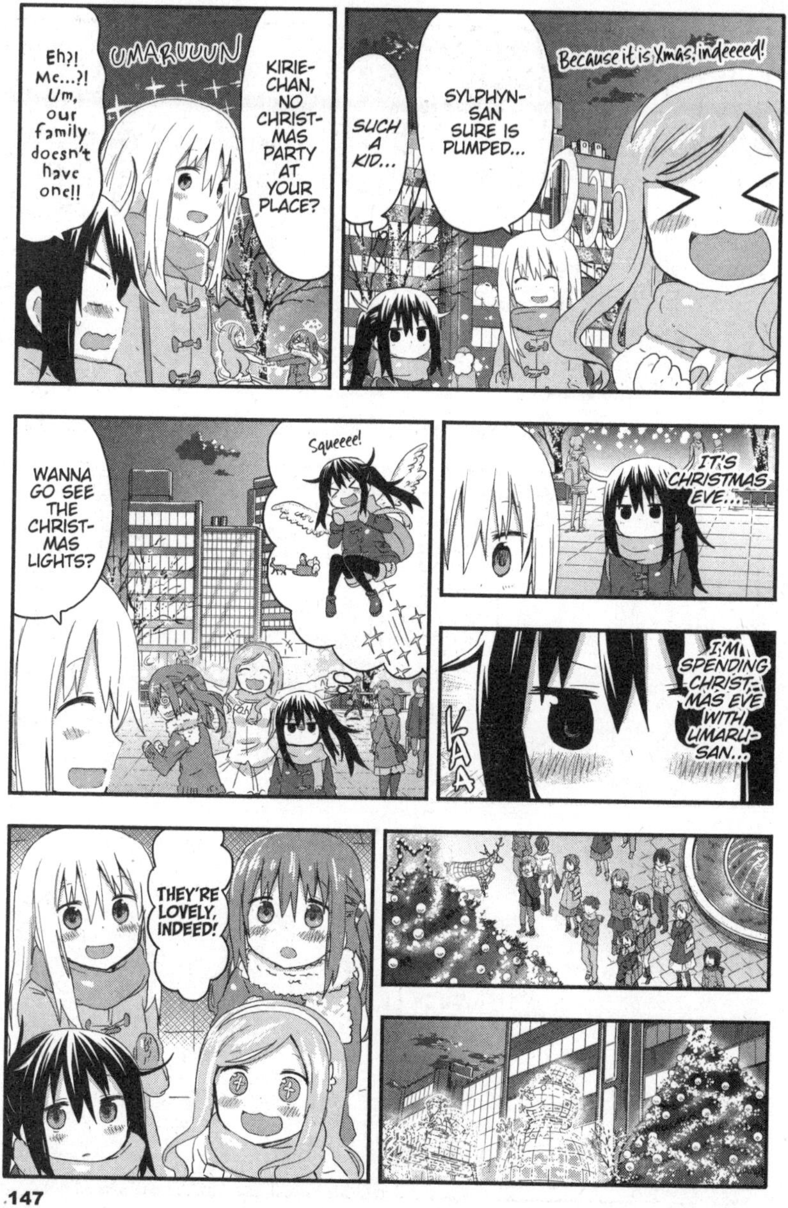

Because it is Xmas, indeeeed!
SYLPHYN-SAN SURE IS PUMPED...
SUCH A KID...
KIRIE-CHAN, NO CHRIST-MAS PARTY AT YOUR PLACE?
UMARUUUN
Eh?! Me...?! Um, our family doesn't have one!!
IT'S CHRISTMAS EVE...
I'M SPENDING CHRIST-MAS EVE WITH UMARU-SAN...
KAA
Squeeee!
WANNA GO SEE THE CHRIST-MAS LIGHTS?
THEY'RE LOVELY, INDEED!

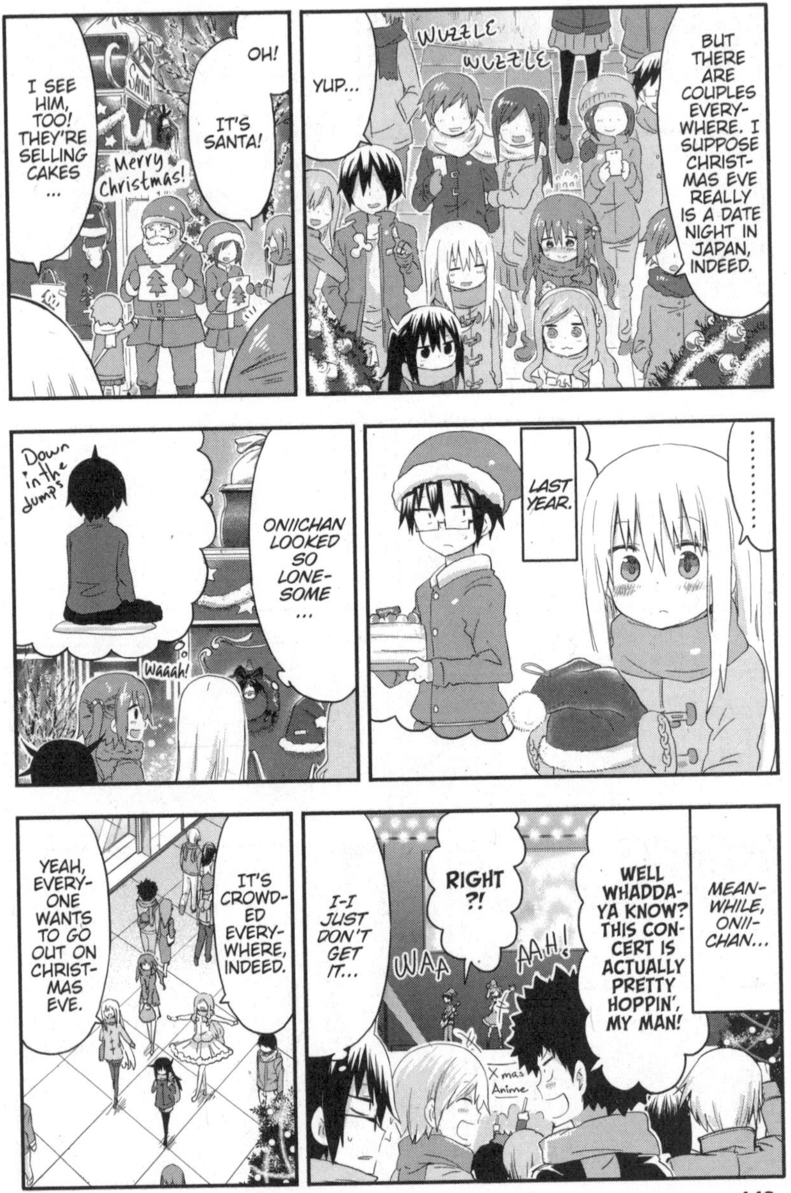
BUT THERE ARE COUPLES EVERY-WHERE. I SUPPOSE CHRIST-MAS EVE REALLY IS A DATE NIGHT IN JAPAN, INDEED.
WUZZLE
WUZZLE
YUP...
OH!
IT'S SANTA!
Merry Christmas!
SANTA
I SEE HIM, TOO! THEY'RE SELLING CAKES ...
......
LAST YEAR.
ONIICHAN LOOKED SO LONE-SOME ...
Down in the dumps
Waaah!
MEAN-WHILE, ONII-CHAN...
WELL WHADDA-YA KNOW? THIS CON-CERT IS ACTUALLY PRETTY HOPPIN', MY MAN!
RIGHT ?!
AAH!
WAA
I-I JUST DON'T GET IT...
X mas Anime
IT'S CROWD-ED EVERY-WHERE, INDEED.
YEAH, EVERY-ONE WANTS TO GO OUT ON CHRIST-MAS EVE.

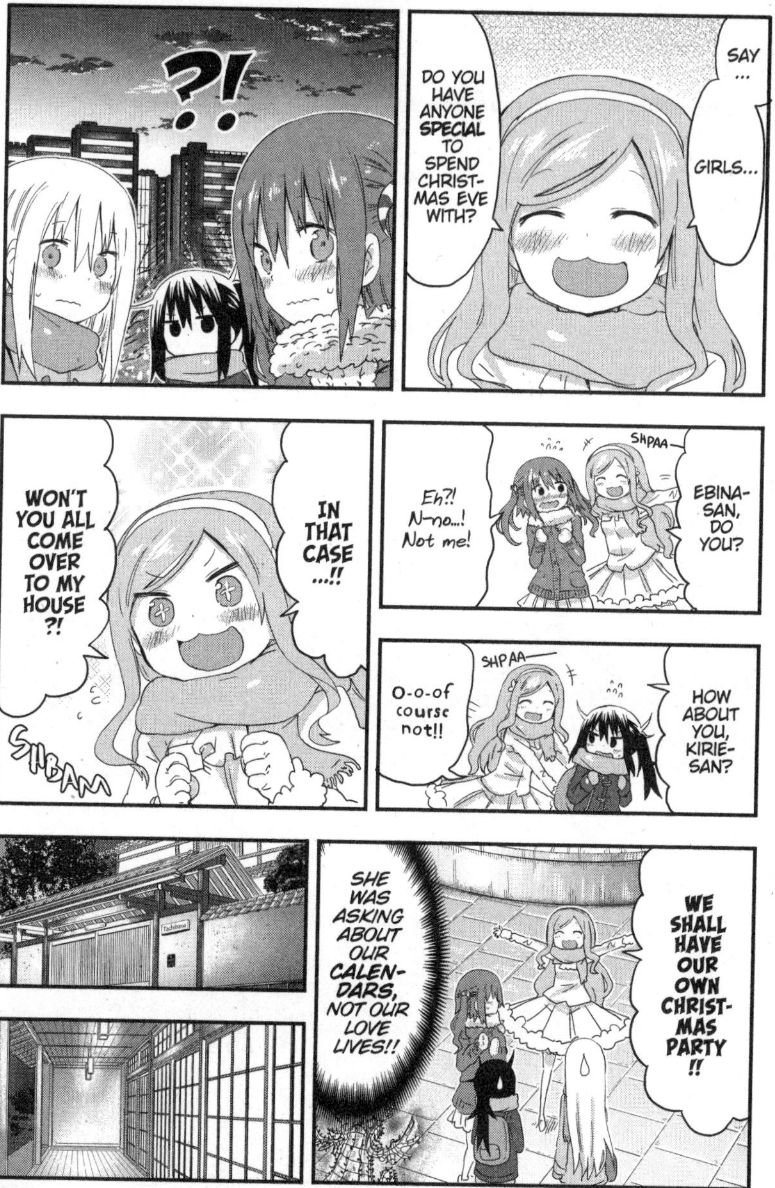
SAY ...
GIRLS...
DO YOU HAVE ANYONE SPECIAL TO SPEND CHRIST-MAS EVE WITH?
?!
EBINA-SAN, DO YOU?
SHPAA—
Eh?! N-no...! Not me!
HOW ABOUT YOU, KIRIE-SAN?
SHPAA—
O-o-of course not!!
IN THAT CASE ...!!
WON'T YOU ALL COME OVER TO MY HOUSE ?!
SHBAM
WE SHALL HAVE OUR OWN CHRIST-MAS PARTY !!
SHE WAS ASKING ABOUT OUR CALEN-DARS, NOT OUR LOVE LIVES!!
Tachibana

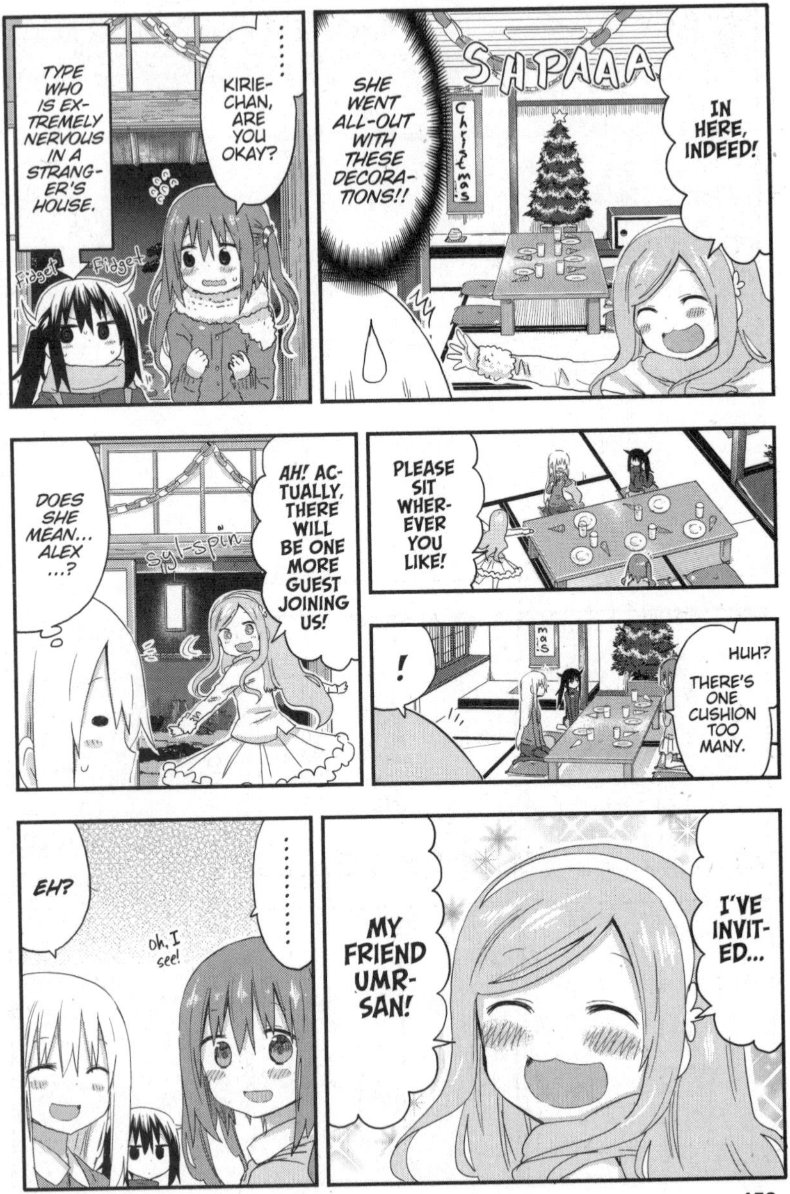
IN HERE, INDEED!
SHPAAA
Christmas
SHE WENT ALL-OUT WITH THESE DECORATIONS!!
......
KIRIE-CHAN, ARE YOU OKAY?
TYPE WHO IS EXTREMELY NERVOUS IN A STRANGER'S HOUSE.
Fidget
Fidget
PLEASE SIT WHEREVER YOU LIKE!
HUH? THERE'S ONE CUSHION TOO MANY.
!
AH! ACTUALLY, THERE WILL BE ONE MORE GUEST JOINING US!
Syl-spin
DOES SHE MEAN... ALEX ...?
I'VE INVITED...
MY FRIEND UMR-SAN!
......
Oh, I see!
EH?

No. 89 Umaru & the Christmas Party: Part 2

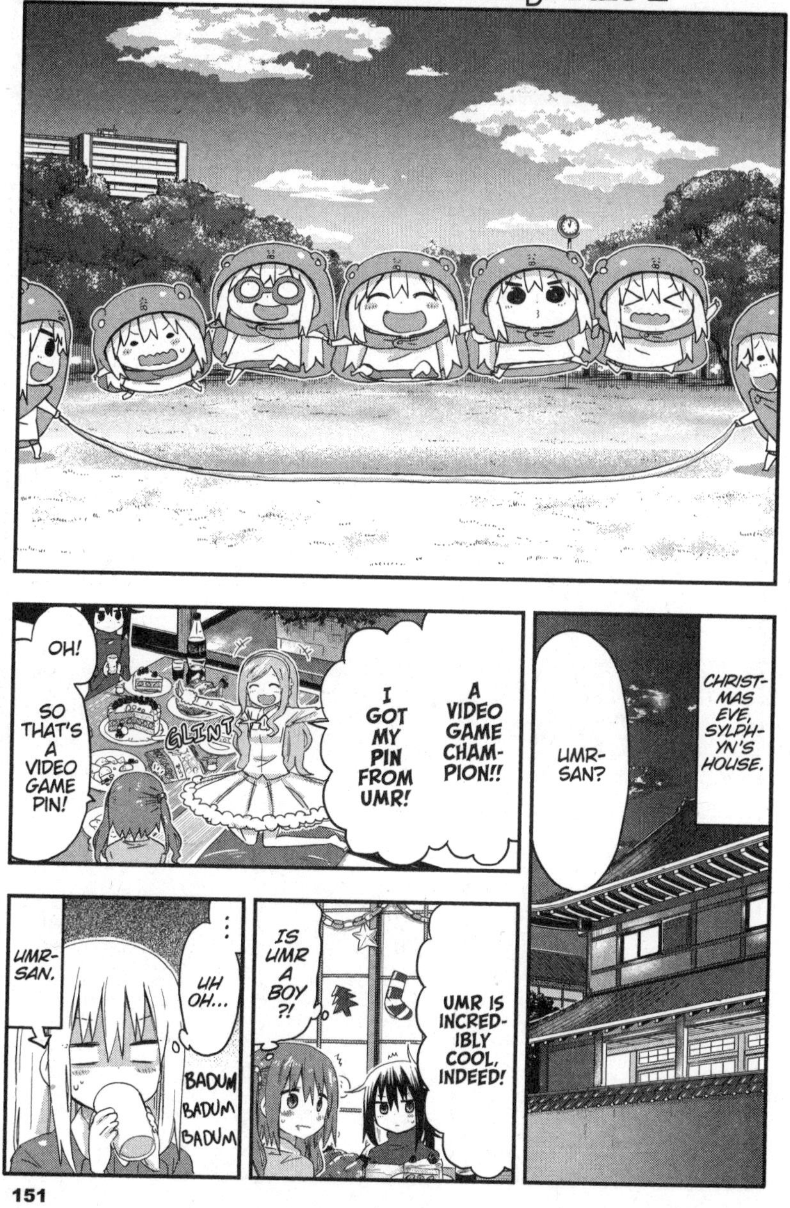

CHRISTMAS EVE, SYLPHYN'S HOUSE.
UMR-SAN?
A VIDEO GAME CHAMPION!!
I GOT MY PIN FROM UMR!
GLINT
OH!
SO THAT'S A VIDEO GAME PIN!
UMR IS INCREDIBLY COOL, INDEED!
IS UMR A BOY?!
...
UH OH...
UMR-SAN.
BADUM BADUM BADUM

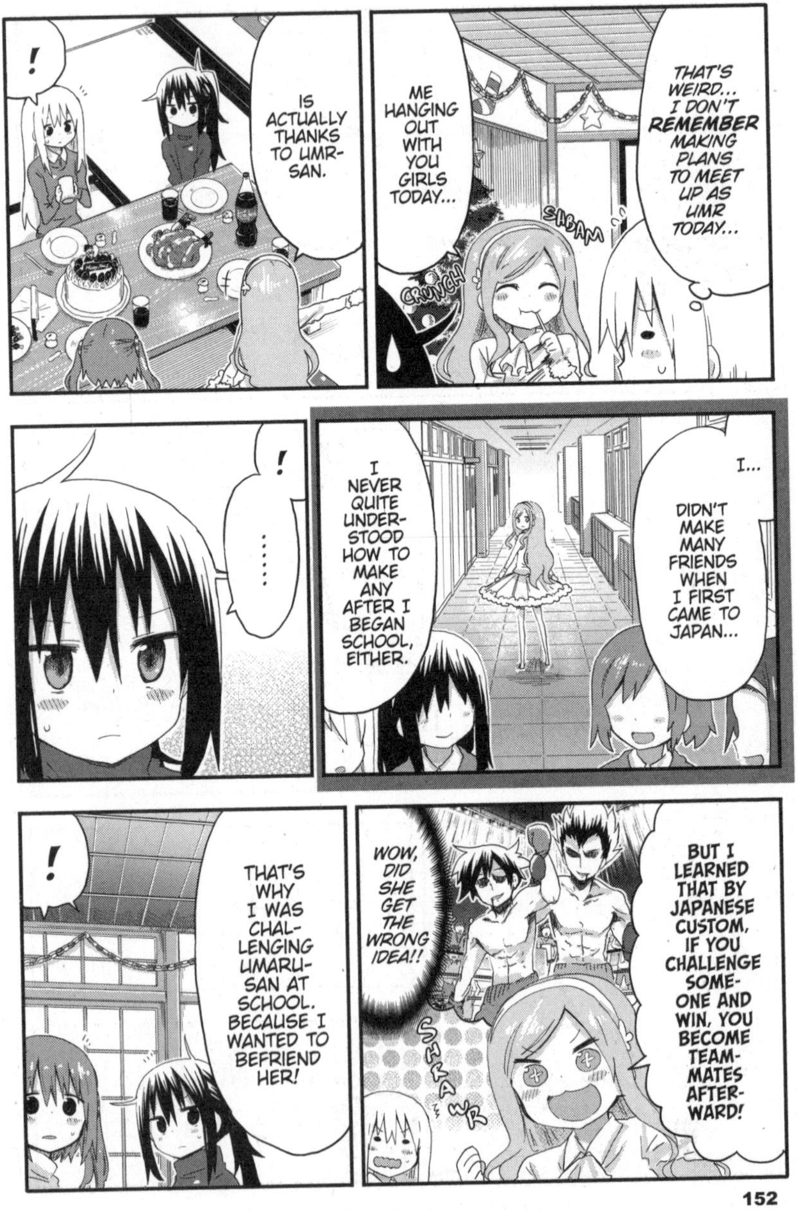
THAT'S WEIRD... I DON'T **REMEMBER** MAKING PLANS TO MEET UP AS UMR TODAY...
SHBAM
ME HANGING OUT WITH YOU GIRLS TODAY...
CRUNCH
IS ACTUALLY THANKS TO UMR-SAN.
!
I...
DIDN'T MAKE MANY FRIENDS WHEN I FIRST CAME TO JAPAN...
I NEVER QUITE UNDER-STOOD HOW TO MAKE ANY AFTER I BEGAN SCHOOL, EITHER.
......
!
BUT I LEARNED THAT BY JAPANESE CUSTOM, IF YOU CHALLENGE SOME-ONE AND WIN, YOU BECOME TEAM-MATES AFTER-WARD!
WOW, DID SHE GET THE WRONG IDEA!!
SHKAWR
THAT'S WHY I WAS CHAL-LENGING UMARU-SAN AT SCHOOL. BECAUSE I WANTED TO BEFRIEND HER!
!

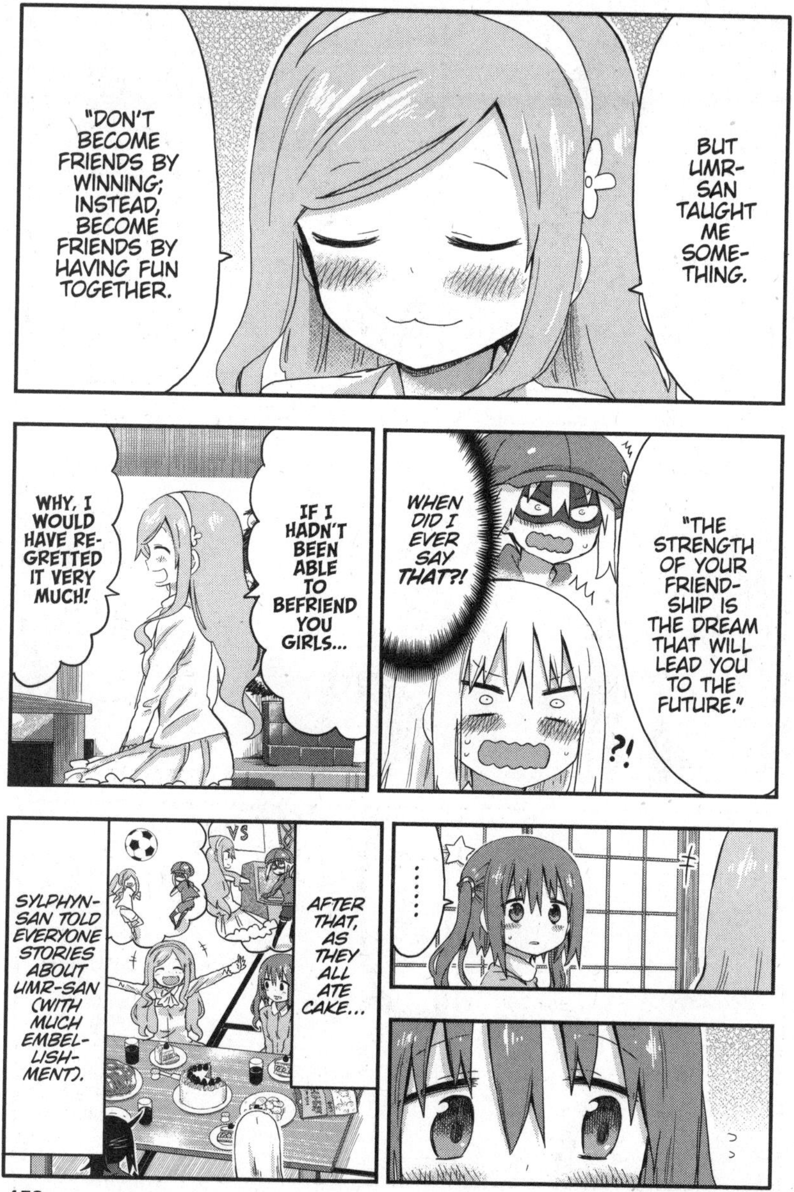
BUT UMR-SAN TAUGHT ME SOMETHING.
"DON'T BECOME FRIENDS BY WINNING; INSTEAD, BECOME FRIENDS BY HAVING FUN TOGETHER.
"THE STRENGTH OF YOUR FRIENDSHIP IS THE DREAM THAT WILL LEAD YOU TO THE FUTURE."
?!
WHEN DID I EVER SAY THAT?!
IF I HADN'T BEEN ABLE TO BEFRIEND YOU GIRLS...
WHY, I WOULD HAVE REGRETTED IT VERY MUCH!
......
AFTER THAT, AS THEY ALL ATE CAKE...
VS
SYLPHYN-SAN TOLD EVERYONE STORIES ABOUT UMR-SAN (WITH MUCH EMBELLISHMENT).

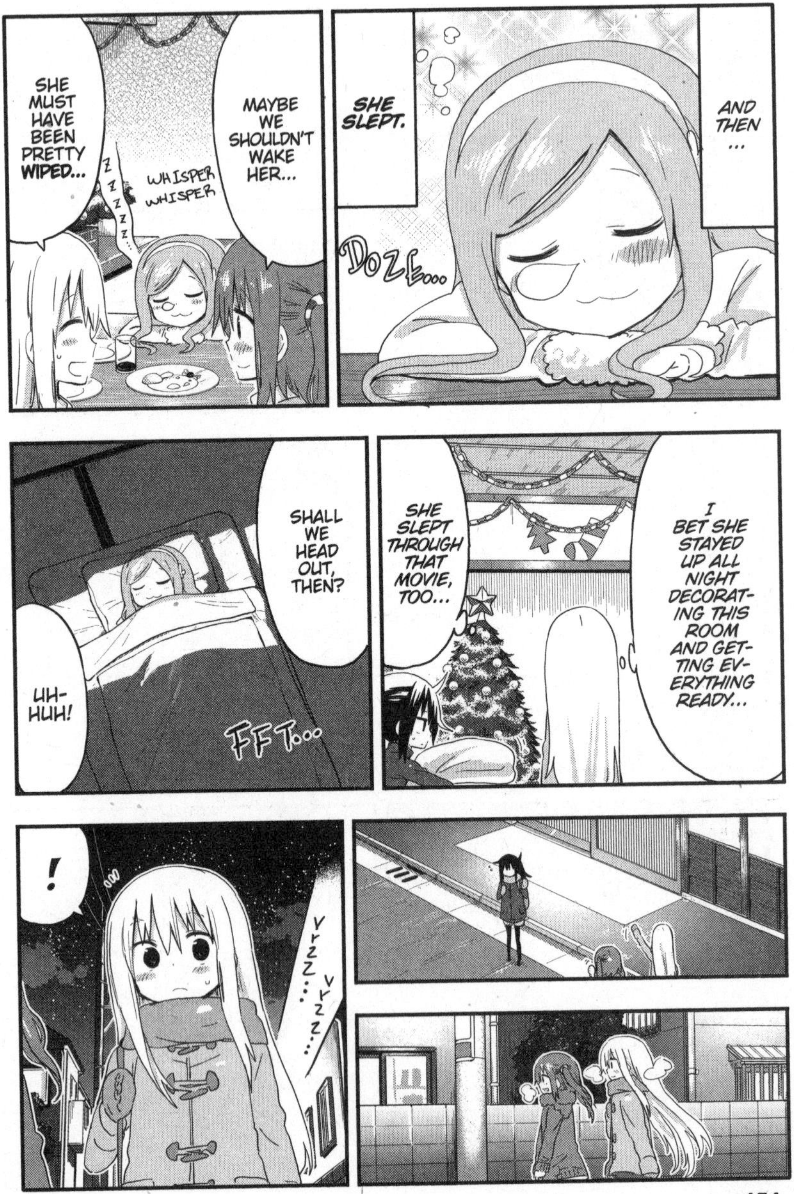
AND THEN ...
SHE SLEPT.
DOZE...
MAYBE WE SHOULDN'T WAKE HER...
WHISPER WHISPER
Z Z Z Z Z...
SHE MUST HAVE BEEN PRETTY WIPED...
I BET SHE STAYED UP ALL NIGHT DECORATING THIS ROOM AND GETTING EVERYTHING READY...
SHE SLEPT THROUGH THAT MOVIE, TOO...
SHALL WE HEAD OUT, THEN?
FFT...
UH-HUH!
VRZZ... VRZZZ...
!

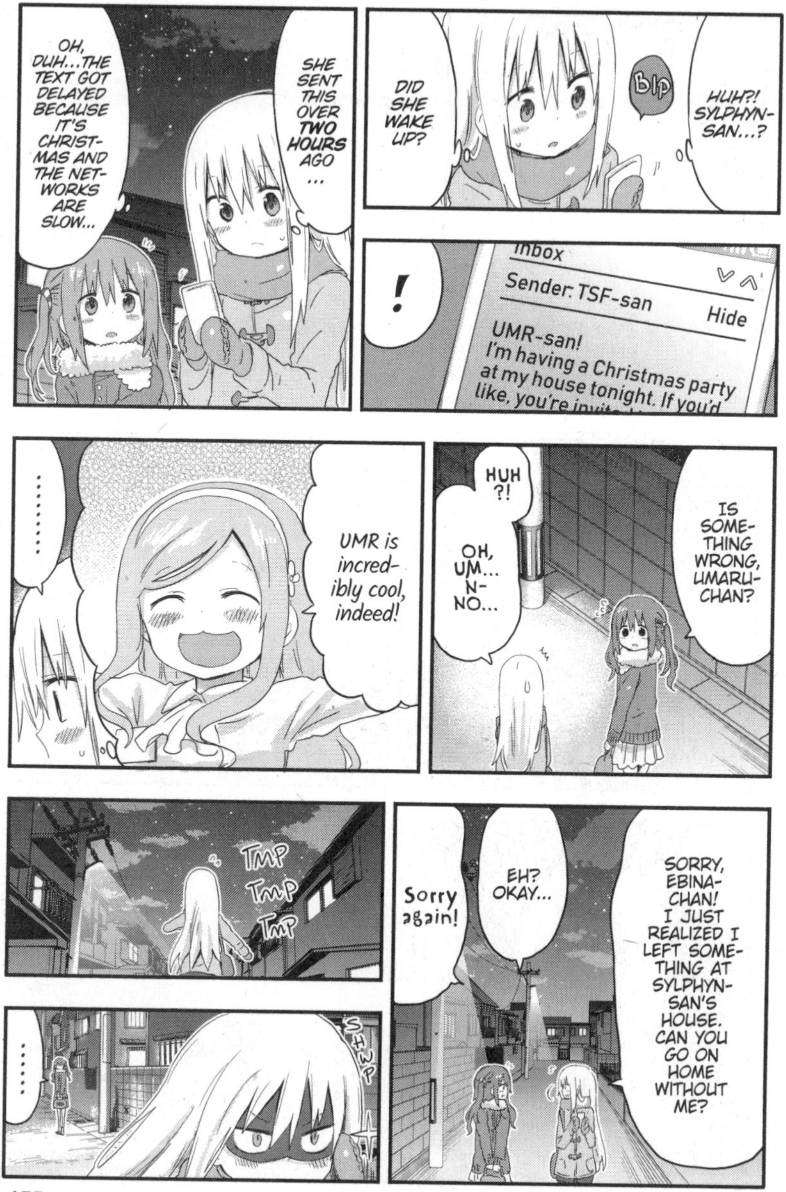
HUH?! SYLPHYN-SAN...?
Blip
DID SHE WAKE UP?
!
Inbox
Sender: TSF-san
Hide
UMR-san! I'm having a Christmas party at my house tonight. If you'd
SHE SENT THIS OVER TWO HOURS AGO...
OH, DUH...THE TEXT GOT DELAYED BECAUSE IT'S CHRISTMAS AND THE NETWORKS ARE SLOW...
IS SOMETHING WRONG, UMARU-CHAN?
HUH ?!
OH, UM... N-NO...
UMR is incredibly cool, indeed!
....
SORRY, EBINA-CHAN! I JUST REALIZED I LEFT SOMETHING AT SYLPHYN-SAN'S HOUSE. CAN YOU GO ON HOME WITHOUT ME?
EH? OKAY...
Sorry again!
TMP
TMP
TMP
SHWP
......

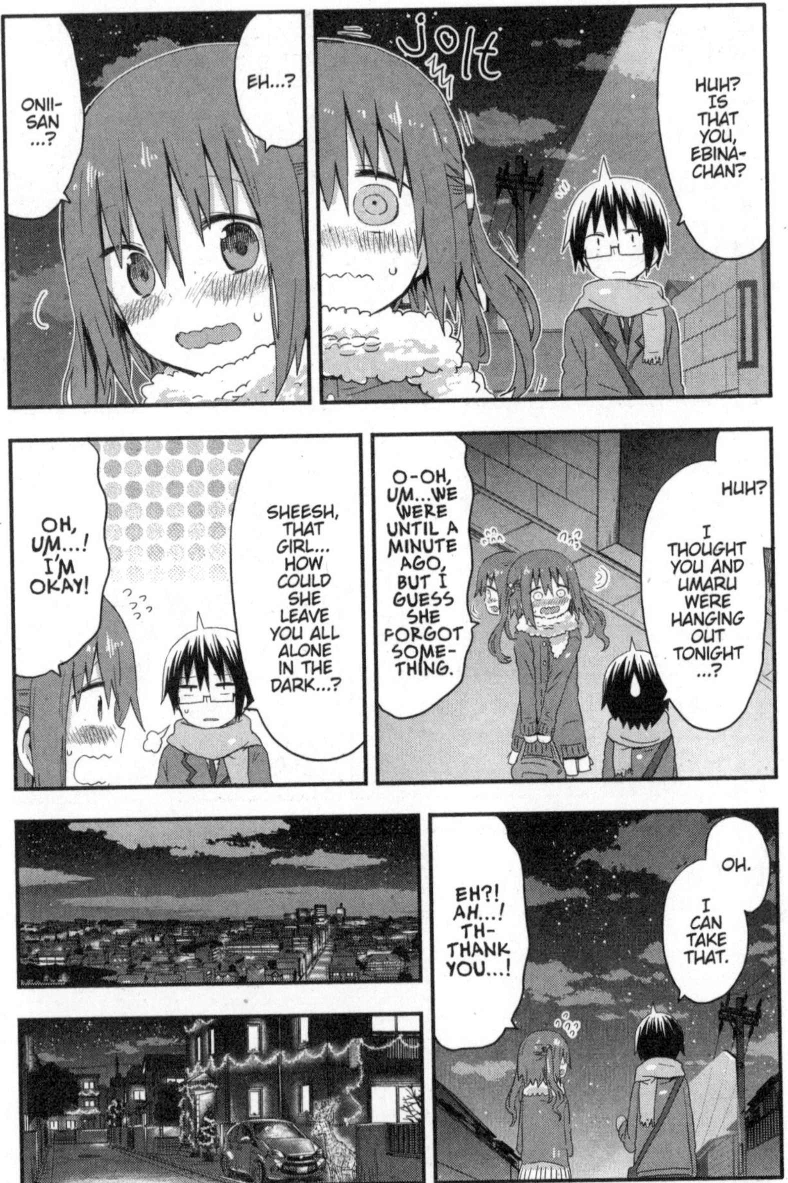
HUH? IS THAT YOU, EBINA-CHAN?
jolt
EH...?
ONII-SAN ...?
HUH?
I THOUGHT YOU AND UMARU WERE HANGING OUT TONIGHT ...?
O-OH, UM...WE WERE UNTIL A MINUTE AGO, BUT I GUESS SHE FORGOT SOME-THING.
SHEESH, THAT GIRL... HOW COULD SHE LEAVE YOU ALL ALONE IN THE DARK...?
OH, UM...! I'M OKAY!
OH.
I CAN TAKE THAT.
EH?! AH...! TH-THANK YOU...!

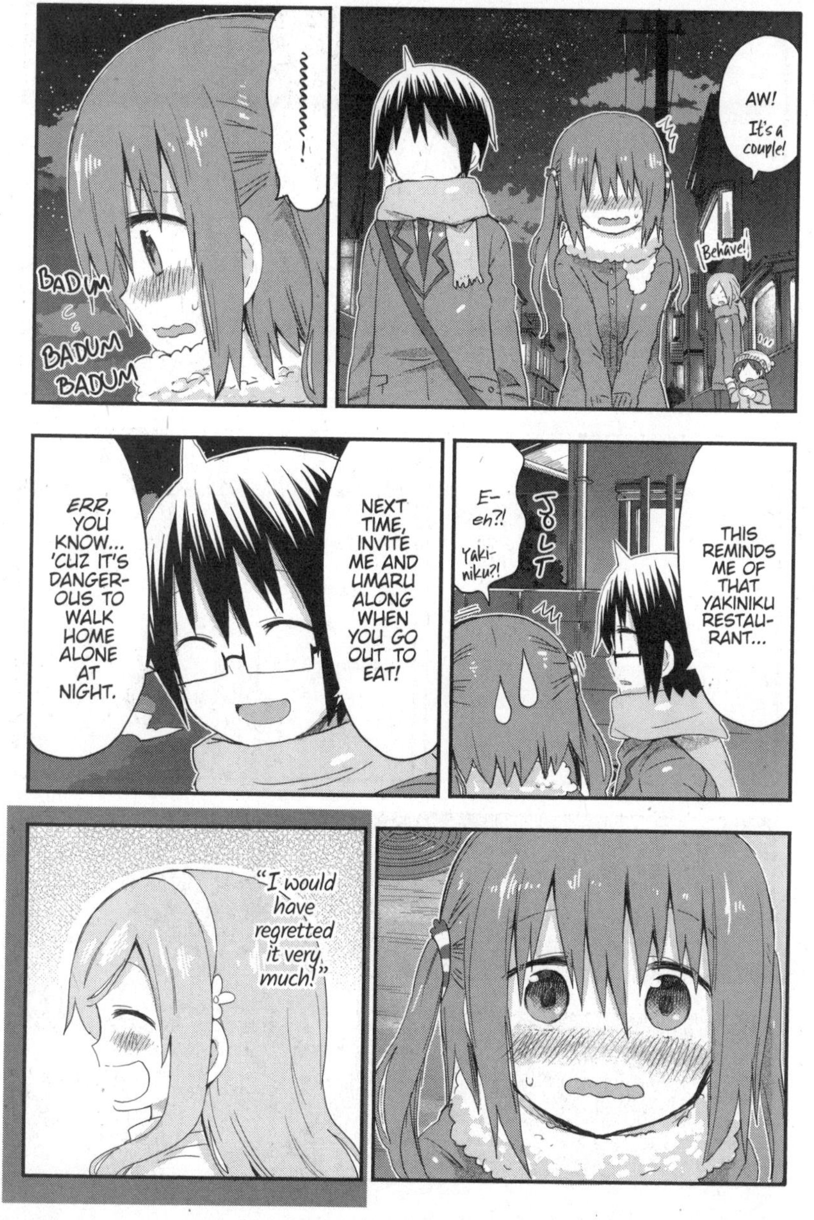
AW! It's a couple!
Behave!
mmm...!
BADUM BADUM BADUM BADUM
THIS REMINDS ME OF THAT YAKINIKU RESTAURANT...
JOLT
E-eh?!
Yakiniku?!
NEXT TIME, INVITE ME AND UMARU ALONG WHEN YOU GO OUT TO EAT!
ERR, YOU KNOW... 'CUZ IT'S DANGEROUS TO WALK HOME ALONE AT NIGHT.
"I would have regretted it very much!"

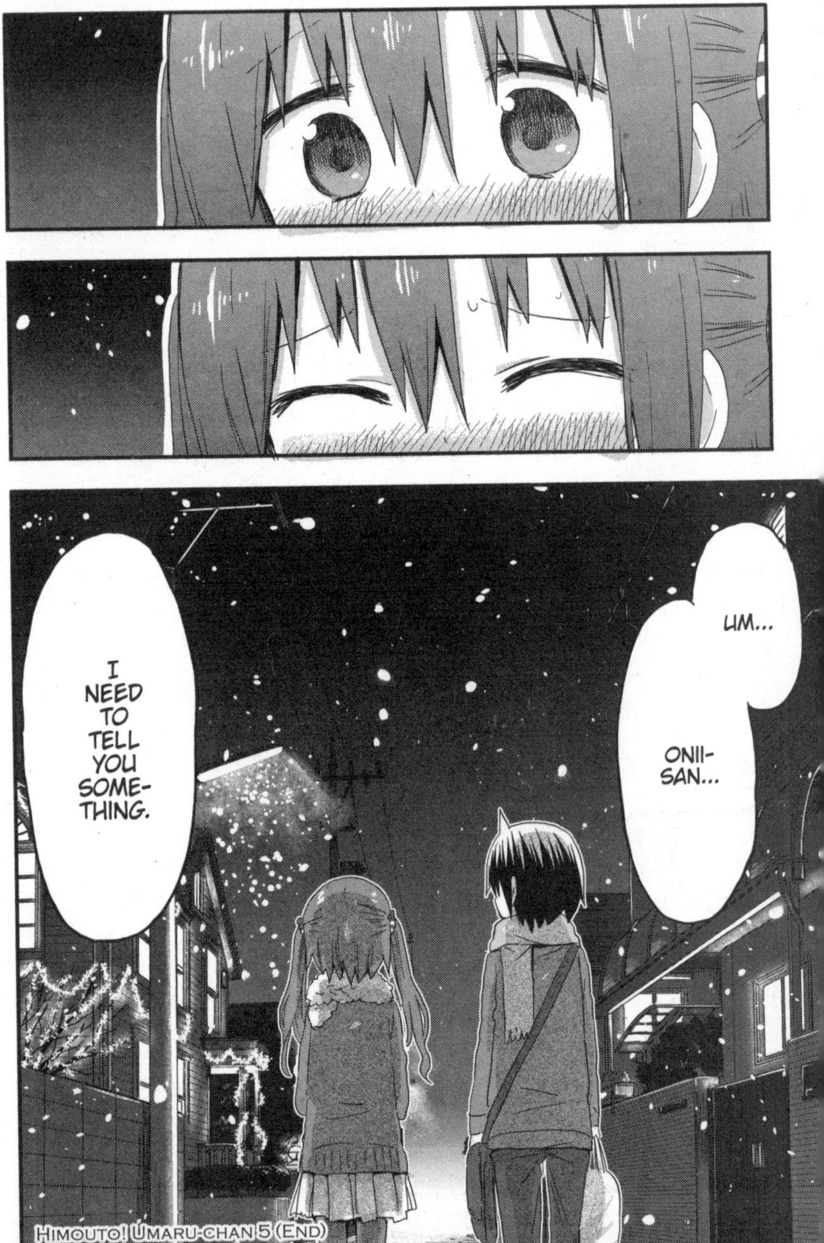
UM...
ONII-SAN...
I NEED TO TELL YOU SOME-THING.
Himouto! Umaru-chan 5 (End)

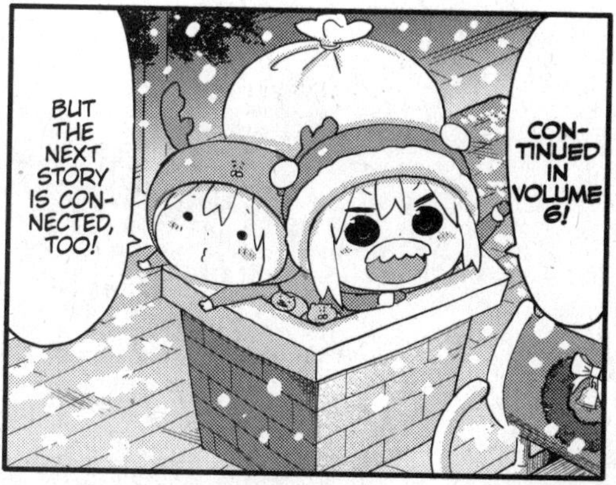
CON-TINUED IN VOLUME 6!
BUT THE NEXT STORY IS CON-NECTED, TOO!

HIMOUTO! UMARU-CHAN

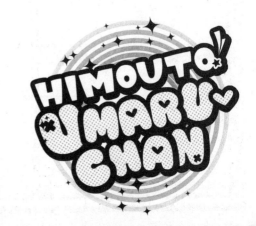

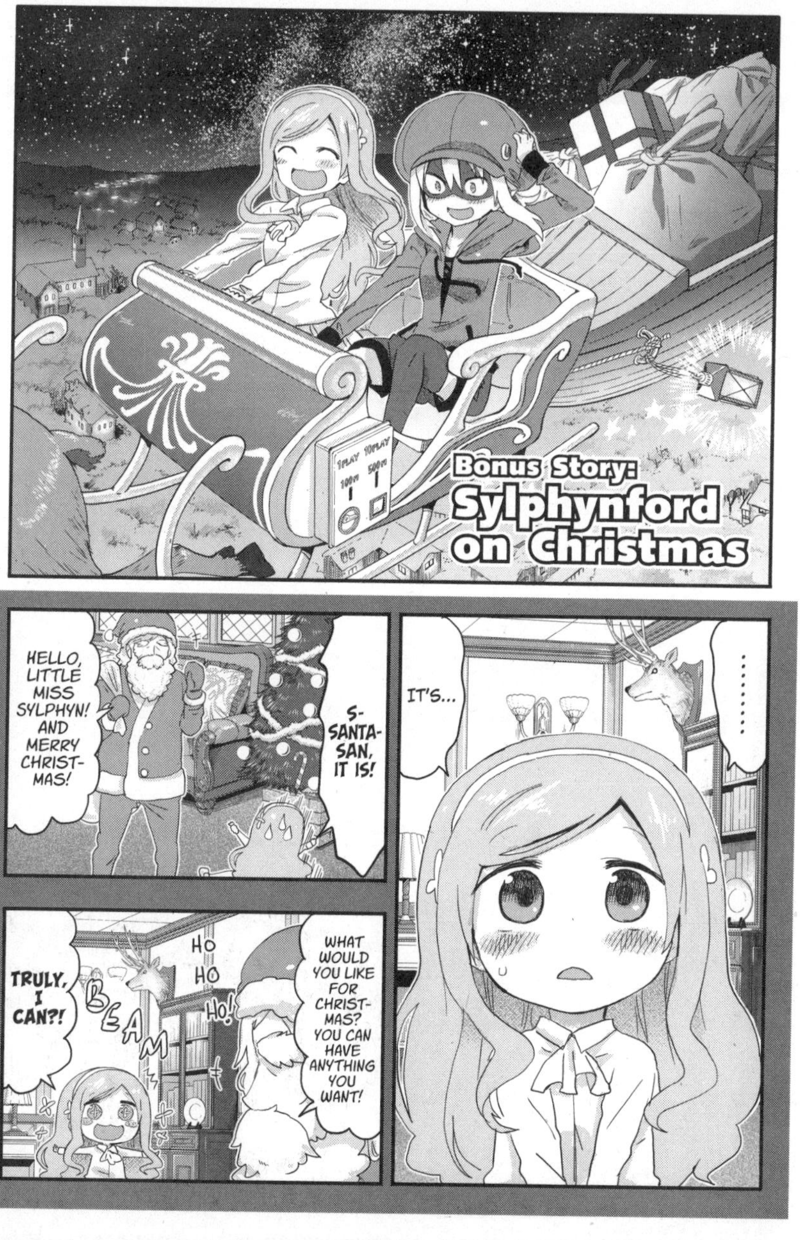

Bonus Story:
Sylphynford on Christmas
....
IT'S...
S-SANTA-SAN, IT IS!
HELLO, LITTLE MISS SYLPHYN! AND MERRY CHRISTMAS!
WHAT WOULD YOU LIKE FOR CHRISTMAS? YOU CAN HAVE ANYTHING YOU WANT!
HO HO HO!
BEAM
TRULY, I CAN?!

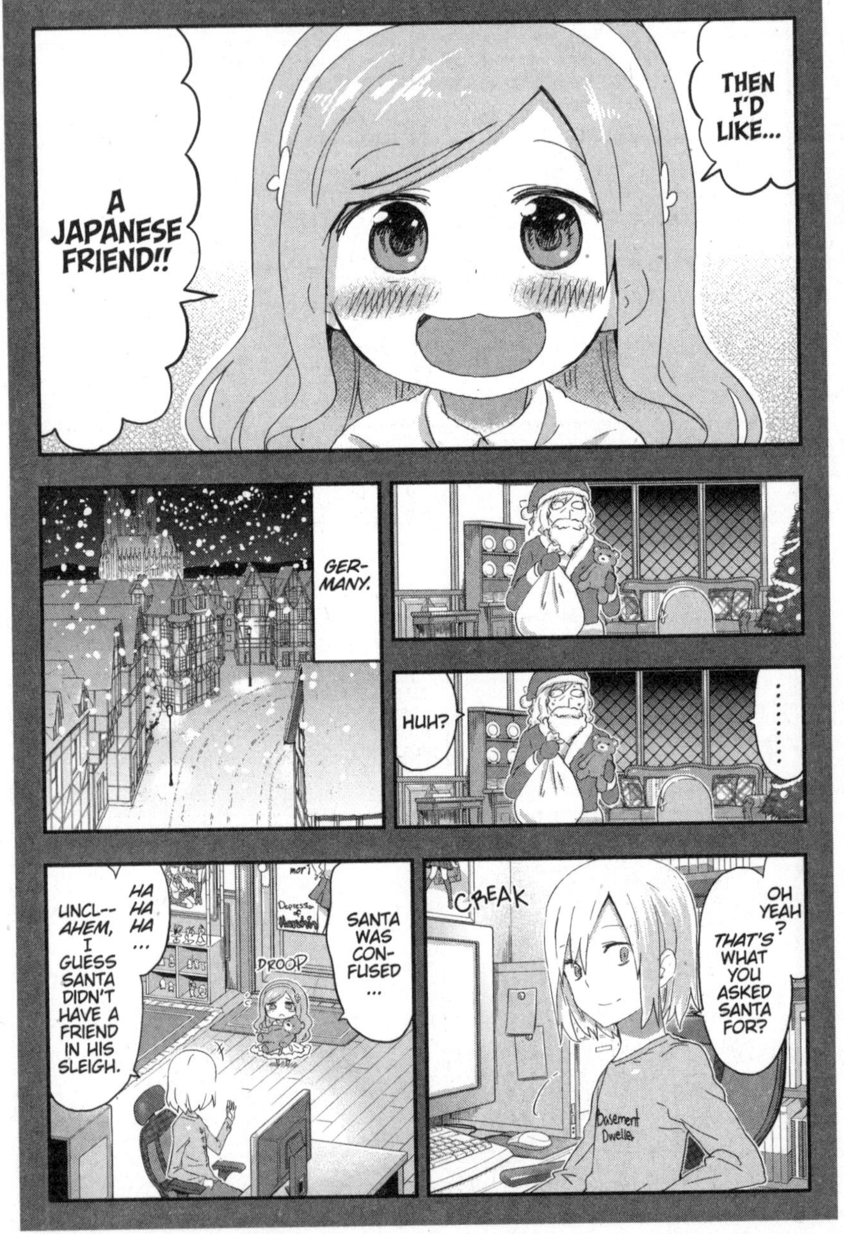
THEN I'D LIKE...
A JAPANESE FRIEND!!
......
HUH?
GER-MANY.
OH YEAH? THAT'S WHAT YOU ASKED SANTA FOR?
CREAK
SANTA WAS CON-FUSED ...
DROOP
HA HA HA ...
UNCL-- AHEM, I GUESS SANTA DIDN'T HAVE A FRIEND IN HIS SLEIGH.

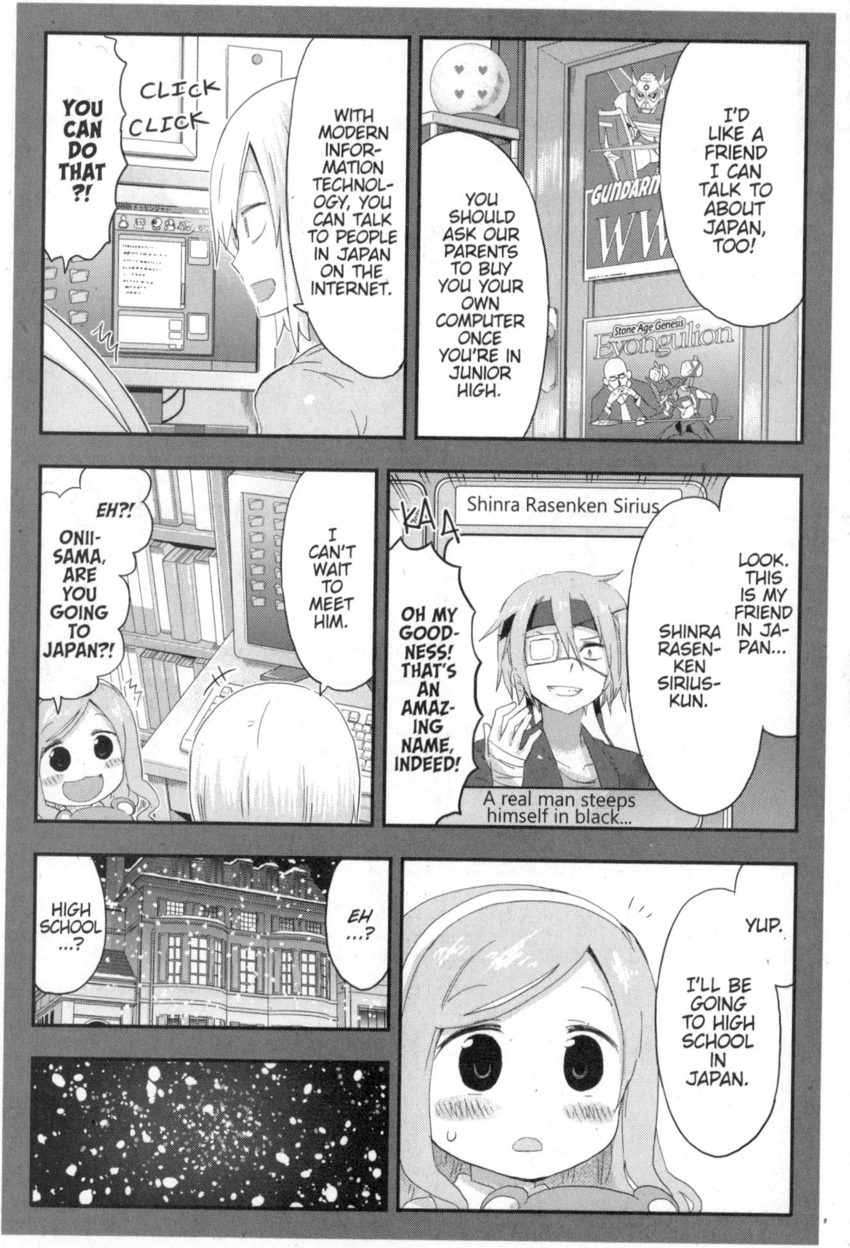
I'D LIKE A FRIEND I CAN TALK TO ABOUT JAPAN, TOO!
Stone Age Genesis Evongulion
YOU SHOULD ASK OUR PARENTS TO BUY YOU YOUR OWN COMPUTER ONCE YOU'RE IN JUNIOR HIGH.
WITH MODERN INFORMATION TECHNOLOGY, YOU CAN TALK TO PEOPLE IN JAPAN ON THE INTERNET.
CLICK
CLICK
YOU CAN DO THAT?!
Shinra Rasenken Sirius
KAA
LOOK. THIS IS MY FRIEND IN JAPAN... SHINRA RASENKEN SIRIUS-KUN.
OH MY GOODNESS! THAT'S AN AMAZING NAME, INDEED!
A real man steeps himself in black...
I CAN'T WAIT TO MEET HIM.
EH?! ONII-SAMA, ARE YOU GOING TO JAPAN?!
YUP.
I'LL BE GOING TO HIGH SCHOOL IN JAPAN.
EH ...?
HIGH SCHOOL ...?

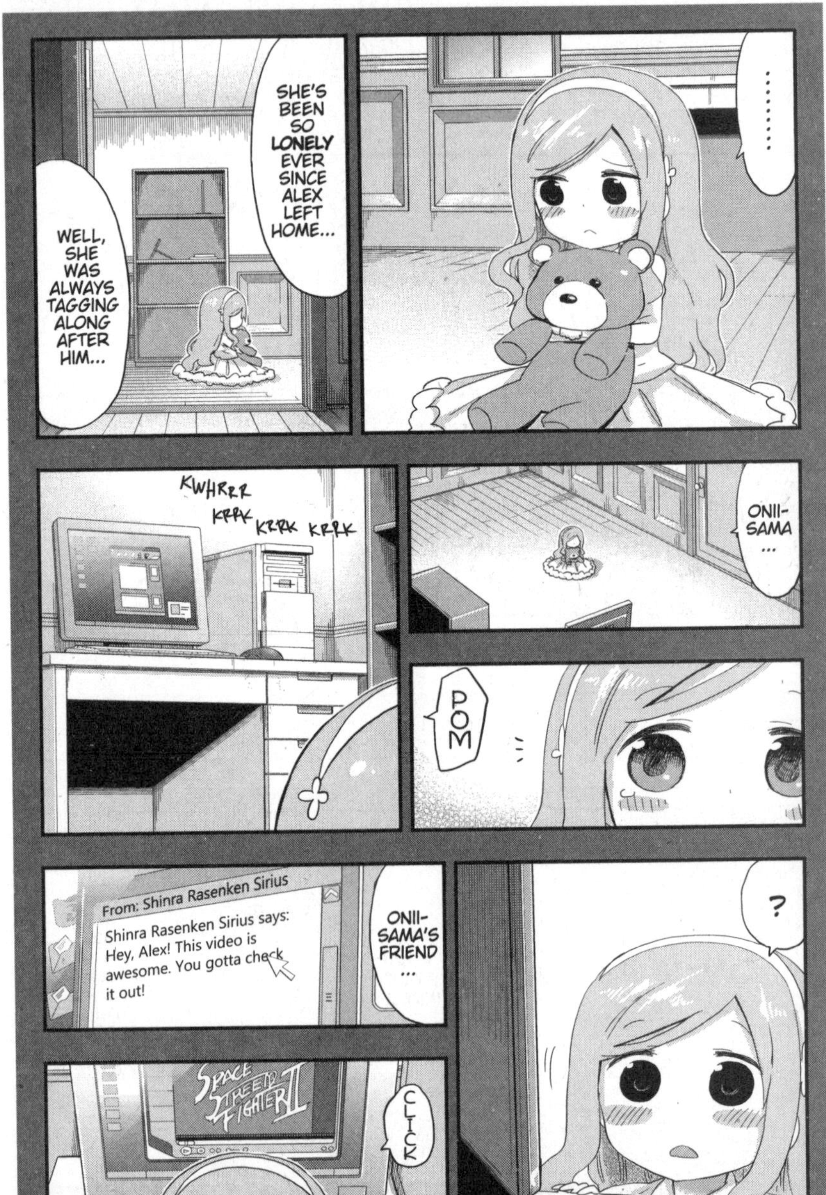
……
SHE'S BEEN SO LONELY EVER SINCE ALEX LEFT HOME...
WELL, SHE WAS ALWAYS TAGGING ALONG AFTER HIM...
ONII-SAMA ...
POM
KWHRRR
KRRK KRRK KRRK
?
ONII-SAMA'S FRIEND ...
From: Shinra Rasenken Sirius
Shinra Rasenken Sirius says: Hey, Alex! This video is awesome. You gotta check it out!
CLICK

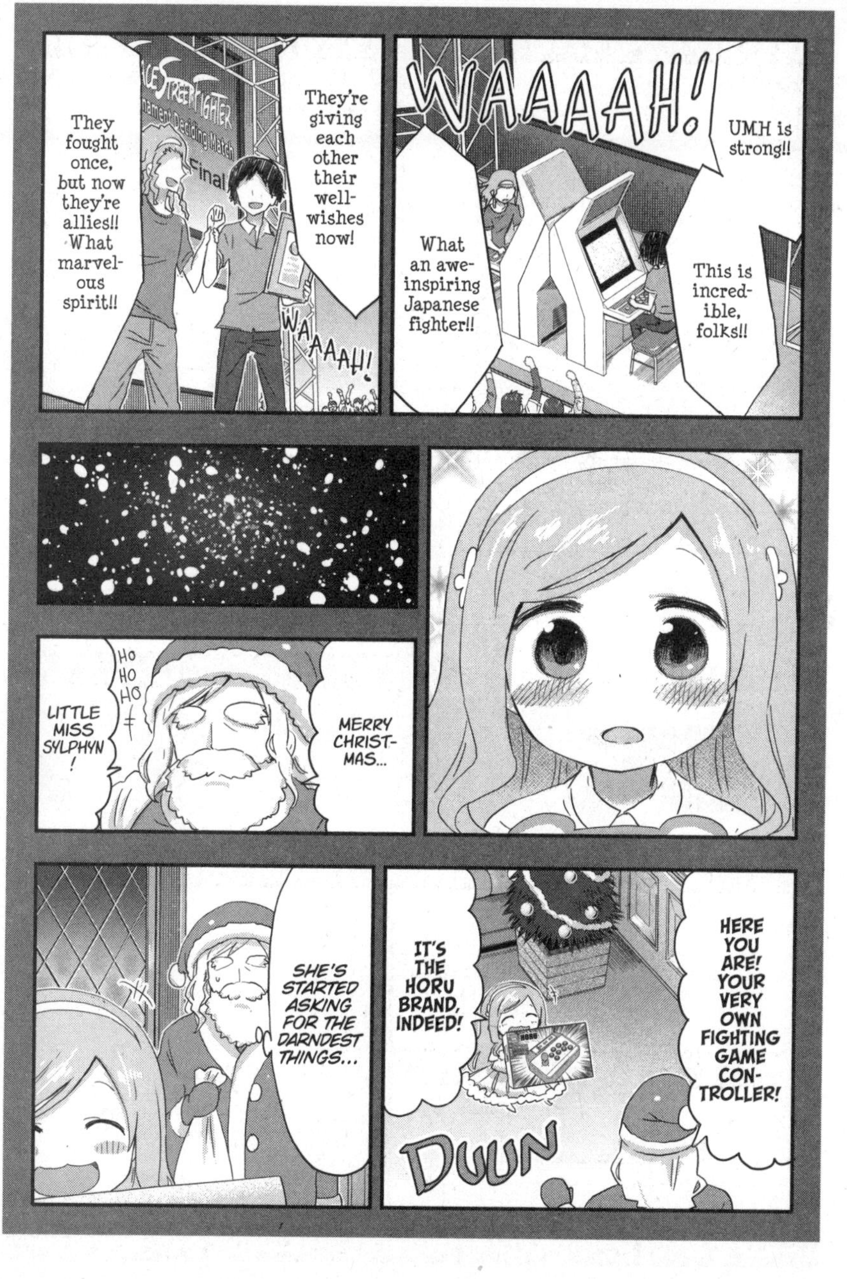
WAAAAH!
UMH is strong!!
This is incredible, folks!!
What an awe-inspiring Japanese fighter!!
They're giving each other their well-wishes now!
They fought once, but now they're allies!! What marvelous spirit!!
WAAAAH!
MERRY CHRISTMAS...
HO HO HO
LITTLE MISS SYLPHYN!
HERE YOU ARE! YOUR VERY OWN FIGHTING GAME CONTROLLER!
IT'S THE HORU BRAND, INDEED!
DUUN
SHE'S STARTED ASKING FOR THE DARNDEST THINGS...

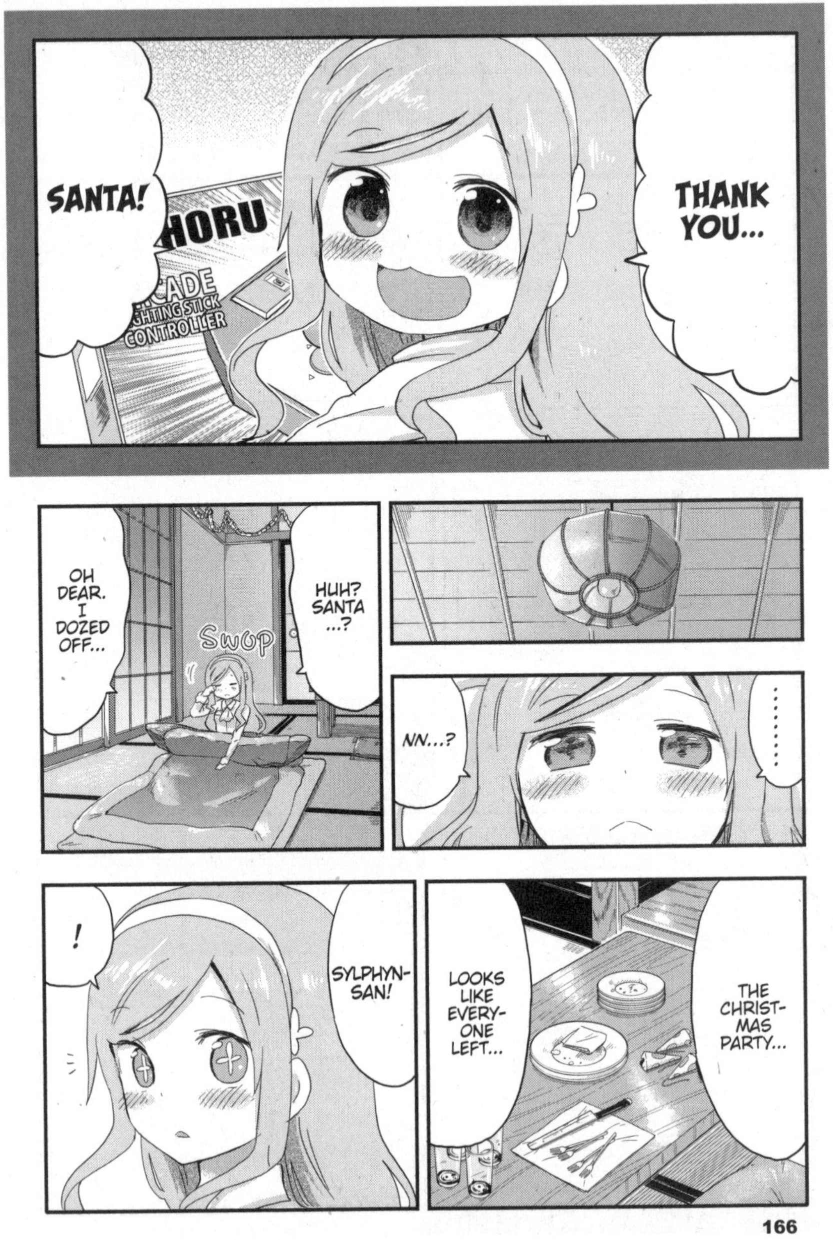
THANK YOU...
SANTA!
HORU
CADE
GHTING STICK
CONTROLLER
......
NN...?
HUH? SANTA ...?
SWOP
OH DEAR. I DOZED OFF...
THE CHRIST-MAS PARTY...
LOOKS LIKE EVERY-ONE LEFT...
SYLPHYN-SAN!
!

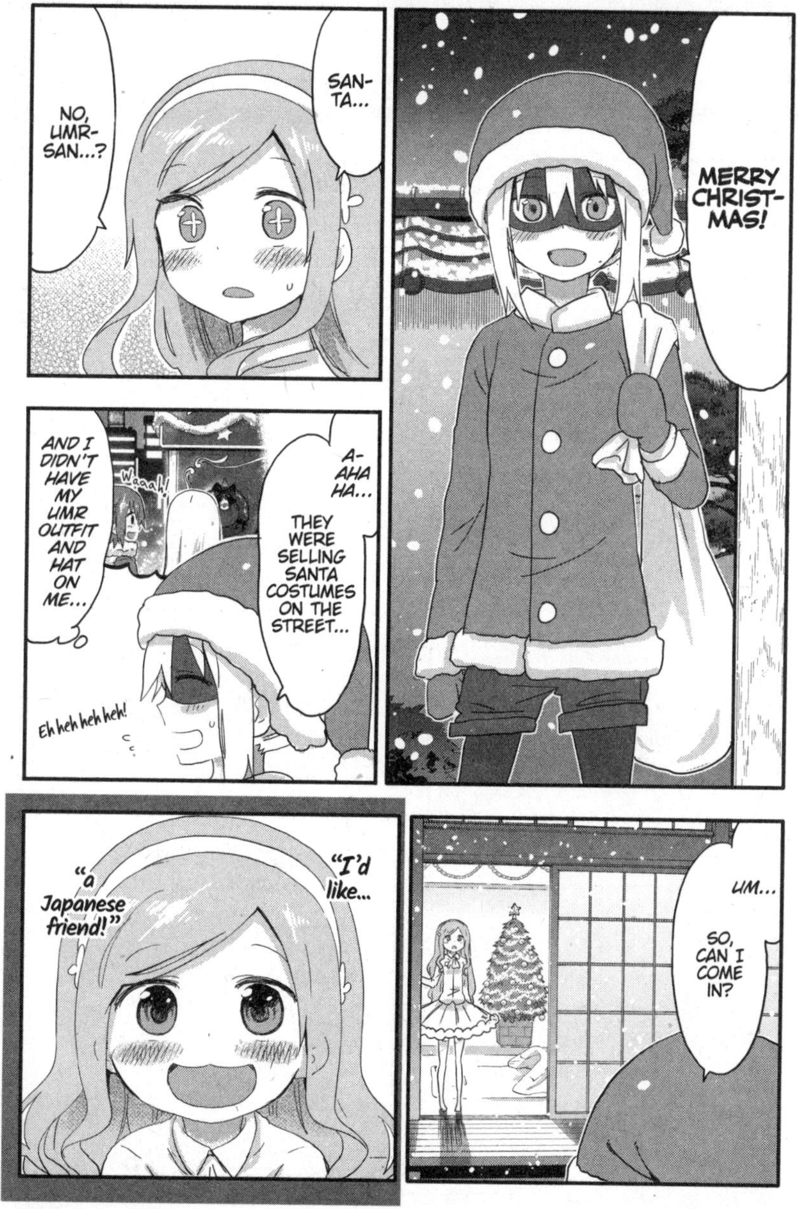
MERRY CHRISTMAS!
SANTA...
NO, UMR-SAN...?
A-AHA HA...
THEY WERE SELLING SANTA COSTUMES ON THE STREET...
AND I DIDN'T HAVE MY UMR OUTFIT AND HAT ON ME...
Waaah!
Eh heh heh heh!
UM...
SO, CAN I COME IN?
"I'd like...
"a Japanese friend!"

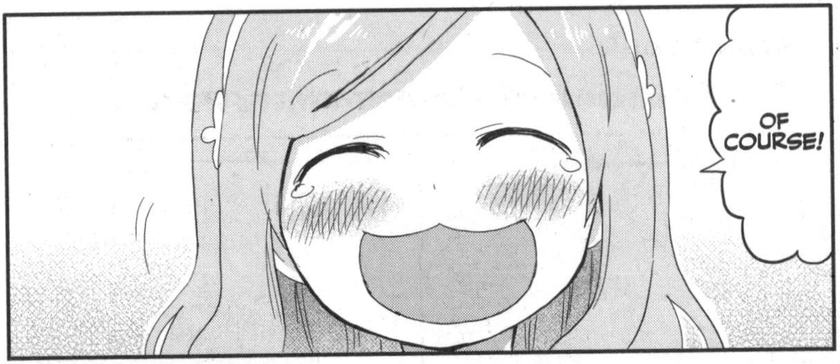
OF COURSE!

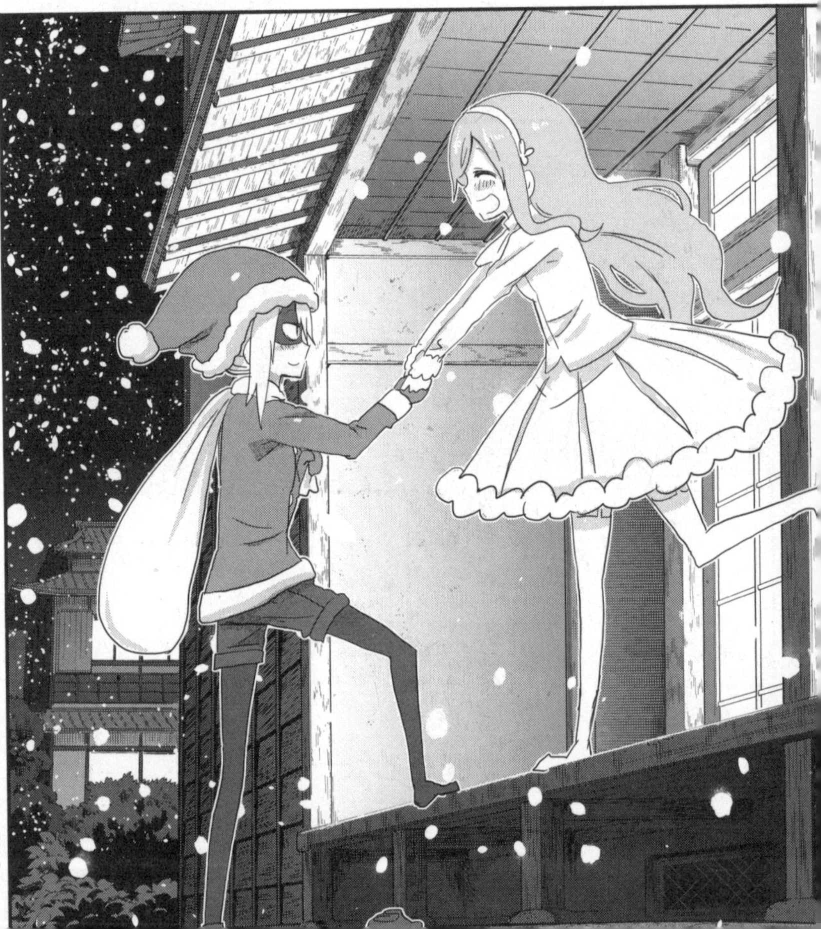

Sylphynford on Christmas (End)

AFTERWORD

The Creation of *Umaru-chan:* Part 5

Final Part!

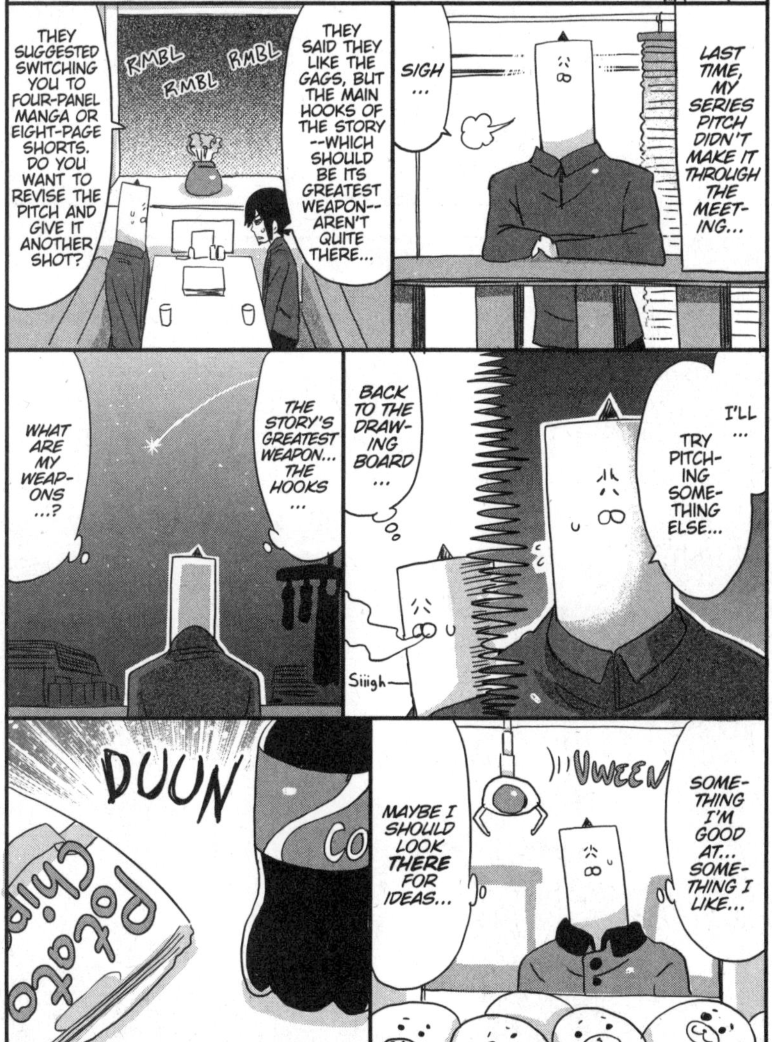

LAST TIME, MY SERIES PITCH DIDN'T MAKE IT THROUGH THE MEETING...
SIGH...
THEY SAID THEY LIKE THE GAGS, BUT THE MAIN HOOKS OF THE STORY --WHICH SHOULD BE ITS GREATEST WEAPON-- AREN'T QUITE THERE...
THEY SUGGESTED SWITCHING YOU TO FOUR-PANEL MANGA OR EIGHT-PAGE SHORTS. DO YOU WANT TO REVISE THE PITCH AND GIVE IT ANOTHER SHOT?
RMBL RMBL RMBL
I'LL... TRY PITCHING SOMETHING ELSE...
BACK TO THE DRAWING BOARD...
Siiigh
THE STORY'S GREATEST WEAPON... THE HOOKS...
WHAT ARE MY WEAPONS...?
SOMETHING I'M GOOD AT... SOMETHING I LIKE...
VWEEN
MAYBE I SHOULD LOOK THERE FOR IDEAS...
DUUN
CO
Potato Chip

At long last, the final part!! Umaru-chan is finally born...!!

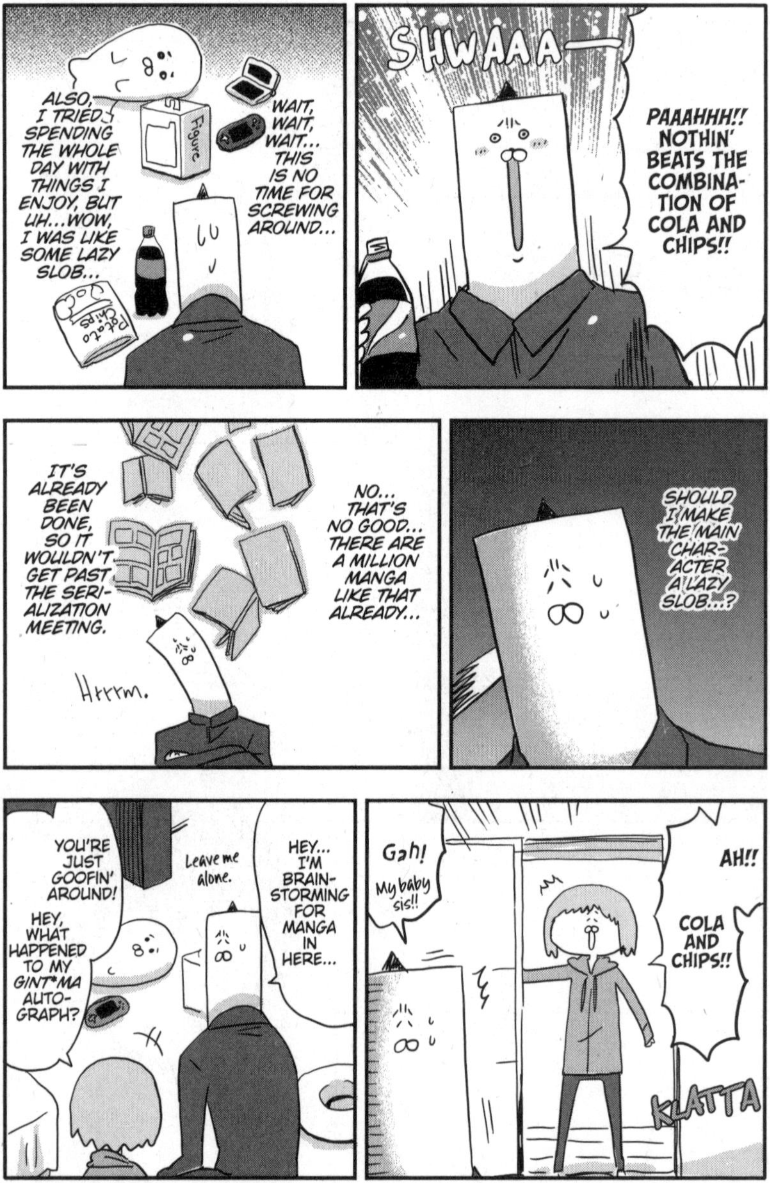
SHWAAA—
PAAAHHH!! NOTHIN' BEATS THE COMBINATION OF COLA AND CHIPS!!
ALSO, I TRIED SPENDING THE WHOLE DAY WITH THINGS I ENJOY, BUT UH...WOW, I WAS LIKE SOME LAZY SLOB...
WAIT, WAIT, WAIT... THIS IS NO TIME FOR SCREWING AROUND...
Figure
Potato Chips
SHOULD I MAKE THE MAIN CHARACTER A LAZY SLOB...?
NO... THAT'S NO GOOD... THERE ARE A MILLION MANGA LIKE THAT ALREADY...
IT'S ALREADY BEEN DONE, SO IT WOULDN'T GET PAST THE SERIALIZATION MEETING.
Hrrrm.
AH!!
COLA AND CHIPS!!
Gah!
My baby sis!!
KLATTA
HEY... I'M BRAINSTORMING FOR MANGA IN HERE...
Leave me alone.
YOU'RE JUST GOOFIN' AROUND!
HEY, WHAT HAPPENED TO MY GINT*MA AUTOGRAPH?

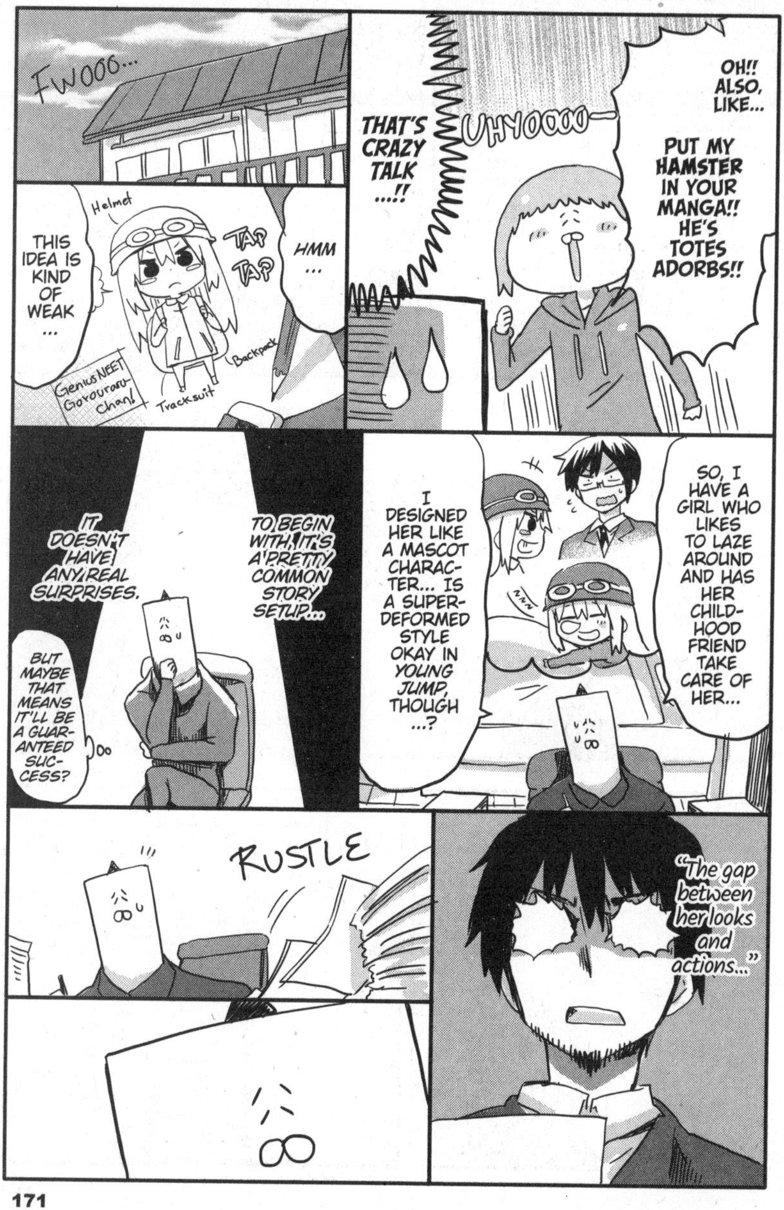

OH!! ALSO, LIKE...
PUT MY HAMSTER IN YOUR MANGA!! HE'S TOTES ADORBS!!
UHYOOOO—
THAT'S CRAZY TALK ...!!
FWOOO...
HMM ...
TAP TAP
THIS IDEA IS KIND OF WEAK ...
Helmet
Backpack
Tracksuit
Genius NEET Gorouraru-Chan!
SO, I HAVE A GIRL WHO LIKES TO LAZE AROUND AND HAS HER CHILDHOOD FRIEND TAKE CARE OF HER...
I DESIGNED HER LIKE A MASCOT CHARACTER... IS A SUPER-DEFORMED STYLE OKAY IN YOUNG JUMP, THOUGH ...?
TO BEGIN WITH, IT'S A PRETTY COMMON STORY SETUP...
IT DOESN'T HAVE ANY REAL SURPRISES.
BUT MAYBE THAT MEANS IT'LL BE A GUARANTEED SUCCESS?
"The gap between her looks and actions..."
RUSTLE

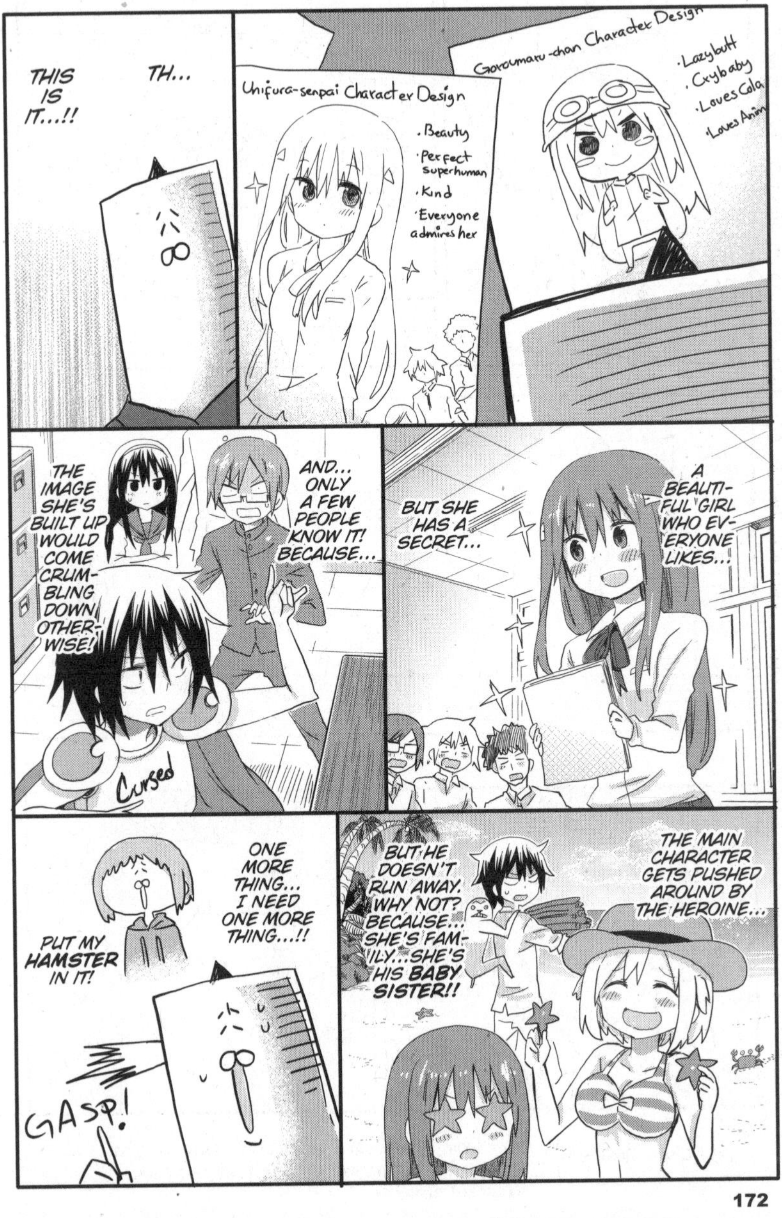
Goroumaru-chan Character Design
·Lazybutt
·Crybaby
·Loves Cola
·Loves Anim
Unifura-senpai Character Design
·Beauty
·Perfect superhuman
·Kind
·Everyone admires her
TH...
THIS IS IT...!!
A BEAUTIFUL GIRL WHO EVERYONE LIKES...
BUT SHE HAS A SECRET...
AND... ONLY A FEW PEOPLE KNOW IT! BECAUSE...
THE IMAGE SHE'S BUILT UP WOULD COME CRUMBLING DOWN OTHERWISE!
Cursed
THE MAIN CHARACTER GETS PUSHED AROUND BY THE HEROINE...
BUT HE DOESN'T RUN AWAY. WHY NOT? BECAUSE... SHE'S FAMILY...SHE'S HIS **BABY SISTER!!**
ONE MORE THING... I NEED ONE MORE THING...!!
PUT MY **HAMSTER** IN IT!
GASP!

※Included in the back of Volume 1!

Just when you thought this afterword was over... Next volume, we continue with the creation of the anime!!

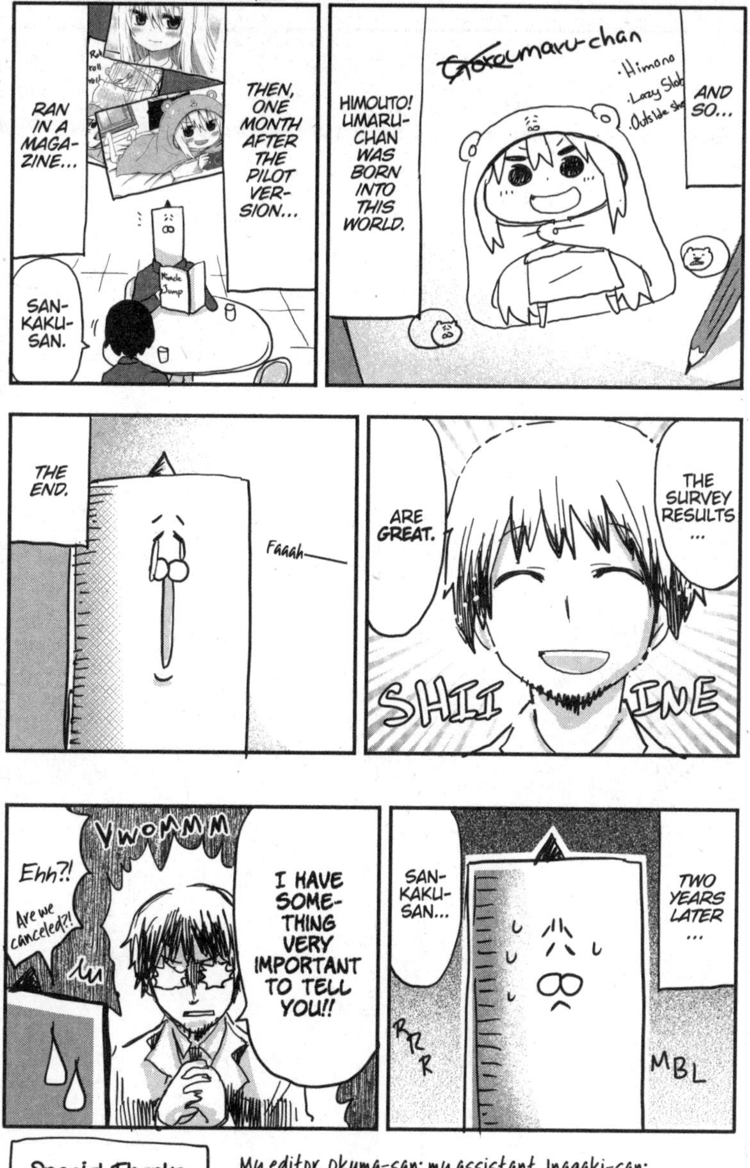
AND SO...
HIMOUTO! UMARU-CHAN WAS BORN INTO THIS WORLD.
~~Gotou~~maru-chan
·Himono
·Lazy Slob
·Outside she
THEN, ONE MONTH AFTER THE PILOT VERSION...
RAN IN A MAGAZINE...
Roll roll roll
SAN-KAKU-SAN.
THE SURVEY RESULTS...
ARE GREAT.
SHIII INE
Faaah—
THE END.
TWO YEARS LATER...
SAN-KAKU-SAN...
RRR
MBL
I HAVE SOMETHING VERY IMPORTANT TO TELL YOU!!
VWOMMM
Ehh?!
Are we canceled?!
Mu

Special Thanks

My editor, Okuma-san; my assistant, Inagaki-san; Kitagawa-san; Yamashita-san; my wife; my mom; Hayashi Yuichi-san

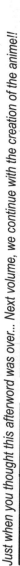

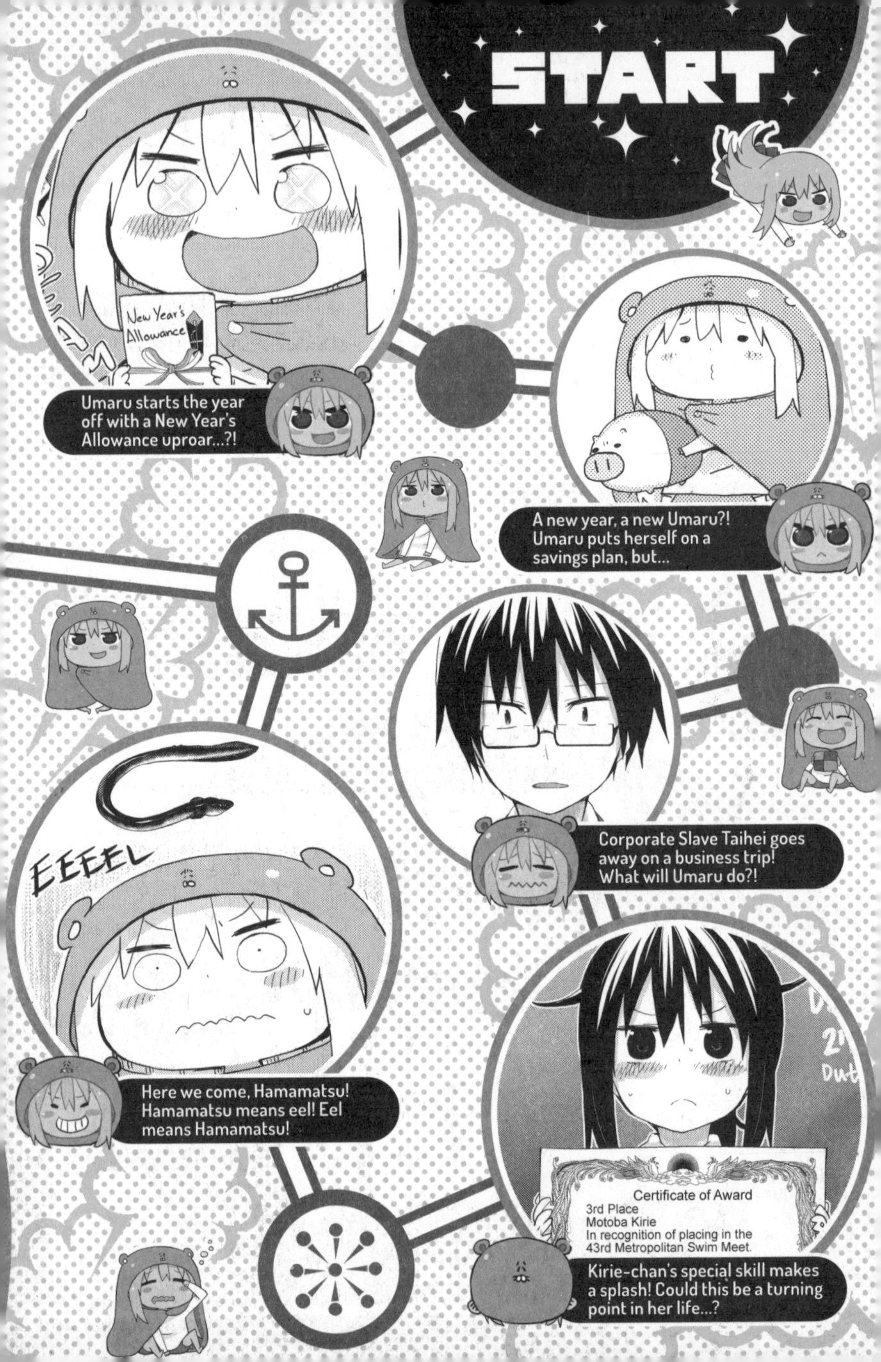
START
New Year's Allowance
Umaru starts the year off with a New Year's Allowance uproar...?!
A new year, a new Umaru?! Umaru puts herself on a savings plan, but...
Corporate Slave Taihei goes away on a business trip! What will Umaru do?!
Certificate of Award
3rd Place
Motoba Kirie
In recognition of placing in the 43rd Metropolitan Swim Meet.
Kirie-chan's special skill makes a splash! Could this be a turning point in her life...?
EEEEL
Here we come, Hamamatsu! Hamamatsu means eel! Eel means Hamamatsu!

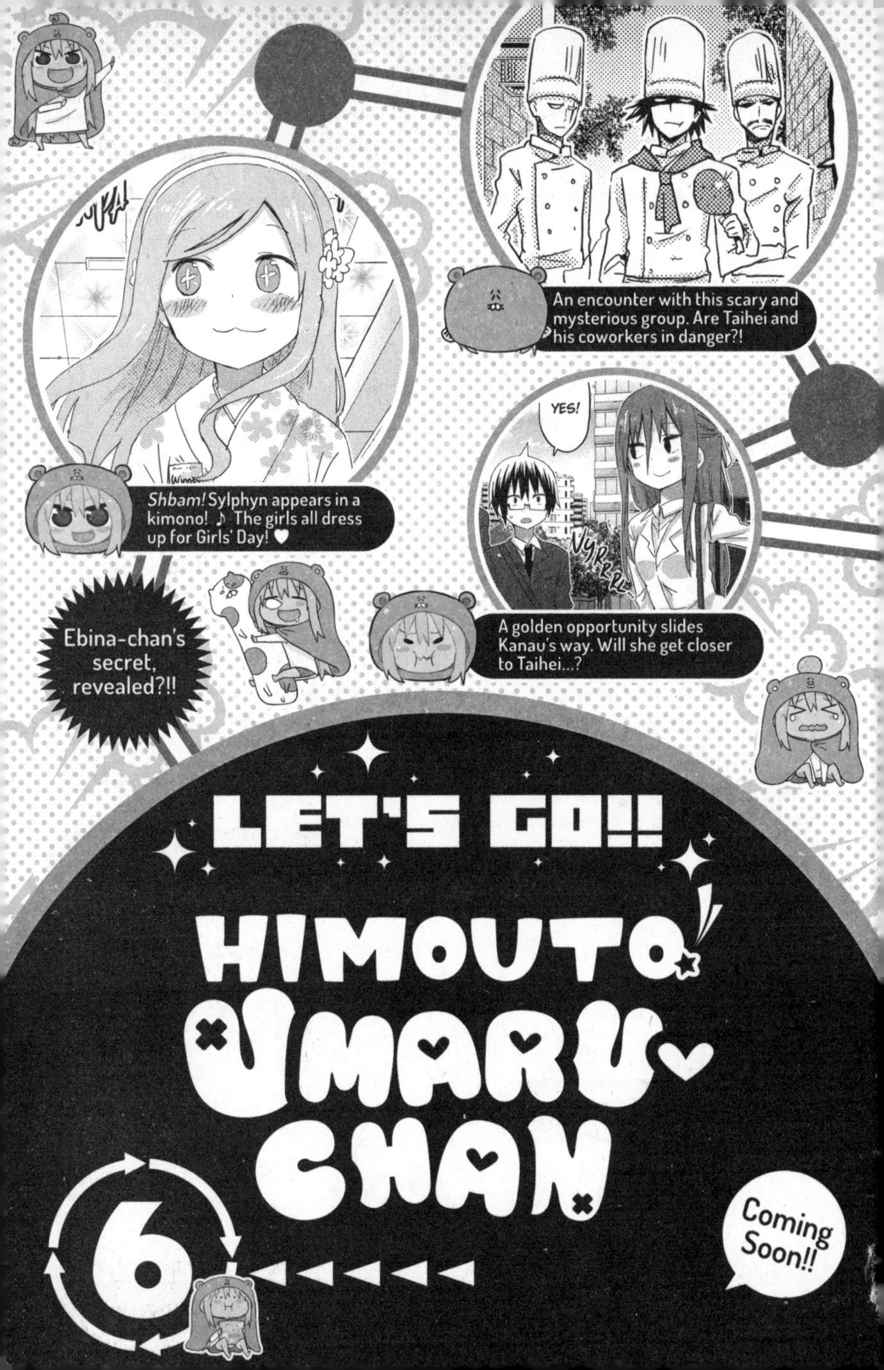

An encounter with this scary and mysterious group. Are Taihei and his coworkers in danger?!
Shbam! Sylphyn appears in a kimono! ♪ The girls all dress up for Girls' Day! ♥
YES!
A golden opportunity slides Kanau's way. Will she get closer to Taihei...?
Ebina-chan's secret, revealed?!!
LET'S GO!!
HIMOUTO! UMARU-CHAN
6
Coming Soon!!

SEVEN SEAS ENTERTAINMENT PRESENTS

Volume 5

HIMOUTO! UMARU-CHAN

story and art by SANKAKUHEAD

TRANSLATION
Amanda Haley

ADAPTATION
Shanti Whitesides

LETTERING AND RETOUCH
Carolina Hernández Mendoza

COVER DESIGN
Nicky Lim

PROOFREADER
Janet Houck

EDITOR
Jenn Grunigen

PRODUCTION MANAGER
Lissa Pattillo

MANAGING EDITOR
Julie Davis

EDITOR-IN-CHIEF
Adam Arnold

PUBLISHER
Jason DeAngelis

Seven Seas press and purchase enquiries can be sent to Marketing Manager
Lianne Sentar at press@gomanga.com. Information regarding the distribution
and purchase of digital editions is available from Digital Manager CK Russell
at digital@gomanga.com.

Seven Seas and the Seven Seas logo are trademarks of
Seven Seas Entertainment. All rights reserved.

ISBN: 978-1-642750-28-7

Printed in Canada

First Printing: April 2019

10 9 8 7 6 5 4 3 2 1

FOLLOW US ONLINE: www.sevenseasentertainment.com

READING DIRECTIONS

This book reads from *right to left*, Japanese style.
If this is your first time reading manga, you start
reading from the top right panel on each page and
take it from there. If you get lost, just follow the
numbered diagram here. It may seem backwards at
first, but you'll get the hang of it! Have fun!!

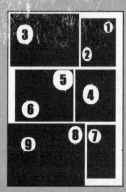